UNSAFE in the IVORY TOWER

UNSAFE in the IVORY TOWER

The Sexual Victimization of College Women

Bonnie S. Fisher
University of Cincinnati

Leah E. Daigle
Georgia State University

Francis T. Cullen
University of Cincinnati

Los Angeles | London | New Delhi
Singapore | Washington DC

For information:

SAGE Publications, Inc.
2455 Teller Road
Thousand Oaks, California 91320
E-mail: order@sagepub.com

SAGE Publications Ltd.
1 Oliver's Yard
55 City Road
London EC1Y 1SP
United Kingdom

SAGE Publications India Pvt. Ltd.
B 1/I 1 Mohan Cooperative Industrial Area
Mathura Road, New Delhi 110 044
India

SAGE Publications Asia-Pacific
  Pte. Ltd.
33 Pekin Street #02-01
Far East Square
Singapore 048763

Printed in the United States of America

Library of Congress Cataloging-in-Publication Data

Fisher, Bonnie, 1959-
Unsafe in the ivory tower : the sexual victimization of college women/Bonnie Fisher, Leah E. Daigle, Francis T. Cullen.
    p. cm.
Includes bibliographical references and index.
ISBN 978-1-4129-5476-1 (cloth: alk. paper)
ISBN 978-1-4129-5477-8 (pbk.: alk. paper)
    1. Sexual harassment in universities and colleges—United States—Statistics. 2. Women—Education (Higher)—United States. I. Daigle, Leah E. II. Cullen, Francis T. III. Title.

LC212.862.F58 2010
378.1'958—dc22   2009037019

This book is printed on acid-free paper.

09   10   11   12   13   10   9   8   7   6   5   4   3   2   1

Acquisitions Editor:	Jerry Westby
Editorial Assistant:	Eve Oettinger
Production Editor:	Karen Wiley
Copy Editor:	Trey Thoelcke
Typesetter:	C&M Digitals (P) Ltd.
Proofreader:	Caryne Brown
Indexer:	Gloria Tierney
Cover Designer:	Edgar Abarca
Marketing Manager:	Jennifer Reed Banando

Brief Contents

Contents

Preface

Unsafe in the Ivory Tower represents the culmination of 15 years of sustained research on the sexual victimization of college women. Leah Daigle joined this collaboration at the mid-point. We entered this field of inquiry expecting to conduct a single project. Alas, we ended up devoting a large portion of our careers to investigating the victimization of college women—a decision we are thankful we made.

At the inception of this journey, it was readily apparent that sexual victimization was part of a broader culture war being fought on and beyond college campuses. We had ideological leanings, of course, but we concluded that we could best contribute to this debate by setting aside our political views. Our goal was not to find what we *wanted* but what *the data revealed*. We trust that our efforts will both provide valuable insights into the study of sexual victimization and inspire others to stand on our shoulders and see much farther than we have seen. We are persuaded that it is through the accumulation of scientific knowledge that it will be possible to unravel the complex sources of sexual victimization and, in turn, to design effective interventions that transform colleges into safer havens for female students.

Over the past 2 decades, Mary Koss has been at the center of research on sexual victimization—and the object of considerable praise and considerable criticism. When we turned to this area of scholarship, we were moved not by her iconic status in the field but by her use of science to map out the extent and nature of sexual victimization among college students. Koss richly deserved the field's attention because she had used innovative methods to collect national-level data that yielded salient empirical results. We were not troubled by the criticism of her work, though some seemed a touch hyperbolic. After all, a key norm of science is organized skepticism. But in the end, it seemed that Koss's critics and, with a few exceptions, her defenders were merely swapping accusations. The time had come, we concluded, to stop the banter and, instead, to undertake the next nationally representative study capable of advancing our understanding of female students' sexual victimization. We believed that our backgrounds in survey methodology and in victimology would enable us to conduct a project of some value.

The most daunting challenge was to figure out how to measure something as complex as sexual victimization. Especially with regard to rape, it is inordinately difficult to capture in a survey format when a sexual advance might have crossed the line from clumsy or bad behavior to a criminal offense. As we explain in detail, we designed a measurement strategy that merged the main advantages of Koss's Sexual Experiences Survey and of the Bureau of Justice Statistics' National Crime Victimization Survey. This instrument was then used in a national study of college women that assessed their experiences with sexual victimization. In addition, we conducted three other national-level projects: an earlier survey of crime victimization on campus (with John Sloan); an investigation using National Crime Victimization Survey methodology to assess rape and sexual assault; and an analysis of how colleges responded to sexual victimization (with Heather Karjane).

Unsafe in the Ivory Tower reports what we have discovered about college women's experiences with sexual victimization. In a way, this is a methodological story—that is, an account of how we tried to use measurement as a means of illuminating a subject that had become embroiled in ideological controversy. More than this, however, *Unsafe in the Ivory Tower* attempts to paint an accurate portrait of the risks that female students face and how they respond when they are sexually victimized. We do not wish to disclose here the details of our findings; read on to learn what we have uncovered! But as a preview, we can share that college women not only face a modest but meaningful chance of being raped and sexually assaulted but also are at risk of unwanted sexual advances, of verbal and visual harassment, and of being stalked. Sexual victimization thus is an integral part of many female students' lives—a reality that is often endured in silence or, usually at most, a secret that is disclosed to one's friends. As a result, sexual victimization comprises a hidden inequality of college life—an unpleasant if not disquieting cost that is imposed unwillingly on college women. It is thus incumbent upon college officials to grasp the potential seriousness of sexual victimization and to take steps to make their campuses safe havens for female students.

We have incurred many debts in bringing *Unsafe in the Ivory Tower* to press, which we are now happy to acknowledge. In fact, we have learned that "it takes a village" to conduct a series of national studies and then to synthesize their diverse findings under one cover. Our fear is that we have received such wide assistance that we will leave out a supporter who richly deserves notice. Our apologies in advance for those we inadvertently fail to mention. Over the years, we have aged and, although wiser in some respects, we are more forgetful in others. We start by expressing our gratitude to our colleagues in the School of Criminal Justice at the University of Cincinnati and Georgia State University. Janice Miller and Jean Gary of the University of Cincinnati often dropped what they were doing and, with their typical friendly and supportive style, assisted us in a variety of ways. The Division of Prevention and Community Research at Yale University and John Jay College of Criminal Justice provided an intellectual home for Bonnie Fisher for the 2007–2008 academic year, a crucial time during which the writing of this book was under way.

As noted, *Unsafe in the Ivory Tower* is based on several national-level studies that we conducted. These studies were generously funded by the National Institute of Justice and the Bureau of Justice Statistics. Bernard Auchter, among others, supplied invaluable guidance in these federally funded investigations. Completing these projects would not have been possible without much support. Joanne Belknap deserves special notice for the integral role she played in the development of our main measure of sexual victimization. Michael Turner merits our appreciation for working closely with us on the primary study and coauthoring writings that inform parts of this book. Others who collaborated or assisted on these projects—and later were often coauthors on publications—include Valerie Bell, Kristie Blevins, Jennifer Hartman, Cheryl Lero Jonson, Heather Karjane, Sharon Levrant, Jamie Newsome, Travis Pratt, Shannon Santana, Kristin Swartz, Megan Stewart, and Brenda Vose. Many colleagues, drawn from different disciplines, gave us invaluable encouragement and concrete help. These include Rosemary Barberet, Michael Benson, Amy Cassidy, Ann Coker, Walter DeKeseredy, George Dowdall, John Eck, Jamie Fargo, Jodi Lane, Chris Krebs, Chris Lindquist, Sandy Martin, Soni Regan, John Sloan, Marti Smith, Lynn Sommers, Tami Sullivan, Brent Teasdale, Sharon Tracy, Tara Warner, Pamela Wilcox, John Wright, John Wozniak, and Therese Zink. Finally, we are indebted to Paul Jonson for providing the wonderful photograph that graces our book's cover. His diligence and artistic talent allowed him to meet the daunting challenge of capturing the sense of being "unsafe in the ivory tower."

We thank the more than 8,000 randomly selected college women who participated in each of our national studies. Without your responses to our many survey questions, we would not have had data to answer our research questions. Your experiences coupled with our interests have helped to further the scientific understanding of the sexual victimization of college women. We also thank the hundreds of students at our respective schools who attentively listened to each of us talk endlessly about the sexual victimization of college women. These students provided valuable insight from a new perspective that provided us with much food for thought.

We must also thank the assistance we have received from the editorial and production staff at SAGE Publications. We extend our deepest gratitude to Jerry Westby. Jerry has shown unwavering support for this enterprise, providing patience and prodding as needed! Without his editorial wisdom and faith in us, this book would not have come to fruition.

When this project was still in the planning stages, a number of scholars kindly reviewed the prospectus and supplied insightful comments. Along with SAGE Publications, we wish to thank these reviewers:

Karin Dudash
Cameron University

Patricia Harris
University of Texas at San Antonio

Lynn C. Jones
Northern Arizona University

Robert Lilly
Northern Kentucky University

Susan Miller
University of Delaware

Damon Mitchell
Central Connecticut State University

Karen Terry
John Jay College of Criminal Justice

Janet Wilson
University of Central Arkansas

Portions of this book were derived from previous reports of our research, as follows:

Portions of Chapters 1 and 2 were derived from Bonnie S. Fisher, Francis T. Cullen, and Michael G. Turner (1999), *The Extent and Nature of Sexual Victimization Among College Women: A National-Level Analysis* (Final Report), Washington, DC: U.S. Department of Justice, National Institute of Justice; Bonnie S. Fisher and Francis T. Cullen (2000), "Measuring the Sexual Victimization of Women: Evolution, Current Controversies, and Future Research," in David Duffee (Ed.), *Criminal Justice 2000 Volumes: Vol. 4—Measurement and Analysis of Crime and Justice* (pp. 317–390), Washington, DC: National Institute of Justice; and Bonnie S. Fisher, Francis T. Cullen, and Michael G. Turner (2000), *The Sexual Victimization of College Women*, Washington, DC: U.S. Department of Justice, Bureau of Justice Statistics.

Portions of Chapter 5 were taken from Leah E. Daigle, Bonnie S. Fisher, and Francis T. Cullen (2008), "The Violent and Sexual Victimization of College Women: Is Repeat Victimization a Problem?" *Journal of Interpersonal Violence, 23,* 1296–1313; and Leah E. Daigle, Bonnie S. Fisher, and Pamela Guthrie (2007), "The Recurrence of Victimization: What Researchers Know About Its Terminology, Characteristics, and Causes," in Robert C. Davis, Arthur J. Lurigio, and Susan Herman (Eds.), *Victims of Crime* (3rd ed., pp. 211–232), Thousand Oaks, CA: Sage.

Portions from Chapter 6 were based on findings published in Bonnie S. Fisher, Leah E. Daigle, Francis T. Cullen, and Michael G. Turner (2003), "Acknowledging Sexual Victimization as a Rape: Results From a National-Level Study," *Justice Quarterly, 20,* 535–574; and Bonnie S. Fisher, Leah E. Daigle, Francis T. Cullen, and Michael G. Turner (2003), "Reporting Sexual Victimization to the Police and Others: Results From a National-Level Study of College Women," *Criminal Justice and Behavior, 30,* 6–38.

Portions of Chapter 7 appear in Bonnie S. Fisher, Francis T. Cullen, and Michael G. Turner (2002), "Being Pursued: Stalking Victimization in a National Study of College Women," *Criminology and Public Policy, 1,* 257–308; and Bonnie S. Fisher and Megan Stewart (2007), "Vulnerabilities and Opportunities 101: The Extent, Nature, and Impact of Stalking Among College Students and Implications for Campus Policy and Programs," in Bonnie S. Fisher and John J. Sloan III (Eds.), *Campus Crime: Legal, Social, and Policy Perspectives* (2nd ed., pp. 210–230), Springfield, IL: Charles C Thomas.

A portion of Chapter 8 was drawn from Bonnie S. Fisher, Francis T. Cullen, and Michael G. Turner (2002), "Being Pursued: Stalking Victimization in a National Study of College Women," *Criminology and Public Policy, 1,* 257–308.

We gratefully acknowledge the permission of the authors and publishers to use this material in our book.

Finally, we cherish the opportunity to express our heartfelt appreciation to those closest to us, whose love, support, and good humor inspired our collective efforts to contemplate and then write *Unsafe in the Ivory Tower.* Thus, this book is dedicated by Bonnie S. Fisher to Nick, Olivia, and Camille Williams, by Leah E. Daigle to Adam, Avery, and Ian Comer, and by Francis T. Cullen to Paula Dubeck and Jordan Cullen.

Bonnie S. Fisher
Leah E. Daigle
Francis T. Cullenc

1

The Discovery of
Sexual Victimization

In the public's mind, the college campus retains the image of an "ivory tower." It is often said that students graduating from college are now entering the "real world," which implies that campus life is detached from the hard obligations and unpleasant experiences found beyond the school's boundaries. When a heinous crime occurs—a coed is slain or a shooting rampage occurs such at Virginia Tech—it is shocking not only because of the nature of the offense but also because of the context in which it transpires. Colleges are supposed to be safe havens—places in which young adults mature through scholarly study and by leading social lives in which risky youthful indiscretions, such as drinking too much, do not have enduring consequences. Tragic victimizations thus are unnerving and prompt us to wonder how such things could ever happen "here." Campus crimes have broader disquieting implications as well. After all, if someone can be victimized in the ivory tower, can the rest of us be certain of our safety in our own homes and communities?

The ivory tower stereotype further shapes how serious campus victimizations are explained. These events are not seen as being bred by the college environment itself—as one might say about the crimes whose roots are deeply implanted in the disadvantages and disorganization found in inner-city neighborhoods. Rather, campus crime is typically attributed to individual pathology—that is, to a "disturbed" student who goes on a rampage or to a criminal intruder who ventures onto the campus to victimize the innocent. These offenders are treated as newsworthy precisely because they are perceived as the exception to the rule—as anomalies within the pristine ivory tower of the college campus.

Stereotypes, of course, not only reflect but also distort reality. In particular, the image of the pathological offender diverts attention from the way in which students' victimization might flow from the everyday routines of college life. Marcus Felson (2002, p. 12) reminds us of the fallacy of assuming that crime is always "part of a larger set of social evils, such as unemployment, poverty, social injustice, or human suffering." His routine activity theory suggests that in most settings, it is risky to fail to provide an "attractive target" with an appropriate level of "guardianship." There usually are enough "motivated offenders" located across society to take advantage of such a situation (Cohen & Felson, 1979). This is one reason that theft is prevalent on college campuses (Fisher, Sloan, Cullen, & Lu, 1998). Unthinking students leave books and cell phones unguarded and, when departing their residence hall rooms, leave the door unlocked if not open. Not surprisingly, their property may well be missing when they return (see, more generally, Mustaine & Tewksbury, 2007).

More significantly, this insight helps us to understand why college campuses are social domains conducive to students' sexual victimization, including rape. There are times when coeds walking alone at night are sexually assaulted by a stranger. But beyond these disturbing crimes, the risk of female students' victimization is ingrained in the very fabric of normal college life. Higher educational institutions are places where large numbers of males and females come into daily contact not only in the classroom but also in social settings—in bars, in fraternity or sorority houses, in residence halls, and in apartments at the school's edge. Encounters in these settings are characteristic of most students' lifestyles and might lead to much-welcomed flirting, dates, and intimate relationships. But predictably, this routine, everyday activity also may lead many women into situations—such as being alone in a room with a male student—where they are, to use Felson's terms, an attractive target with no guardianship. In these circumstances, women risk facing unwanted sexual advances that can escalate into assault if not rape. Scholars have used the terms such as *acquaintance rape* and *date rape* to describe this type of rape victimization.

This book explores how sexual victimization makes women unsafe in the ivory tower. When female students embark on a college career, they bear the unwarranted cost of the threat and reality of being raped, sexually assaulted, harassed, and stalked. For many years, this cost remained hidden from public view. Victims were left to suffer in silence; their voices were not heard and their pains were ignored.

As we show in this chapter, however, the sexual victimization of women, including on college campuses, gradually was "discovered." This discovery was hastened by highly publicized prosecutions that raised consciousness—both in society generally and on college campuses—about sexual victimizations in which the perpetrator was not a stranger but known to the victim. Scholars, starting most notably with Mary Koss, also played an integral role in providing empirical data showing the prevalence of female students' victimization. In particular, the finding that many females were being raped sparked demands that colleges do more to protect their coeds. This claim also triggered a countervailing movement, led mostly by conservatives, that attributed the attention accorded women's victimization to a feminist plot to make college campuses politically correct. These commentators accused researchers, such as Koss, of misreading, if not fudging, their data so as to invent a problem that did not really exist.

Thus, in the pages ahead, we trace this debate—this "culture war"—over women's sexual victimization. This discussion is the broader context that surrounds any research, including ours, into how college students' bodies are violated by others. As we move through the remainder of this book, we try to push ideology aside and present empirical evidence on the nature, extent, and consequences of sexual victimization on the nation's campuses. In so doing, we show that rape and other forms of sexual victimization comprise a real problem that warrants attention and appropriate efforts at prevention.

Before proceeding, let us pause briefly to clarify terminology. First, we are interested in the sexual victimization experiences of female students across postsecondary institutions—from 2-year schools to universities with graduate programs. We use various terms synonymously to refer to this universe of institutions. Most often we call them *colleges*, but at times we utilize terms such as *universities, institutions,* and *schools.* Second, we employ the term *sexual victimization* to refer to acts with sexual purpose or content that violates women's bodies and/or minds. This would include rape and *sexual assault*, a term reserved for unwanted sexual contact that does not involve penetration. Sexual victimization also covers sexual coercion, verbal and visual harassment, and (as we explain in Chapter 7) most stalking behavior. Sexual victimization can be attempted, completed, or threatened. Third, we use the concept of *acquaintance rape* to cover rapes by a perpetrator the victim knows but is neither formally dating nor enmeshed with in an ongoing intimate relationship. The term *date rape* refers to rapes that occur on a date or by a dating partner.

Beyond Real Rape

In 1987, Susan Estrich, then a law professor at Harvard University, published *Real Rape.* Estrich began this volume with a chilling account of a rape she had experienced in 1974, shortly before she entered law school. As she was exiting her automobile in a parking lot, she was abruptly pushed back inside and raped. Her money and car were stolen. When the police arrived, they sized up the situation. Was her account believable? She had no bruises. But her story rang true. She seemed like a "nice girl," and the perpetrator was a stranger—and a black man at that. They were willing to take her to the police station and have her repeat her story. Later, after a trip to the hospital, she returned to the station to look at mug shots of suspected rapists. Her car was recovered, without tires. Nobody was ever prosecuted for the crime.

Estrich noted that, in a way, she was a fortunate rape victim. "I am lucky because everyone agrees that I was 'really' raped. . . . no one doubts my status as a victim. No one suggests that I was 'asking for it.' No one wonders, at least out loud, if it was really my fault" (1987, p. 3). This is because she experienced a "real rape"—a sexual penetration to which she "obviously" did not give her consent. A real rape has certain markers: the perpetrator is a stranger; the act is committed in a public setting; the victim shows signs of resistance or of being overpowered—torn clothes, a bloodied face, bodily bruises.

Ironically, however, Estrich's book was not about real rape. Rather, she conveyed her victimization as a way of illuminating another kind of victimization, which she termed "simple rape." (As noted, others would call this acquaintance or date rape.) Victims of these assaults typically are raped in private settings and by people they know. On the crucial issue of their consent to the sexual act, their testimony that they said "no" often is not sufficient. For victims to be believed, a witness must be present or they must suffer sufficient physical harm that their effort to resist the sexual act cannot be challenged. "To use resistance as a substitute for intent," observed Estrich (1987, p. 96), "unnecessarily and unfairly immunizes those men whose victims are afraid enough, or intimidated enough, or frankly smart enough not to take the risk of resisting physically."

The point of Estrich's book was to show that "a 'simple' rape *is* a real rape" (1987, p. 7, emphasis added). Her goal was to change the way in which sexual victimization is understood or "socially constructed." In this view, a rape is a crime regardless of whether it is perpetrated by a stranger or an acquaintance, occurs in a private or a public setting, or leaves a woman battered or free of bruises.

This is not to say that the issue of consent is unproblematic. Sexual encounters with acquaintances or dating partners may evolve over an evening's time. Men may misinterpret a woman's willingness to engage in some sexual acts as an expression of her willingness to have intercourse. Cues meant to communicate a lack of consent might not be expressed clearly or fully understood. Research shows that even women who have been legally raped do not always define their nonconsensual sexual victimization as the crime of rape (see, e.g., Fisher, Daigle, Cullen, & Turner, 2003b; Kahn, Jackson, Kully, Badger, & Halvorsen, 2003).

Nonetheless, this ambiguity on the issue of consent is not a license to ignore that many women, some repeatedly, experience acquaintance or "simple" rapes. As Estrich noted, these victims—and how well they survived a potentially disquieting victimization—matter too. Further, attempts to downplay these nonconsensual victimizations as an "unfortunate misunderstanding" risk nourishing the acceptability of "rape myths." As Chapleau, Oswald, and Russell (2003, pp. 601–602) explain, "rape myths are stereotypical or false beliefs about the culpability of victims, the innocence of rapists, and the illegitimacy of rape as a serious crime" (see also Payne, Lonsway, & Fitzgerald, 1999). These antisocial beliefs—what criminologists call "techniques of neutralization" (Sykes & Matza, 1957)—give potential perpetrators the justification or permission to engage in forced sex (e.g., "when a woman says 'no' she really means 'yes'"; "she was asking for it").

It is noteworthy that writing in the mid-1980s, Estrich took notice of one positive development. "For the first time," she observed, "colleges are recognizing and trying to deal with date rape on their campuses" (1987, p. 7). To Estrich, "this discovery of date rape is surely an important part of the effort to change the way men and women in our society think about nonconsensual sex." (p. 7). Two decades later, our book is, in a way, a product of this discovery and an attempt to document the extent of the ways in which female college students are sexually victimized.

Sexual Victimization in Context

Estrich's *Real Rape* was not a solitary call for action but part of a larger chorus demanding that female victims be accorded equal protection under the law. Most generally, her book appeared as the civil rights movement was well under way and had expanded its focus beyond racial equality to include gender equality. This campaign argued for the extension of rights to females across social, economic, and political domains—to provide women equal access to higher education, to participation in sports, to employment, and to financial remuneration. Advocates further insisted that the nation's women be free from the control of men not only in public sectors but also in private sectors such as the home and bedroom.

In this latter regard, special efforts were made to recognize and publicize "intimate violence"—the ways in which women were victimized physically in private settings (Gelles & Straus, 1988). Most of this attention was given to domestic violence and to sexual victimization, especially date or acquaintance rape. Writings in this area tended to be informed by three central themes.

First, an attempt was made to show how violence against women, often disquieting in its ruthlessness and effects, had been hidden behind closed doors, rendering victims invisible (Belknap, 1996). In *Domestic Tyranny*, Elizabeth Pleck (1987, p. 182) notes that there "was virtually no public discussion of wife beating from the turn of the century until the mid-1970s." In the *Journal of Marriage and the Family*, the first article on family violence did not appear until 1969, 3 decades after the forum's inception (Pleck, 1987). Similar observations were made about sexual victimization (Brownmiller, 1975; Estrich, 1987; Warshaw, 1988). Second, commentators decried the failure of the criminal justice system to treat women as true victims and to protect them from male perpetrators. The promise of equal protection under the law in the United States was unmasked as an empty promise to half the nation's population. Third, violence against women was portrayed as a fundamental by-product of sex inequality and the sexist beliefs that supported this patriarchal system. Male violence, including rape, was not due to a few pathological "bad apples" but to a "bad barrel" that allowed men to use physical power to maintain control over women and to take what they wanted. Such dominance was so hegemonic that ideology had arisen (such as "rape myths") that justified women's coercion. In *The Beauty Myth*, Naomi Wolf (1991, p. 167) expressed this view:

> Cultural representation of glamorized degradation has created a situation among the young in which boys rape and girls get raped *as a normal course of events*. The boys may even be unaware that what they are doing is wrong; violent sexual imagery may well have raised a generation of young men who can rape women without even knowing it. (emphasis in the original)

Attributing male violence against women to patriarchy politicized these issues. Showing the extent of, and failure to prevent, females' victimization became feminist causes integral to the women's movement for equal rights. Many women were inspired not only to write books and articles but also to take to the streets to demand changes. Advances were achieved more quickly in the area of domestic violence, where advocates succeeded in opening shelters for battered women and forcing police departments to arrest male abusers. Sexual victimization, however, also earned attention. Thus, statutes were passed outlawing marital rape (husbands had been legally raping wives with impunity) and the use of past sexual history to discredit rape victims testifying against their perpetrators (rape shield laws). Awareness of date and acquaintance rape also occurred.

This politicization, however, had another consequence. It meant that women's victimization would not be seen as a neutral, bipartisan matter but as part of a culture war between the political left and right. Efforts on college campuses to "raise consciousness" about acquaintance and date rape, to warn that "every man is a potential rapist," and to implement prevention programs were portrayed as radical feminism run amok (Roiphe, 1993). The illumination of wife battering was similarly suspected as a disingenuous leftist attempt to attack the traditional nuclear family in which authoritative fathers worked and nurturing mothers raised children. As Pleck (1987, p. 197) notes:

> The New Right identified domestic violence legislation with feminism, which in turn they associated with an attack on "motherhood, the family, and Christian values." They hoped to restore the family as an institution separate from the public world. At the same time, they wanted to win the state over to their own view of morality. This New Right favored federal legislation to outlaw abortion, [to] prohibit teenagers from receiving birth control information, and to reinstate prayer in public schools.

As we will return to fairly soon, the study of sexual victimization, especially acquaintance and date rape, is now always undertaken in a politicized context. Those conducting research risk the criticism that the supposed scientific data they produce are, in reality, a product of their feminist ideology. Because many of those moved to probe the nature and extent of sexual victimization are females if not also feminists, this criticism has a surface appeal. In the end, however, research findings should be assessed based on their scientific merits and not discredited by ad hominem attacks from those harboring alternative political sentiments and, as is often the case, no data of their own.

The Hidden Figure of Rape

On June 3, 1991, the cover of *Time* showed a black and white picture of a college coed, allegedly sexually victimized, partially overlaid with the title, in stunning red, "Date Rape." Inside, the cover story probed how the very concept of rape was being broadened to include this type of sexual victimization (Gibbs, 1991a). Issues around consent were explored. When is it given and not given? When is a "no" really a "no"? It was observed that, while most rapes are never reported, women were now rising up in protest against their victimization—especially on college campuses (Gibbs, 1991b). This sentiment was captured by the *Time* reporter, Nancy Gibbs (1991a, pp. 48, 49):

> Women charge that date rape is the hidden crime; men complain that it is hard to prevent a crime they can't define. Women say it isn't taken seriously; men say it is a concept invented by women who like to tease but not take the consequences. . . . This attitude sparks rage among women who carry scars received at the hands of men they knew. . . . Date rape is not about a misunderstanding, they say. It is not about a woman's having regrets in the morning for a decision she made the night before. It is not about a "decision" at all. Rape is rape, and any form of forced sex—even between neighbors, co-workers, classmates, and casual friends—is a crime.

Time's interest in rapes by dates and acquaintances signaled that this phenomenon had emerged from hiding and was now a public policy issue—something that public officials, from prosecutors to campus officials, could no longer ignore. The national consciousness about such intimate violence, including on college campuses, was heightened by two prominent criminal cases, one transpiring before and the other after the *Time* report.

In 1991, William Kennedy Smith—a member of the celebrated Kennedy clan—was accused of an acquaintance rape. On Good Friday of that year, Smith had sex with a woman, whom he had met that evening at a bar, on the lawn of his Palm Beach home. Bruises, the emotional reaction of the woman, and a lie detector test she took led investigators to believe her charge of rape (Gibbs, 1991a). Three other women claimed that Smith previously had assaulted them, but their testimony was not allowed at the December trial. With the nation's attention riveted on this case, Smith was found not guilty.

The outcome for Mike Tyson, former heavyweight boxing champion, was not so sanguine. In July of 1991, Tyson was accused of luring Desiree Washington, the 18-year-old Miss Rhode Island participant in the Miss Black America pageant, into his Indianapolis hotel room. He claimed that he was explicit in his intent—what he wanted sexually—from the moment they met that afternoon at a publicity event. She countered that she was awakened by his telephone call later in the evening (1:36 a.m.) and enticed into his limousine with the promise of making rounds at parties populated by celebrities. With no witnesses or compelling physical evidence (she waited 24 hours to report the assault), the outcome hinged on the jury's judgment of whom to believe. He was portrayed as a predator; she was portrayed as someone who taught Sunday school and was an honor student. But small factors seemed influential. Before heading to Tyson's limousine, she had grabbed her camera. Who, jury members wondered, would bring a camera to an impending sexual rendezvous? In the end, in February of 1992, Tyson was convicted (Nack, 1992). He would serve 3 years in prison.

In the intervening years, other celebrated accusations of rape, including on college campuses, would grab national attention and increase consciousness about sexual victimization: Kobe Bryant's tryst with a resort employee in Eagle, Colorado; the Duke University lacrosse team scandal; the sexual victimization of female cadets at the Air

Force Academy; and so on. These cases are important for their dialectical quality. They reflect a social context and awareness that make them possible, but they also nourish the conditions that make future investigations and cases likely. Still, in the end, disclosures of alleged sexual misconduct are only suggestive. They are the smoke that indicates that a fire must be raging unseen and underneath—hidden from full public view. But they do not prove that a given problem is sufficiently disquieting to warrant special policy consideration.

Determining the true dimensions and seriousness of a potential social problem thus must move beyond the telling of "atrocity tales" to the collection of hard data—of objective statistical estimates based on rigorous scientific research (see Best, 1990). The stubborn reality, however, is that developing reliable estimates of sexual victimization is a daunting challenge. One option might be to rely on crimes reported to the police, which are compiled and published annually by the Federal Bureau of Investigation (FBI) in *Crime in the United States: Uniform Crime Reports* (UCR). As is well known, because most rape victims do not report their victimization, such "official statistics" vastly underestimate the extent of the problem. That is, many such offenses remain hidden from law enforcement officials and thus never appear in the FBI's yearly volume. Another option might be to rely on the National Crime Victimization Survey (NCVS), which asks a sample of the public if they have been victimized, specially asking about rape and sexual assault. Victimization surveys have their own methodological difficulties, but they are designed to capture offenses people experience but do not report to law enforcement officials. In the case of rape and sexual assault, however, the questions on the NCVS have serious limitations that prevent their yielding reliable estimates. We discuss this matter in more detail in Chapter 2.

Specially Designed Victimization Surveys

Given that existing national data collected by the U.S. federal government did not allow for reliable estimates of sexual victimization, what could researchers do? Methodological barriers are, in a sense, the mother of invention. Thus, to capture the "hidden figure" of rape and other types of sexual victimization, scholars developed a third approach: they designed self-report surveys specifically devoted to measuring this realm of victimization.

Notably, early attempts at such surveys date back to at least the 1950s. Research at this time by Clifford Kirkpatrick and Eugene Kanin (1957; Kanin, 1957), for example, attempted to define and empirically measure "erotic aggressiveness" or "erotic offensiveness" by males against females in dating-courtship relationships on a university campus. Their methods are still relevant to today's sexual victimization research.

They developed and distributed a self-report "schedule" to female students enrolled in one of 22 "varied" university classes during the academic year (September 1954 to May 1955). Their questionnaire distinguished five degrees of erotic aggressiveness: attempts at (1) "necking," (2) "petting above the waist," (3) "petting below the waist," (4) "sex intercourse," and (5) "sex intercourse with violence or threats of violence." The questions focused on the extent to which the respondents were "offended" by intimacy level, frequency, and number of men during the academic year (Kirkpatrick & Kanin, 1957, p. 53). In essence, this was a victimization survey. Among the 291 female students, they found that a large portion had experienced a sexual victimization. During the academic year, 55.7% of women reported being offended at least once at some level of erotic intimacy, with 6.2% stating that they had been subjected to "aggressively forceful attempts at sex intercourse in the course of which menacing threats or coercive infliction of physical pain were employed" (p. 53).

Given that their investigation was undertaken in the 1950s, Kirkpatrick and Kanin's research did not trigger a movement to study women's sexual victimization. In fact, their work was largely neglected until rediscovered 2 decades later when, sensitized to females' victimization by a changed social context, scholars returned to this topic. Still, their research is important in showing a finding that would tend to be repeated in later studies: specially designed surveys generally reveal that sexual victimization is not a rare event and is more widespread than found by the FBI's official crime statistics and by the NCVS's sexual victimization estimates.

Much of the sexual victimization research—including Kirkpatrick and Kanin's and the research of those that would follow—has been conducted using college student samples, in part because of their convenience and in part because this is a social domain in which such victimization is elevated. In contrast, Diana Russell (1982) undertook a now-classic project that surveyed adults living in the community. Thus, she randomly selected 930 adult female residents in San Francisco from a probability sample of households. Sixty-four percent of the original sample of 2,000 completed the interview. Sensitive to the possible effects of the gender of the interviewer, Russell employed professionally trained female interviewers; their race and ethnicity were matched to those of each respondent. Whenever possible, she had them interview selected respondents in person and in a private setting. The interviews were conducted during the summer of 1978.

Several features of this study are noteworthy because they informed subsequent investigations—including the pathbreaking study of Mary Koss and our own research (both of which are discussed later). First, previous research had provided respondents, if at all, with only a brief or ambiguous definition of rape. In contrast, Russell's definition of rape was patterned after the legal definition of extramarital rape in California as "forced intercourse (e.g., penile-vaginal penetration) or intercourse obtained by threat of force, or intercourse completed when a woman was drugged, unconscious, asleep, or otherwise totally helpless and hence unable to consent" (1982, p. 84).

Second, Russell sought to measure whether a person had been raped by using several "behaviorally specific" questions with respect to rape (e.g., "38 questions on sexual assault and abuse," p. 85). A behaviorally specific question is one that does not simply ask, "Have you been raped?" Rather, it describes a victimization incident in graphic language that covers the elements of a criminal offense (e.g., someone "physically forces you . . . to have sexual intercourse"). Notably, researchers have found that when surveys use multiple, behaviorally specific questions, the respondents disclose more sexual victimization (see Crowell & Burgess, 1996, p. 35). Her approach thus shaped the content of the questions employed in the most significant surveys that later scholars would develop. So that the nature of behaviorally specific questions is clear, we present the examples of items used on Russell's survey in Table 1.1.

Table 1.1 Examples of Russell's Questions Used to Elicit Experiences of Rape or Attempted Rape[1]

1. Did a ____[2] ever physically force you, or try to force you, to have any kind of sexual intercourse (besides anyone you've already mentioned)?

2. Have you ever had any unwanted sexual experience, including kissing, petting, or intercourse with a ____[2] because you felt physically threatened (besides anyone you've already mentioned)? IF YES: Did [3] (any of them) either try or succeed in having any kind of sexual intercourse with you?

3. Have you ever had any kind of unwanted sexual experience with a ____[2] because you were asleep, unconscious, drugged or in some other way helpless (besides anyone you've already mentioned)? IF YES: Did [3] (any of them) either try or succeed in having any kind of sexual intercourse with you?

4. At any time in your life, have you even been the victim of a rape or attempted rape?

SOURCES: Fisher and Cullen (2000); Russell (1982).

NOTES:
1. Russell only provided the wording for these four of her 38 questions.
2. The interviewers asked the respondents these questions three times: first about strangers, second about acquaintances or friends, and third about dates, lovers, or ex-lovers.
3. Russell used the pronoun he here because she had already asked the respondents about any unwanted sexual experiences with females.

Third, for every episode of rape and attempted rape elicited, the interviewer administered a separate questionnaire. Included was a "description of the assault sufficiently detailed to ensure that one of the criteria for defining the assault as a rape or attempted rape had been met" (Russell, 1982, p. 86). Fourth, for the first three questions in Table 1.1, she asked if they had been perpetrated by (1) strangers; (2) acquaintances or friends; and (3) dates, lovers, or ex-lovers.

Russell's development and use of behaviorally specific questions based on the legal criteria for rape set a new standard for the operationalization of rape—one that the best of subsequent research would build on. Her approach potentially reduced measurement error inherent in previous studies. Thus, the use of a legal-based definition of rape meant that she was likely to have assessed victimizations that would qualify legally as a crime. The use of behaviorally specific questions both increased the likelihood that respondents would be cued to victimization incidents that had occurred and diminished the likelihood that respondents would "read into" and thus differentially interpret the victimization questions they were asked to answer. Russell suggested the importance of using follow-up questions to further explore or to "confirm" responses to initial questions about sexual victimization experiences, thus minimizing the possibility of counting as rape incidents those that did not qualify legally for this categorization. Finally, by asking about victimizations perpetrated not only by strangers but also by intimates, she potentially cued respondents to include acquaintance and date rapes that might otherwise have gone unreported to the interviewer.

All these factors—the number of questions asked, the manner in which they were presented, and her follow-up questions—likely contributed to Russell's reported rape estimates (1982, p. 85). She found that 41% of the women reported experiencing at least one completed or attempted extramarital rape during their lifetime. This was a remarkable discovery; it suggested that 4 in 10 women would experience the risk of rape in their lives.

Russell also explored victimization experiences over the past year (12 months prior to interview). In this limited time, 3% of the women reported that they had experienced a completed rape or attempted rape. Further, Russell was among the first researchers to compare her survey results with those reported in the FBI's UCR and the NCVS (then called the National Crime Survey) and to question why statistical discrepancies existed. She tried, for example, to make her incidence rape rates as comparable as she could to the UCR and the NCVS rates. She reported that her rates were higher than both the UCR and the NCVS. Although Russell's rape estimation and extrapolation procedures and her response rate have been criticized, this critical line of thinking about government-produced "official" rape estimates helped to give direction to future researchers (see Gilbert, 1997, pp. 121–123).

Koss's Sexual Experiences Survey

In 1976, Mary Koss started her career by exploring a new area of research, which she referred to as "hidden rape." At that time, the term *date rape* had not been coined. In part, this was, as Koss (1988a, p. 189) later noted, because "there was no convincing evidence that rape or rape-like behavior occurred among 'normal' people." In 1978, she received federal funding to undertake her first research project on this topic. She surveyed 4,000 students attending Kent State University in Ohio, the college where she was an assistant professor. She investigated college students largely for reasons of convenience—that is, for their ready accessibility. But it would prove a wise choice. "As it turns out," Koss observed, "this 'decision' to use college students was fortuitous because the college years happen to coincide with the greatest period of risk for rape" (p. 190).

Koss's research eventually was described in a piece on date rape in the feminist publication *Ms.* magazine. It was "the first national magazine article to address this issue" (1988a, p. 190). Subsequently, editors at *Ms.* approached Koss about conducting a national study that would assess sexual victimization more widely and thus present a truly complete portrait of the risks female students faced. In 1983, the National Institute of Mental Health (NIMH) agreed to sponsor the study, but only on the condition that the survey "be scientific, not politicized or sensational" and nationally representative. To guard against any biases creeping into the project, a separate company was employed to "design a plan for choosing a group of schools that would fairly represent the diversity of higher education settings and students" (p. 190). Recall that this potentially controversial, federally sponsored study was being undertaken during the administration of President Ronald Reagan, who inspired the rebirth of conservative politics.

One of Koss's major contributions to this investigation, which would take 3 years to plan and finish, was her measure of sexual victimization called the Sexual Experiences Survey. This instrument is now widely known in the field by its acronym: the SES. It was this measure that would be used to estimate, in particular, the extent to which college women had experienced rape and attempted rape. The findings would prove controversial—taken by feminists as evidence of the serious risks women faced and by critics as evidence that exaggerated the problem of rape so as to serve political ends. Below, we describe the nature of the SES and of Koss's findings. In the following section, we examine more fully the controversy her study inspired.

WHAT THE SEXUAL EXPERIENCES SURVEY (SES) MEASURES

In her first study at Kent State University, Koss had developed an initial version of the SES (Koss & Oros, 1982). With her colleagues, she revised this initial scale for her national-level study sponsored by *Ms.* and the NIMH (Koss & Gidycz, 1985; Koss, Gidycz, & Wisniewski, 1987). The SES was composed of the 10 questions presented in Table 1.2. The respondents were instructed to answer "yes" or "no" to each of them. These items were intended to measure a range of sexual aggression a woman might have experienced, including completed rape and attempted rape. Specifically, let us describe what the SES assessed:

- *Sexual Contact:* a yes response to Questions 1, 2, or 3.
- *Sexual Coercion:* a yes response to Questions 6 or 7.
- *Attempted Rape:* a yes response to Questions 4 or 5.
- *Completed Rape:* a yes response to Questions 8, 9, or 10.

The respondents were classified according to the highest degree of sexual victimization that they reported (e.g., if a person answered "yes" to Questions 2 and 9, she was counted as experiencing rape and not sexual contact). Note that two of the types of sexual victimization on the SES are criminal—completed rape and attempted rape—and one is not—sexual coercion. Sexual contact may be criminal (Question 3) or not (Questions 1 and 2), depending on whether the offender used physical force. In any

Table 1.2   Sexual Experiences Survey (SES)

1. Have you given in to sex play (fondling, kissing, or petting, but not intercourse) when you didn't want to because you were overwhelmed by a man's continual arguments and pressure?

2. Have you had sex play (fondling, kissing, or petting, but not intercourse) when you didn't want to because a man used his position of authority (boss, teacher, camp counselor, supervisor) to make you?

3. Have you had sex play (fondling, kissing, or petting, but not intercourse) when you didn't want to because a man threatened or used some degree of physical force (twisting your arm, holding you down, etc.) to make you?

4. Have you had a man attempt sexual intercourse (get on top of you, attempt to insert his penis) when you didn't want to by threatening or using some degree of force (twisting your arm, holding you down, etc.), but intercourse *did not* occur?

5. Have you had a man attempt sexual intercourse (get on top of you, attempt to insert his penis) when you didn't want to by giving you alcohol or drugs, but intercourse *did not* occur?

6. Have you given in to sexual intercourse when you didn't want to because you were overwhelmed by a man's continual arguments and pressure?

7. Have you had sexual intercourse when you didn't want to because a man used his position of authority (boss, teacher, camp counselor, supervisor) to make you?

8. Have you had sexual intercourse when you didn't want to because a man gave you alcohol or drugs?

9. Have you had sexual intercourse when you didn't want to because a man threatened or used some degree of physical force (twisting your arm, holding you down, etc.) to make you?

10. Have you had sex acts (anal or oral intercourse or penetration by objects other than the penis) when you didn't want to because a man threatened or used some degree of physical force (twisting your arm, holding you down, etc.) to make you?

SOURCE: Koss, Gidycz, and Wisniewski (1987).

event, the salient point is this: by incorporating all of these types of sexual victimization, Koss's work could provide insights on experiences that may not be criminal but nonetheless victimize women.

Importantly, similar to Diana Russell's study, Koss employed *behaviorally specific* language in the SES to measure the specific types of sexual victimization. According to

Koss (1993a, p. 209), the use of behaviorally specific questions places "before the respondent detailed scenarios for the type of experiences the interviewer seeks to identify." Thus, rather than ask a respondent "have you been raped?" the SES used graphic, descriptive language. See, for example, Question 9 in Table 1.2. It starts off by asking: "Have you ever had sexual intercourse when you didn't want to?" This establishes penetration and lack of consent. Question 9 then proceeds to make clear that the lack of consent was due to physical coercion: "because a man threatened or used some degree of physical force." It then closes by defining physical force so that the respondent is aware as to what such force might entail: "(twisting your arm, holding you down, etc.) to make you."

As noted, measuring a complex act, such as rape, through a survey instrument is quite difficult. In a thoughtful way, however, Koss was using an advanced approach to try to minimize the likelihood that a respondent would misunderstand what was being asked. In methodological terms, Koss was employing descriptive, behaviorally specific items to reduce measurement error. Using a more general statement that merely asks about being "raped" is open to diverse interpretations. What the investigator and the respondent each believes falls under the umbrella of this concept may be quite different. Indeed, in her study, Koss (1989) found that nearly three-fourths of college women who met the legal definition for rape failed to use this term as the label for their experiences.

In this latter regard, Koss wished to avoid the claim that she might bias the results by allowing her own definition of what constitutes a rape to creep into the SES. She wisely defined rape according to the 1980 Ohio Revised Code. Thus, the rape questions in the SES (Questions 4, 5, 8, 9, and 10 in Table 1.2) are explicit as to the legal criteria for rape: type of penetration, force or threat of force, and no consent. To operationalize penetration, Koss used the term *sexual intercourse* and, as can be seen in Question 4 that measures attempted rape, the respondent was told exactly what this means ("get on top of you, attempt to insert his penis"). To measure other forms of penetration that the Ohio rape law also encompasses, the SES asked about experiencing "sex acts—anal or oral intercourse or penetration by objects other than the penis" (see Question 10). Force or threat of force was operationalized as physical force, and examples were provided for the respondent (e.g., "twisting your arm"; see Question 9). Lack of consent was defined for the respondent as "when you didn't want to" (for example, see Question 8).

The details of the SES might at first seem tedious, but these intricacies had crucial implications. Koss and her colleagues were attempting to develop sound estimates of how much sexual victimization the college women in their sample had experienced. In any scientific study, the results can be due either to *empirical reality* or to *methodological artifact*. If the methods used are rigorous, then we have confidence that the study has produced results that reflect the empirical reality of what actually is happening in the real world. If the methods used are flawed, our confidence diminishes, and we have reason to worry that the study has produced results that reflect biased methods and not objective reality. In this instance, the key methodological issue was *measurement*. Was it possible to develop a scale that could accurately measure the extent of sexual victimization— experiences that were rarely disclosed to local police or campus officials?

Indeed, much was at stake in Koss's investigation. She was attempting to decipher whether the sexual victimization of college women, including rape and attempted rape, was a serious or a trivial problem. If Koss's study yielded the conclusion that a substantial proportion of these women were being victimized, it would be a bombshell. It would suggest that she had uncovered a serious issue that hitherto had been hidden from public view. It would raise questions about why women were being subjected to such aggression and why nobody was doing much to address it.

WHAT DID KOSS FIND?

As noted, Koss and her colleagues conducted a national-level study of college women. They used a two-stage sampling design to choose schools and then students. In the first stage, to select schools, they used a cluster sampling design to sample every Xth cluster, according to the portion of total enrollment accounted for by the region. Ninety-three colleges and universities were selected; 32 agreed to participate. Then, in the second stage, from these schools, classes were randomly selected into the sample (for the details of the sampling design, see Koss et al., 1987, pp. 163–165). The 10-question SES was part of a 330-question self-report questionnaire titled the "National Survey of Inter-Gender Relationships." It was administered by post–master's degree psychologists (men and women) to those students who attended the selected classes that day. The response rate was 98.5%. The study was conducted during the 1984–1985 academic year.

Koss measured sexual victimization during two periods in women's lives. First, to estimate the prevalence of sexual victimization, she asked the respondents about their experiences *since age 14.* Second, to obtain 1-year estimates, she asked respondents about their experiences *since the previous academic year,* from September to September (for freshmen, this would have been their senior year in high school). The first measure thus probed sexual victimization since moving into the teenage years when dating was likely to begin. The second measured assessed the likely experiences of the respondents while they were college students.

What did Koss find? We present her results first for the prevalence of sexual victimization since age 14:

- More than half of the women (53.7%) reported some form of sexual victimization since age 14.

- Nearly 15% (14.4%) had experienced sexual contact.

- More than one in ten (11.9%) had experienced sexual coercion.

- A bit more than that (12.1%) had experienced attempted rape, and 15.4% had been raped.

- Taken together, these latter two figures meant that since age 14, more than one in four members of the sample (27.5%) had suffered a victimization that met the state of Ohio's legal definition of rape.

And what was the extent of victimization in the 1-year period?

- Almost half (46.3%) of the women experienced some form of sexual victimization in the past year.
- More than one in five (23.2%) had experienced sexual contact.
- More than one in ten (11.5%) had experienced sexual coercion.
- One in ten (10.1%) had experienced an attempted rape, and 6.5% had been raped.
- Taken together, these latter two figures meant that in the past year, 16.6% of the sample had suffered a victimization that met the State of Ohio's legal definition of rape.
- This also meant that the 1-year rate for attempted and completed rape was 166 per 1,000 students. Concretely, a college of 10,000 female students would have, *in any one year,* an estimated 1,666 rape victims walking its campus.

Koss also wondered how her results compared with the major national victimization study administered by the federal government. Again, this is now known as the National Crime Victimization Survey (NCVS); then it had the slightly shorter title of the National Crime Survey (NCS). To avoid a biased comparison, Koss and her colleagues (1987) recalculated their data to include only those incidents that met the definition of rape employed by the NCS, which limited rape to penile-vaginal penetration (and excluded acts such as oral and anal intercourse and sexual intercourse made possible by intentionally incapacitating a victim). Even under this more restrictive definition, Koss et al. (1987, p. 168) concluded that the rape victimization rate computed from their survey was "10–15 times greater than rates that are based on the NCS." This finding was truly startling, for it suggested that rape victimization was extensive and thus a serious social problem.

In essence, Koss was arguing that using behaviorally specific, legally based measures of sexual victimization captured an empirical reality masked in previous studies that were plagued by methodological artifacts. Methodological details, conveyed in the section of research articles and books that readers often skip, were placed by Koss at the center of the debate over how many women were raped or otherwise sexually victimized. Good measurement, she showed, revealed a disquieting reality: many women were raped and victims of other types of sexual victimization, and most of these victimizations had remained hidden from public view.

One in Four: Publicizing the Rape Epidemic

Koss's national Sexual Experiences Survey quickly earned—and we believe richly deserved—the status as a classic social science study. In each generation, there are only a few empirical works that not only are of high quality but also define how other scholars will pursue a line of inquiry. Koss's work did so. The SES, and subsequent modified versions of it, would be used in many sexual victimization studies both inside and outside the United States (see, e.g., DeKeseredy & Schwartz, 1998; Lane & Gwartney-Gibbs, 1985; Schwartz & Pitts, 1995).

But unlike most academic research, Koss's findings did not remain buried in the arcane, if not musty, pages of an obscure academic journal. Due to its involvement in Koss's study, *Ms.* magazine reported the findings in an article authored by Ellen Sweet (1985). This article carried the title "Date Rape," again using a term that was still sufficiently unfamiliar at this time to be eye-catching. The subtitle was even more telling, because it pointed to the real message of Koss's research: "The Story of an Epidemic and Those Who Deny It."

Sweet begins her piece with a story about a woman she calls Judy, who was a junior at Yale University when sexually assaulted:

> Once we were inside, he kissed me. I didn't resist. I was excited. He kissed me again. But when he tried for more, I said no. He just grew completely silent. I couldn't get him to talk to me any more. He pinned me down and ripped off my pants. *I couldn't believe it was happening to me.* (p. 56; emphasis in the original)

Given the dearth of awareness of date rape at the time, Judy's reaction was not anomalous. There is "so much silence that surrounds this kind of crime," observed Sweet, "that many women are not even aware that they have been raped" (p. 56). Few victims, including Judy, notify the police; many blame themselves. According to Sweet, "as long as such attacks continue to be a 'hidden' campus phenomenon, unreported and unacknowledged by many college administrators, law enforcement personnel and students, the problem will persist" (p. 57). How can this silence be pierced? Research is an invaluable weapon. "Statistics alone will not solve the problem of date rape," Sweet noted, "but they could help bring it out into the open" (p. 58). Sweet thus pointed to the disquieting results of Koss's "*Ms.* Study." These hard facts illuminated the "epidemic" of hidden date rape: "One quarter of women in college today have been victims of rape or attempted rape, and almost 90 percent of them knew their assailants" (p. 58).

Koss's study was publicized even more widely by a popular trade book, based on her data, by reporter Robin Warshaw (1988). The title, *I Never Called It Rape,* echoed the themes of the *Ms.* article, conveying the message that many women who were raped were still unaware about their right not to be coerced into sex. There was a need to puncture rape myths and to raise the consciousness of women, especially those victimized sexually who were prone to self-blame. The back cover of the book carried the message that this was a "ground-breaking report on the hidden epidemic of date and acquaintance rape"; the book would offer "essential new information and insight along with avenues for prevention and healing." Indeed, Warshaw saw her volume as a call to action. Thus, she subtitled her work, *The* Ms. *Report on Recognizing, Fighting and Surviving Date and Acquaintance Rape.*

Most telling, Warshaw memorably captured the essence of Koss's work by voicing this key finding: "1 in 4 women surveyed were victims of rape or attempted rape." (p. 11). Recall that in the *Ms.* article, Sweet had highlighted the same finding. This takeaway statistic was easily remembered and thus would often be repeated in academic

writings and popular discourse. In many ways, it became an unquestioned social fact—
a reality that seemed based on science and that was not to be challenged.

No research, however, should be so easily accepted. A core norm of science is "organized skepticism" (Merton, 1973). Journal articles, such as Koss's, have a good measure
of credibility; after all, they are not mere opinion but are based on a field's research
standards and must pass peer review before earning publication. Still, organized skepticism is an invaluable prescription because it guards against uncritically accepting
findings that conform to our preexisting biases. The challenge in science is to probe for
a study's potential weaknesses so as to illuminate the next set of investigations that
might use more finely calibrated ways of studying the phenomenon—in this case
sexual victimization.

Unfortunately, this did not occur. Koss's SES was perhaps too readily accepted as a
sacrosanct scale for measuring sexual victimization—to be used without question by
subsequent researchers rather than subjected to methodological scrutiny. Her findings
often were accepted uncritically because they provided a portrait of empirical reality
that many readers, especially those with feminist leanings, "knew to be true"—that is,
that many women were victims of male sexual aggression. At this point, her followers
did not wish to waste time on additional studies or to question the intricacies of Koss's
methods. Rather, for them, the 1-in-4 finding meant that an urgent, hitherto hidden
crisis was continuing unabated. With so many women at risk of sexual victimization—
an untreated "epidemic" in Warshaw's words—it was time to act; it was time to take to
the streets and to insist that programs be implemented to halt the violence being
imposed on women.

In this context, it is perhaps not surprising that Koss's research, when it was subjected to critical scrutiny, would be accused of being hopelessly biased by her supposed
feminist ideology. However, whatever her political sentiments, these should not be con-
flated with the rigorous science underlying her study, especially with regard to the
measurement of sexual victimization. Although Koss's work had its weaknesses—
what study does not?—these were not inspired by her ideology. From the inception of
her project, her commitment was to using the best methods available to measure the
sexual experiences of women. Nonetheless, Koss would be pulled into a broader culture
war in which her view of reality would be stridently challenged.

Two Critiques

Mary Koss contributed to the discovery of sexual victimization by furnishing rigorous
scientific evidence that estimated the extent of the problem. Her study gained credence
because scientific data are hard to dispute. It is one thing to claim that there is a
problem; it is quite another to provide empirical data firmly demonstrating its
existence and magnitude. In the subsequent years, two serious criticisms of her work
and, more generally, of claims of an epidemic of sexual victimization on college campuses
would appear—one by Neil Gilbert and another by Katie Roiphe. Defenders of Koss's
SES and of her study have depicted Gilbert and Roiphe as conservative scholars with

their own hidden agenda. Although we are more sympathetic to Koss's position, we also believe that issues raised by Gilbert and Roiphe are legitimate and warrant careful consideration.

GILBERT: THE DANGERS OF ADVOCACY RESEARCH

In a more general analysis of "problems" that, on closer inspection, prove unfounded, Barry Glassner (1999) suggests that Americans are often "afraid of the wrong things" and thus are enmeshed in a "culture of fear." In this context, Neil Gilbert accuses feminist scholars of engaging in an ideologically inspired social construction of reality that is meant to spread fear about sexual victimization. He argues that feminist investigations are an example of "advocacy research." In its most "honorable" form, advocacy researchers engage in "studies that seek to measure social problems, heighten public awareness of them, and recommend possible solutions" (Gilbert, 1997, p. 101). In his view, this "standard of advocacy . . . has eroded since the 1960s" (p. 103). Now, to call attention to their favorite concerns, advocates use "emotive statistics— startling figures that purport to uncover 'hidden crises' and 'silent epidemics'" (pp. 104–105). According to Gilbert, feminist researchers, such as Mary Koss, are exemplars of this practice. After all, have not they purported to uncover that "hidden rape" is of epidemic proportions? Are not they the ones who claim that one in four college women have experienced rape or attempted rape?

Gilbert (1997, p. 123) contends that ostensibly high rates of rape are an artifact of faulty measurement strategies that, among other things, define "a problem so broadly that it forms a vessel into which almost any human difficulty can be poured." The feminists' goal, he argues, is to show that sexual victimization is so pervasive that it must reflect structures of inequality in society—inequality that, in turn, is in need of fundamental social change. "They tend not only to see their client group's problems as approaching epidemic proportions but to attribute the underlying causes to oppressive social conditions—such as sexism," observes Gilbert (1997, pp. 112–113). "If 5 percent of females are sexually abused as children, the offenders are sick deviants; if 50 percent are sexually abused as children, the problem is the way that males are regularly socialized to take advantage of females."

Once again, then, we return the issue of methodology—that seemingly mundane, if not boring, part of social science that, in this case, is the source of vigorous, if not inflammatory, dispute. Thus, Gilbert's (1991, 1992, 1997) central thesis is that Koss's research, based on the SES, is erected on *faulty measurement* that has exaggerated the extent of rape. He contends further that her findings have been uncritically accepted because they reinforce feminist notions that entrenched patriarchal relationships in America generate widespread sexual exploitation of women. Gilbert rests his case on two main charges.

First, of the five questions in the SES used to measure rape, two involved a man attempting or completing forced intercourse "by giving you alcohol or drugs" (see Table 1.2). Koss used this phrasing to operationalize those acts that qualify as rapes under the Ohio Revised Code, which reads "for the purpose of preventing resistance the offender substantially impairs the other person's judgment or control by administering any drug or intoxicant to the other person" (Koss et al., 1987, p. 166). Notably, 44% of the rape victims in Koss's study were counted as victims because they answered "yes" to these two questions that involved rape accomplished through purposeful intoxication.

Gilbert characterizes these two rape questions as "awkward and vaguely worded" because they lack any notion of the man's intention, how much alcohol the respondent ingested, and whether the alcohol or drugs led the respondent not to offer her consent. For example, what does having sexual intercourse with a man because he "gave you drugs or alcohol" mean? Did he order a beer or wine for the respondent? Was the respondent too intoxicated to consent to sexual intercourse (Gilbert, 1991, p. 59)? Gilbert goes so far as to suggest that perhaps "the woman was trading sex for drugs, or perhaps a few drinks lowered her inhibitions so that she consented to an act that she later regretted" (1997, p. 116). He contends that the question could have been worded more clearly to denote "intentional incapacitation of the victim" (1997, p. 117). The larger point, of course, is that an unknown number of respondents might have answered "yes" to these two items even though their sexual experiences did not qualify legally as a rape (see also Muehlenhard, Sympson, Phelps, & Highby, 1994).

Second, Gilbert questions more fundamentally whether the SES items developed by Koss and associates are, in any methodologically rigorous way, capable of validly measuring rape victimization. Two troubling anomalies are found in Koss and associates' data. First, nearly three-quarters (73%) of the women categorized as rape victims in the study did not, when asked, believe they had been raped. Second, about 4 in 10 women counted by Koss as rape victims stated that they subsequently had sexual relations with the person who had purportedly raped them (Gilbert, 1997, p. 116). Gilbert argues that it is highly unlikely that such a large portion of college-educated women would be so uninformed or sexually inexperienced as (1) to misinterpret when they had, in fact, been raped and/or (2) to become involved again with a "rapist." The more plausible interpretation, contends Gilbert, is that Koss's SES is hopelessly flawed, cueing respondents to answer "yes" to questions measuring rape even though the nature of their sexual experience would not, if examined in detail, qualify legally as a rape.

Koss has offered reasonable rebuttals to Gilbert's criticisms. For example, Koss and Cook (1993) note that even when the two items involving rape due to alcohol and drugs are removed from statistical calculations, the extent of rape in Koss's sample remains disquietingly high (9.3% of the sample experiencing, in one year, attempted or completed rape). Further, Koss does not find it so implausible that many women, raised with a limited conception of rape as involving only attacks by strangers, might fail to define forced intercourse by an acquaintance as a rape. It also is possible that women might subsequently have sexual relations with their attacker because they blamed themselves for the previous encounter or because this person again attacked them. We might add a contextual factor: Koss's national study was conducted in 1984–1985, a time period before acquaintance and date rape had earned much attention. The fact that many college students of this era might not have been sensitized to the illegal nature of physically coercive sex is perhaps not surprising.

ROIPHE: THE MORNING AFTER

A second prominent critical analysis was written by Katie Roiphe in her 1993 book, *The Morning After: Sex, Fear, and Feminism on Campus.* Quite remarkably, Roiphe authored this volume not long after graduating from Harvard University in 1990. Its appeal rested in her presenting a critical analysis of campus feminism that lay substantially in her own recent personal experiences with political correctness during college. Her views were an odd mixture of neoconservative polemic and a rugged feminism that sought to reaffirm female individual self-efficacy or agency.

Accepting Gilbert's research without question, Roiphe (1993, p. 51) criticizes the "*Ms.* survey" conducted by Koss and its conclusion that "one in four college women is the victim of rape of attempted rape." This statistic, in Roiphe's view, not only was deconstructed by Gilbert's scathing rebuttal to Koss but also did not comport with her own personal experiences. She relayed her doubts:

One in four. I remember standing outside the dining hall in college looking at a purple poster with this statistic in bold letters. It didn't seem right. If sexual assault was really so pervasive, it seemed strange that the intricate gossip networks hadn't picked up more than one or two shadowy instances of rape. If I was really standing in the middle of an epidemic, a crisis, if 25 percent of my female friends were really being raped, wouldn't I know it? (pp. 51–52)

What, then, to believe? Roiphe (1993, p. 54) argues that, in the least, Gilbert's research "shows that these figures are subjective, that what is being called rape is not a clear-cut issue of common sense." For her, "whether or not one in four college women has been raped . . . is a matter *of opinion, not a matter of mathematical fact*" (p. 54, emphasis added). She goes so far as to claim that "someone's rape may be another person's bad night" (p. 54). Definitions of rape, apparently among researchers and women who have had a supposed bad night, "become entangled in passionate ideological battles" (p. 54). The current rape crisis is thus not an objective reality but socially constructed by those with a broader political agenda. And who might they be—who "is identifying this epidemic and why"? (p. 55). "Someone," Roiphe notes, "is 'finding' this rape crisis and finding it for a reason" (p. 55).

The culprits, of course, are the "rape-crisis feminists" who have infiltrated the nation's campuses (p. 73). In Roiphe's view, "rape is a natural trump card for feminism" (p. 56). Especially when claimed to be pervasive, rape is prima facie evidence of patriarchy and men's use of violence to control women. Pointing to the 1-in-4 statistic places university administrators on the defensive and forces them, without further discussion, to fund special feminist programs aimed at curtailing assaults against female students. In short, rape-crisis feminists are empowered by claims of high rates of sexual victimization.

But according to Roiphe, this embrace of victimhood comes at a high cost. It spreads a culture of fear on campuses that exaggerates any objective risk of victimization. It also ironically legitimates sexist "anachronistic constructions of the female body," especially about "female purity" (p. 71). Indeed, "all the talk about empowering the voiceless dissolves into the image of the naïve girl child who trusts the rakish man" (p. 71). Roiphe prefers a stronger feminism—one in which women shed their innocence and the umbrella of protections placed over them and instead take control of their lives, including, if necessary, dealing with "bad decisions" and the "morning after."

> At the most uncharted moments in our lives we reach instinctively for the stock plots available to our generation. . . . Now, if you're a woman, there's another role readily available: that of the sensitive female, pinched, leered at, assaulted daily by sexual advances, encroached upon, kept down, bruised by harsh reality. Among other things, feminism has given us this. A new stock plot, a new identity spinning . . . around . . . passivity and victimhood. This is not what I want, not even as a fantasy. (1993, p. 172)

We will leave it to others to rebut Roiphe's claim that rape-crisis feminism has done more harm than good. Our concern is with her narrower claim, but one upon which the foundation of her argument rests: that rape statistics are merely a matter of "opinion" and not of "mathematical fact." In our view, the key issue is about mathematics—or, in our terms, about the quality of the measurement strategies used to assess the extent of sexual victimization among college women. As we will show in a later chapter, Roiphe's argument that she would have known if her classmates were being sexually assaulted appears misguided. Many victims do, in fact, tell their friends when victimized. More than this, her critique of Koss's *Ms.* study and 1-in-4 statistic conflates Koss's commitment to science with the agenda of campus feminists that flourished, some years later, during Roiphe's Harvard University days.

Recall that Koss constructed the first version of her Sexual Experiences Survey well in advance of the *Ms.* study and at a time, in the late 1970s, when feminism's roots were just starting to take hold on colleges campuses (Koss & Oros, 1982; see also Koss, 1988a; Koss et al., 2007). In fact, Koss could not have joined the rape-crisis-feminist club if she had wanted to do so; it did not exist! From the beginning, her motivation was not to artificially inflate rape statistics but to develop an instrument, the SES, that could measure sexual practices that, according to existing state laws, met the criteria of rape (and other forms of sexual victimization). The fact that her study uncovered much hidden rape and sexually coercive victimization was hardly foreordained. Students answering her SES in 1984–1985 were from across the nation—many of them, in fact, from sections of the United States virtually untouched by feminism. Koss did not select the schools sampled, and her data collectors were not radical feminists sent into the field with the mission of urging respondents to get even with their male perpetrators by disclosing their victimization. To be sure, organized skepticism requires that Koss's SES measure and its findings be subjected to critical scrutiny. But it would be imprudent to ignore the central thrust of her study—that sexual victimization is more prevalent than previously imagined—on the assumption that Koss's findings are ideologically tainted.

What's Ahead

There are three important lessons to take from this discussion. First, the study of sexual victimization on college campuses is conducted in the context of an ongoing culture war between feminists and their critics (for a recent example, see Mac Donald, 2008). Each side has a stake in the research findings, with feminists anticipating high prevalence rates and critics preferring low prevalence rates. Second, measurement matters. Especially in an ideologically heated context, research will have credibility only to the extent that its design and measures are above reproach. Even then, results that offend those of one ideological persuasion or the other will be criticized. The best defense to these attacks is a rigorous methodology. Third, Gilbert's and Roiphe's criticisms should not be accepted whole cloth but neither should they be dismissed out of hand for their excesses. At the core of their criticisms is the reminder that even classic studies, including Koss's, have features that potentially produce measurement error. When questions are raised—such as whether wording choices on questions inflate the reporting of rape—the challenge is not to defend the original study but to move beyond and improve what was done. Koss herself has done so (see Koss et al., 2007). So have we.

In fact, this book is the by-product of our attempt to develop a methodologically rigorous measure of sexual victimization and then to undertake a large-scale, national study that would allow us to bring fresh data to the question of the extent and nature of sexual assault on college campuses. We learned from the research of Koss, but, as the saying goes, we have tried to "see farther" by "standing on the shoulders of a giant." But, ultimately, our allegiance was not to Koss or, for that matter, to any side of the culture war on this issue. Rather, our intent was to push aside ideology and to pursue the measurement of empirical reality to the best of our abilities. In the end, our data show that to varying degrees, many female students are unsafe in the ivory tower.

In Chapter 2, we review our methodological adventure into the realm of college student sexual victimization. That chapter conveys how we endeavored to develop a newer way of assessing rape and other types of sexual victimization. Although we integrate much of the existing research into our discussions, the contribution of our book is that we report original data from our project. In Chapter 3, we start our tour through the various dimensions of student sexual victimization. There, we take up the issue so much at the core of the debate over Koss's SES findings: exploring the risk of rape that students face. In Chapter 4, we move beyond the issue of rape to examine how else female students are sexually victimized. This includes probing the extent of sexual coercion, unwanted sexual contact, and noncontact sexual abuse. Chapter 5 illuminates the often neglected issue of revictimization. The data reveal that, to a significant extent and within a limited period of time, women are victimized more than once. We report the factors that place female students at risk of both initial sexual victimization and then of revictimization. In Chapter 6, our attention turns to "victim secrets." As we have seen, an important issue is whether victims acknowledge that they have been raped and are willing to report their victimization to campus or law enforcement officials. We investigate the extent to which some women disclose their victimizations while others do not—and why this is so. Chapter 7 then switches focus away from sexual victimization per se and onto the closely related topic of stalking. Stalking shares much in common with other types of sexual victimization because a male's unwanted, continuing pursuit of a female typically is fueled by sexual attachment and can evoke fear of harm. Finally, Chapter 8 concludes with a discussion of the policy implications of the portrait we have painted of the extent and sources of sexual victimization. Is it possible to make the ivory tower safer? And, if so, how might this worthy goal be achieved?

2

Beyond the Culture Wars

The Measurement of Sexual Victimization

We are unlikely participants in the debate over sexual victimization on college campuses. As the controversy over this issue percolated and then boiled over, we largely sat on the sidelines as observers. We were not culture warriors anxious to enter the fray. Rather, our interests were initially tangential. We had been involved in a broader project that examined crime on campuses, with a special focus on its nature, explanation, prevention, and role in public policy issues (Fisher, 1995; Fisher et al., 1998). As we delved into this research, it became apparent that sexual victimization was potentially a key component of campus crime. As a result, this was a topic that could not be ignored.

But what could we add to this debate? At first, it seemed that our lack of ideological fervor might disqualify us from contributing meaningfully. In the debates that were raging, we had, so to speak, no intellectual dog in this hunt. This is not to say, of course, that we did not have political leanings (mostly progressive). Still, we had no personal investment in confirming, for example, whether the prevalence of rape was high or low.

Upon reflection, however, we thought that our scholarly detachment from the culture war surrounding sexual victimization might be an advantage. It would be hubris to claim that our science is completely value free and untainted by who we are and what we think. Even so, we could enter this field of inquiry with no agenda in mind and with nothing special to prove or disprove. Rather, our task would be to figure out if we could study the topic in a way that would help to resolve the extant debates by producing more solid estimates of the extent to which female students risked sexual victimization.

While studying the research, we concluded that a new measurement strategy was needed. After scrutinizing the literature, we concluded that two main methods of measuring sexual victimization existed but that both had shortcomings if used alone. However, by placing these two strategies together, it seemed possible to create a new and more rigorous measure of rape and other types of sexual victimization.

As we discuss in detail below, we agreed with Koss that behaviorally specific questions are essential to cue respondents to the kind of acts that constitute victimization. However, we were persuaded by critics such as Gilbert that saying "yes" to such questions might not necessarily mean that a woman had been raped or otherwise sexually coerced. The National Crime Victimization Survey had a solution to this problem, which involved using two steps in the interview to determine whether a victimization had been experienced and, if so, which type. In the first step, a respondent was presented with a set of "screen questions" probing whether various victimizations had been experienced. If the respondent answered in the affirmative, then a second step was triggered: a follow-up incident report was used in which the respondent was asked more detailed questions. A series of follow-up questions were employed to determine what happened during a specific incident and how it should be categorized (e.g., rape, sexual assault, some crime other than rape). Why not, then, just rely on the existing NCVS if its two-step process allows for better measurement? Well, as we will see, the screen questions used by the NCVS to cue a respondent to recall a possible victimization are limited in number and not explicitly behaviorally specific like those used in the Sexual Experiences Survey or, as we discuss in more detail later in this chapter, in the National Women's Study, the National Violence Against Women Study, and the National College Women Sexual Victimization Study. As discussed below, the NCVS includes short descriptive cues into its victimization screen questions.

We thus reached the conclusion that we should borrow the best we could from Koss (and similar researchers) and from the NCVS. This meant using a two-step process to measure the victimization of college women:

- Step 1: Use behaviorally specific questions to cue a respondent to recall if she had been sexually victimized. These are called *screen questions*.

- Step 2: If a screen question is answered "yes," then have the interviewer complete a detailed incident report. The answers to the incident report, not to the behaviorally specific screen questions, would determine whether the incident would be counted as a sexual victimization and, if so, then what type of victimization would be said to have occurred.

Let us be clear. We do not argue that our approach to measuring sexual victimization is, or should be, the final methodological word in this area. All studies, including ours, have shortcomings and measurement error. At any given era in the advancement of knowledge, the goal is to devise the best measures possible that yield the most accurate data available. But the goal of science is not to sanctify any study as sacred and beyond criticism. Rather, each advance hopefully is pregnant with the next advance. Only in this way will science become more exacting and knowledge of the world less imperfect.

With this caveat stated, we are convinced that our methodological approach was innovative and perhaps worthy of being called a breakthrough in this area of inquiry. In any event, this approach informed the subsequent national study that we undertook called the National College Women Sexual Victimization Study. Admittedly, that is a mouthful! Therefore, we refer to it by its acronym in the rest of this book: the NCWSV Study. However, because acronyms are easily forgotten and confused with others that will be cited, we will occasionally include the full title of our study so as to avoid any confusion.

This investigation—our NCWSV Study—forms an important part of the chapters that follow. Wherever relevant, we cite other research as well. However, we use this book as a conduit for conveying what our study found and, in particular, the portrait it paints of sexual victimization on the nation's college campuses.

We spend the remainder of this chapter presenting in detail how we developed our sexual victimization measure. We first explore the intricacies of the National Crime Victimization Survey. We then proceed to illuminate how we merged the methods from this survey with those of Koss and others, such as Dean Kilpatrick and his colleagues and Patricia Tjaden and Nancy Thoennes. These latter scholars undertook important national-level studies that have shaped the field and our thinking. Admittedly, some readers might find this upcoming excursion into the depths of measurement somewhat tedious. But as we have seen in the debate over college students' sexual victimization, measurement details are salient because they influence (1) what data will be produced and (2) whether the "rape crisis" is seen as a real problem that has been ignored or as a socially constructed, ideologically inspired myth. In the end, methods matter.

The National Crime Victimization Survey

The major victimization survey in the United States is the National Crime Victimization Survey, known by its acronym the NCVS. It was originally termed the National Crime Survey—that is the NCS. These two surveys—the NCS and the NCVS—have been major sources of information about sexual victimization, although they have also been widely criticized for potentially underestimating the amount of rape in America. The NCS was redesigned into the NCVS during the late 1980s and early 1990s, in part to address this shortcoming in the measurement of sexual victimization (see Bachman & Taylor, 1994; Canter & Lynch, 2000). Annual estimates of rape and sexual assault from the redesigned NCVS were made available starting in 1993.

The NCVS is administered under the auspices of the Bureau of Justice Statistics (BJS). Like its NCS predecessor, the redesigned NCVS is a national household-based survey of an individual's experiences with crime victimization, whether or not the incidents were reported to law enforcement officials. Using a stratified multistage cluster sample, the NCVS collects victimization data from a sample of 90,000 individuals living in housing units (Bureau of Justice Statistics, 1997, Appendix II). The survey employs a rotating panel design of housing units, with each unit being in the sample for 3.5 years; new households are constantly being added to the sample as other households complete their time in the sample. All household members age 12 and older are interviewed by male and female interviewers every 6 months during this period (seven times in all). The first interview is not employed in the reported estimates but is used only to bound the second interview, thus establishing a 6-month reference period for respondents. Thereafter, the previous interview serves as the bound for the subsequent interview. The first and fifth interviews are done in person; all others are conducted by telephone. Further, the NCVS uses computer-assisted telephone interviewing (CATI).

We should caution that in very recent years, financial constraints have resulted in changes in how often the NCVS is undertaken (see Lauritsen, 2005; Rand & Catalano, 2007). Although the survey's underlying methodology was not altered, these methodological cutbacks may mean that estimates from recent years cannot be compared reliably to estimates from previous years (Lauritson, 2009).

How the NCVS Measures Victimization

The major feature of the NCVS is that victimization is measured in a *two-step process*. As noted above, the respondents are first read a series of *screen questions* on whether a victimization may have occurred and, if so, they are then interviewed through a lengthy *incident report* about what did occur. In the NCVS, the interviews include seven individual-level screen questions. The intent of the screen questions is to cue respondents, or jog their memory, as to whether they had experienced a criminal victimization within the 6-month reference period. For this reason, these questions are intended not to be redundant and are designed to elicit a "yes" or "no" regarding victim incidents (Lynch, 1996a, 1996b). When a respondent says "yes" to any screen question, the interviewer then asks him or her "what happened?" (i.e., "briefly describe the incident[s]"). The interviewer in turn asks "how many times" that type of incident occurred during the reference period. Examples of screen questions are furnished in Table 2.1, which can be found in the following section on screen questions.

At the conclusion of the screen questions, the interviewer administers an incident report for each time a respondent mentioned an incident had occurred. This incident report contains detailed questions about the nature of the incident (e.g., month, time, and place of incident; characteristics of the offender; police reporting behavior). It includes questions that ask whether the offender hit, tried to attack, or threatened the respondent, how the respondent was attacked or threatened, and whether injuries were suffered. In short, the incident report is a way of collecting a great deal of information about what occurred during any incident.

Most important—indeed, essential to understand for our purposes—*the NCVS uses the incident report to determine, and thus count, whether a victimization has occurred*. Again, the purpose of the screen questions is to cue the respondent to remember victimization events. Answering "yes" to a screen question only allows the respondent to gain entry into the incident report. At this point, the respondent must answer "yes" to more detailed questions and/or give a verbal account describing a victimization to be counted as having experienced a particular type of victimization. An example of how incident report questions are used to categorize a victimization is presented later in Table 2.2.

Notably, most sexual victimization surveys use only a one-step process, essentially measuring victimization through a series of "cueing" questions that are meant to prompt respondents to recall victimization incidents. This was the case with the classic studies by Russell (1982) and Koss and colleagues (1987) discussed in Chapter 1. The risk of this one-step approach—that is, of not having an incident report—is that it may include reports of victimization that, on closer scrutiny, would not qualify legally as a rape or other type of sexual victimization. Recall that this was Gilbert's (1997) criticism of Koss's research—that her behaviorally specific items may have prompted a "yes" response even though not all of these acts were likely, in reality, to be attempted or completed rapes.

The advantage of the NCVS is that the incident-report questions in essence confirm or validate what occurred to the respondent and led the person to answer "yes" to a screen question. This follow-up thus potentially allows for a more valid categorization of incidents as to (1) whether they took place and, if so, as to (2) what type of victimization transpired. Despite this advantage, the quality of the NCVS as a measure of sexual victimization is contingent on how well the screen questions cue respondents and whether the incident report validly classifies what respondents experienced in the course of a victimization incident. These issues occupy much of our attention in the sections to follow.

The First Step in Measuring Sexual Victimization: The NCVS Screen Questions

In the original NCS, the respondents were asked four screen questions that assessed whether they had been attacked or otherwise physically threatened. The NCS assumed that this broad-based inquiry into being attacked would prompt respondents who had suffered an attack involving rape to answer "yes" to one of these four questions. As critics correctly pointed out, however, the respondents were never asked directly or explicitly if they had experienced a completed or attempted rape (Eigenberg, 1990; Koss, 1992, 1993a). The use of an indirect means on the NCS to "cue" respondents as to their rape, critics argued, would almost certainly mean that some rape or attempted rape victims would not respond "yes" to any of the four screen questions.

Accordingly, the NCS was held to be biased in the direction of underestimating the true incidence of rape and attempted rape victimization (see, e.g., Koss, 1992, 1993a, 1996). Nearly all studies of rape in the United States have reported estimates much higher than those found by the NCS (see Bachman & Taylor, 1994). Moreover, the NCS measured only one type of sexual victimization, rape, and thus did not assess sexual assault.

Given these considerations, the major redesign efforts of the NCS were concentrated in the cueing strategy used in the screening interview (see Bureau of Justice Statistics, 1994a; Canter & Lynch, 2000). The purpose, of course, was to ensure that all those who had been raped or otherwise sexually assaulted would indicate this when first screened. For unless this occurred, then some unknown percentage of victims would never proceed to the second step in the process, the incident report, where a victimization is counted as actually happening. Two important changes were made.

First, new screen questions were added to the NCVS that directly asked respondents about "rape, attempted rape, and any other type of sexual attack" and about "forced or unwanted sexual acts." Second, all the original NCS screen questions were reworded and new cues or information about a potential victimization incident were added. The purpose of adopting more specific cues in the screen questions was to expand the frame of reference for the respondents so as to better stimulate their recall of an incident, thus helping to reduce underreporting because of forgotten incidents.

Thus, the revised NCVS screen questions begin with a reference to a type of criminal victimization that may have been experienced (e.g., "were you attacked or threatened"), which is followed by a list of short cue responses about the potential victimization. This list includes cues regarding specific places or situations in which the victimization could have occurred (e.g., "at work or at school"), objects that could have been used (e.g., "with any weapon, for instance, a gun or knife"), actions that could have been associated with the victimization (e.g., "face-to-face threats"), and people who potentially might have perpetrated the criminal act (e.g., "a relative or family member") (Bureau of Justice Statistics, 1994a). Each of these cues is intended to diminish the effects of subjective interpretations of the questions and to help the respondent structure the recall task before answering the question, "Did any incidents of this type happen to you?" (see Table 2.1).

Table 2.1 lists the four screen questions used on the NCVS to screen for potential incidents of rape and sexual assault. The interviewer asks each respondent these screen questions. The interviewer also is instructed to "briefly describe incident(s)" that the respondent noted. This verbatim account is recorded by the interviewer but is not part of the data files that the Bureau of Justice Statistics—again, known as the BJS—archives at the Inter-University Consortium for Political and Social Research at the University of Michigan. The numbers used in Table 2.1—40a, 41a, 42a, and 43a— correspond to the question numbers used on the NCVS.

In the research literature, most discussion of the NCVS has centered on Questions 41a, 42a, and 43a in Table 2.1 (see Bachman & Taylor, 1994; Koss, 1992, 1996). BJS uses these questions to screen for all types of personal crimes that the NCVS measures (Perkins, Klaus, Bastian, & Cohen, 1996). For our purposes, we also included the first question in Table 2.1 (Question 40a) because it specifically asks the respondent about being threatened in different places. Note that verbal threats are part of the NCVS's definition of rape and sexual assault (see next section). This means that the NCVS uses incidents involving only threats—as opposed to limiting counts to attempted or completed acts—in its estimates of rape and sexual assaults.

Table 2.1 Specific NCVS Individual-Level Screen Questions Designed to Elicit Reports of Rape and Sexual Assault

---

40a. (Other than any incidents already mentioned,) since _____, Year _____, were you attacked or threatened OR did you have something stolen from you— (a) At home including the porch or yard—(b) At or near a friend's, relative's, or neighbor's home—(c) At work or school—(d) In places such as a storage shed or laundry room, a shopping mall, restaurant, bank, or airport—(e) While riding in any vehicle— (f) On the street or in a parking lot—(g) At such places as a party, theater, gym, picnic area, bowling lanes, or while fishing or hunting—OR (h) Did anyone ATTEMPT to attack or ATTEMPT to steal anything belonging to you from any of these places?

41a. (Other than any incidents already mentioned,) has anyone attacked or threatened you in any of these ways *(Exclude telephone threats)*— (a) With any weapon, for instance, a gun or knife—(b) With anything like a baseball bat, frying pan, scissors, or stick—(c) By something thrown, such as a rock or bottle— (d) Include any grabbing, punching, or choking—(e) Any rape, attempted rape or other type of sexual attack—(f) Any face to face threats—OR (g) Any attack or threat or use of force by anyone at all? Please mention it even if you are not certain it was a crime.

42a. People often don't think of incidents committed by someone they know. (Other than any incidents already mentioned,) did you have something stolen from you OR were you attacked or threatened by *(Exclude telephone threats)*— (a) Someone at work or school—(b) A neighbor or friend—(c) A relative or family member—(d) Any other person you've met or known?

43a. Incidents involving forced or unwanted sexual acts are often difficult to talk about. (Other than any incidents already mentioned,) have you been forced or coerced to engage in unwanted sexual activity by—(a) Someone you didn't know before—(b) A casual acquaintance—OR (c) Someone you know well?

SOURCES: Fisher and Cullen (2000); Perkins, Klaus, Bastian, and Cohen (1996, pp.124–125).

NOTE: Question numbers are from the individual screen questions in the basic screen questionnaire.

Again, the screen questions are, in essence, gatekeepers to the respondent proceeding on to the next step to complete an incident report. As a result, the wording of each question is important to the reporting of an incident. In the second question in Table 2.1 (Question 41a), respondents are explicitly asked about rape, attempted rape, and other types of sexual attack (instead of the omnibus "attack you" or "try to attack you" question that was used in the original NCS screen questions). The term *types of sexual attack* is a broad cue to respondents and may work to capture a range of sexual victimization incidents that can then screen into an incident report for further clarification.

Critics of the second question point out that this type of question rests on several assumptions: the respondent knows how rape is defined, perceives what happened to her or him as rape, and remembers the experience with this conceptual label. Underreporting may occur if rape victims fail to realize that their victimization qualifies as a crime and avoid using the term *rape* to describe their experience. Recall that in her study (discussed in Chapter 1), Koss (1988b) found that only 27% of the college women labeled their experiences with forced, unwanted intercourse as rape.

Although the BJS employs Question 42a on the NCVS instrument to screen for all types of personal crimes, this question could be used to screen for rape and sexual assault because it makes reference to potential offenders who could sexually victimize a respondent. Given that a majority of rapes and other forms of sexual victimization are committed by someone the victim knows, this question helps to dispel notions that the survey is only measuring incidents committed by strangers (see Crowell & Burgess, 1996; Koss, 1992). Although the phrase "attacked or threatened" used in this question is an indirect way to ask about rape or sexual assault, it is broad enough to capture a range of incidents that may, or may not, be sexual victimizations (or even victimizations of any kind) once the incident-level responses are taken into account to classify the incident. In this respect, the question could encourage reporting. Use of the term, however, assumes that the respondents will make the connection between being attacked or threatened and unwanted sexual experiences (Koss, 1992). If the respondents do not make this connection, then the gatekeeping function of this question may hinder respondents on the NCVS from reporting a rape or sexual assault incident.

Question 43a on the NCVS explicitly provides the respondents, especially hesitant ones, with a second chance to report a sexual victimization; this is also the case for respondents who do not use the term *rape* or *sexual assault* to label their respective incidents. Within this question, a general definition of what is being measured is provided to the respondent so that she or he knows what type of experience the interviewer is asking about. The question is behaviorally specific; it twice specifically asks respondents about incidents involving "forced or unwanted sexual acts" and about the respondent being "forced or coerced to engage in unwanted sexual activity." The terms used are explicit, yet they are broad enough to include a range of incidents that can be clarified in the incident report. As a gatekeeping question, it could cue or otherwise encourage respondents to report their victimization incidents to the interviewer. Koss (1992) points out several other advantages to this line of questioning that include minimizing the street-violence context within the item. She also suggests, however, that this question might be strengthened if the respondents were told to mention the incident even if they were not certain it was a crime (e.g., see Question 41a).

How well do these four questions screen for incidents whose final classification is a rape or a sexual assault? It is clear that the revisions undertaken were an improvement over the NCS. There are a host of reasons that caution has to be exercised in making comparisons across the two methods (which we will not go into here). But the research is clear that the NCVS produces higher estimates of victimization generally and for rape in particular (Lynch, 1996a). Thus, Taylor and Rand (1995) reported that the revisions resulted in NCVS-method rates that were 323% higher for completed rape and 96% higher for attempted rape than the NCS-method rates. Similarly, a study that employed a split sample test of the two designs revealed a 250% increase in rape estimates using the NCVS methods compared with the NCS methods (Lynch, 1996a).

Still, what cannot be fully determined is whether, even with the revisions, the four NCVS screen questions are able to cue all respondents who have been sexually victimized to report this fact to the survey interviewer. Again, other scholars—such as Russell, Koss, and others to be discussed shortly—argue that behaviorally specific, graphic questions prompt more women to report to interviewers victimizations that are rapes. As such, we cannot estimate how many incidents were not cued by these incident questions and thus never reached the incident report.

It is important to point out that this problem is not unique to the measurement of sexual victimizations. Let us say, for example, that there is a family outing in which too much beer has been consumed and too much taunting between brothers in their 20s has taken place. Angered by a comment, one brother swings at the other, says "I'll kill you!" and has to be restrained from further violence by those present. Six months later, the "victim" in this attack is interviewed as part of the NCVS. His response to Question 40a should be "yes," but he may not conceive of this spat with his brother as an attack. If not, he would answer "no." Alternatively, let us say he was asked: "Has anyone you know, such as your brother, taken a swing at you, even if he did not hit you?" In this case, he might say, "Oh, yeah, my brother did take a swing at me during an outing last summer." In short, more graphic language might prompt a "yes" whereas more general language did not.

Ideally, if a two-step measurement process is used, screen questions should err on the side of being overinclusive. Why? Because there is still an incident report to complete that will probe more fully what occurred and whether the act in question should be counted as an actual victimization. By contrast, narrowly worded screen questions—as some would still characterize those used by the NCVS—prematurely exclude potential victims from the survey. They never are asked what really happened in an incident report.

The Second Step in Measuring Sexual Victimization: The NCVS Incident Report

This all seems fairly complicated, doesn't it? For better or worse, that is the nature of measuring complex acts committed by human beings. Here, matters get even more involved because there is a second step in the NCVS. We have alluded to the incident report a number of times already; now we will discuss it in some detail.

MEASURING RAPE: COMPLETED, ATTEMPTED, OR THREATENED

Forced sexual intercourse includes both psychological coercion and physical force. Forced sexual intercourse means vaginal, anal, or oral penetration by the offender(s). This category also includes incidents where the penetration is from a foreign object such as a bottle. Includes attempted rapes, male as well as female victims, and both heterosexual and homosexual rape. Attempted rape includes verbal threats of rape. (Bureau of Justice Statistics, 1997, p. 149)

The above quotation is how the NCVS defines *rape*. This definition incorporates the legal definition of rape found in legislation passed in the 1970s and 1980s in response to calls for "rape reform" (see Spohn & Horney, 1992). Koss (1996) criticizes the NCVS's definition for being ambiguous with respect to the term *psychological coercion*. She suggests that this term is probably meant to refer to verbal threats of bodily harm or rape, which she notes are crimes. She warns, however, that the term may suggest to respondents "such situations as those involving false promises, threats to end the relationship, continual nagging and pressuring, and other verbal strategies to coerce sexual intercourse" (p. 60), which, as she points out, are undesirable but not crimes.

In any event, as presented in detail in Table 2.2, there are four ways in which the respondent in an incident report can be counted as having experienced a completed rape. Do not be too challenged by the details; bear with us a bit longer. The point of reviewing the NCVS measurement process is to show the complexities of interviewing someone and trying to use structured questions to categorize what kind of criminal victimization, if any, occurred.

In essence, Table 2.2 presents the ways that the NCVS uses to operationalize its definition of rape. Even if the respondents indicate on the screen question that they have been sexually victimized, they do not count as victims unless they answer one of these four sequences of questions in the incident report in a manner consistent with the NCVS's measurement criteria for rape. For example, an answer of "don't know" on a key question may cause an incident not to be counted as a rape victimization.

First, the respondents who answer "yes" to Question 24 in Table 2.2 about being hit or attacked may, in response to the subsequent question regarding how they were attacked, state that they were raped. Note that the interviewer asks this as an open-ended question (see Footnote 5 in Table 2.2). Second, the respondents may answer "yes" to Question 24 but then state that something other than rape occurred when they were attacked. However, when asked whether they suffered any injuries, they may note that they were raped.

Third, if a respondent says "no" to the initial three bodily harm questions (Questions 24, 25, and 26 in Table 2.2), she or he is then asked what actually happened. If the respondent mentions "unwanted sexual contact with force," then the interviewer asks, "Do you mean forced or coerced sexual intercourse including attempts?" If the respondent answers "yes," then the interviewer changes the "no" response to a "yes" for the question, "Did the offender hit you, knock you down, or actually attack you in any way?" The interviewer then proceeds as in the first example of how rape is operationalized. Fourth, the interviewer employs a similar process as the last means of operationalizing completed rape if the respondent says that she or he was threatened with "unwanted sexual contact with force."

Note that in these question sequences, it is assumed that there is a shared definition among the respondents about the word *intercourse*, and that the respondents know the kinds of penetration this word covers. Koss (1992, p. 73) points out, however, that it is "unknown whether women who have had forms of unwanted penetration other than

Table 2.2 Operationalizing Completed Rape in the NCVS Incident Report

Initial Question	Conditional Response	Skip Question				Final Type of Crime Classification
24. Did the offender hit you, knock you down, or actually attack you in any way?	Yes →	29. How were you attacked? Any other way? Mark (X) all that apply[1]		Raped[2] →		Completed rape
24. Did the offender hit you, knock you down, or actually attack you in any way?	Yes →	29. How were you attacked? Any other way? Mark (X) all that apply.	Something other than rape →	31. What were the injuries you suffered, if any? Anything else? Mark (X) all that apply[3]	Raped[4] →	Completed rape
24. Did the offender hit you, knock you down, or actually attack you in any way?	No →	27. What actually happened? Anything else? Mark (X) all that apply[5]	Unwanted sexual contact with force →	Do you mean forced or coerced sexual intercourse including attempts?[6]		Competed rape
25. Did the offender TRY to attack you?						
26. Did the offender THREATEN you with harm in any way?						

(Continued)

Table 2.2 (Continued)

Initial Question	Conditional Response	Skip Question		Final Type of Crime Classification
24. Did the offender hit you, knock you down, or actually attack you in any way?	No →	28a. How did the offender TRY to attack you? Any other way?	*Unwanted sexual contact with force* →	Do you mean forced or coerced sexual intercourse including attempts?[7] → Completed rape
25. Did the offender TRY to attack you?	No →	28b. How were you threatened? Any other way? *Mark (X) all that apply.*		
26. Did the offender THREATEN you with harm in any way?	Yes →			

SOURCE: Fisher and Cullen (2000).

NOTES:

1. The interviewer asked this question as an open-ended question and then listened to the respondent's reply, marking any and all items shown on the list. Included in the list were the following: raped, tried to rape, sexual assault other than rape or attempted rape, shot, shot at (but missed), hit with gun held in hand, stabbed/cut with knife/sharp weapon, attempted attack with knife/sharp weapon, hit by object (other than gun) held in hand, hit by thrown object, attempted attack with weapon other than gun/knife/sharp weapon, hit, slapped, knocked down, grabbed, held, tripped, jumped, pushed, and so on.

36

2. If raped, the interviewer asks the respondent: "Do you mean forced or coerced sexual intercourse?" If no, the interviewer asks the respondent "What do you mean?"

3. The interviewer asked this question as an open-ended question and then listened to the respondent's reply, marking any and all items shown on the list. Included in the list were the following: none, raped, attempted rape, sexual assault other than rape or attempted rape, knife or stab wounds, gunshot, bullet wounds, broken bones or teeth knocked out, internal injuries, knocked unconscious, bruises, black eyes, cuts, scratches, swelling, chipped teeth, or other.

4. If raped, the interviewer asks the respondent: "Do you mean forced or coerced sexual intercourse?" If no, the interviewer asks the respondent "What do you mean?"

5. The interviewer asked this question as an open-ended question and then listened to the respondent's reply, marking any and all items shown on the list. Included in the list were the following: something taken without permission, attempted or threatened to take something, harassed, argument, abusive language, unwanted sexual contact with force (grabbing, fondling, etc.), unwanted sexual contact without force (grabbing, fondling, etc.), forcible entry or attempted forcible entry of house/apartment, forcible entry or attempted forcible entry of car, damaged or destroyed property, attempted or threatened to damage or destroy property, or other.

6. If the respondent says "yes," the interviewer is instructed to go back to Question 24 and change it to a "yes" response, delete entries for questions 25, 26, and 27, and then proceed accordingly (see Row 1).

7. If the respondent says "yes," the interviewer is instructed to go back to Question 24 and change it to a "yes" response, delete entries for questions 25, 26, and 28, and then proceed accordingly (see Row 1).

vaginal, and whether men who have been sodomized, will respond to this wording." Her point is well taken; well-designed experiments in which wording is systematically varied will be needed to further examine the possibility Koss raises.

In addition to completed rape, the NCVS includes measures of attempted rape and verbal threats of rape. There are six ways to operationalize attempted rape and two ways to operationalize verbal threat of rape. Recall that the BJS definition of attempted rape used on the NCVS includes verbal threats of rape. Note that few other studies include verbal threats when counting attempted rapes (see, e.g., Koss et al., 1987).

Four of the six ways to operationalize attempted rape use the identical series of questions employed to operationalize completed rape, with the exception that the respondent either (1) answers "yes" that an attack was tried or physical harm threatened, and/or (2) volunteers that a rape was attempted. There are also two questions that explicitly ask if the offender tried to attack the respondent ("yes" or "no" response) (see NCVS Question 25) and how the offender tried to attack or threatened the respondent (see NCVS Questions 28a and 28b). In the latter question, if the respondent says she or he was verbally threatened with rape and some other type of bodily harm, then the incident is classified as an attempted rape. Similarly, the series of questions that begins with asking the "threaten you with harm in any way" question (see NCVS Question 26) follows a similar line of questioning and responses for an attempted rape classification.

Verbal threats of rape follow the same question series as those for attempted rape. If the respondent says "verbal threat of rape" when asked how the offender tried to attack or threatened the respondent, the incident is classified as a verbal threat of rape. In the NCVS, these are counted under the "attempted rape" estimates.

MEASURING SEXUAL ASSAULT

In the redesign of the NCS, sexual assault was incorporated into the NCVS to measure a type of sexual victimization other than rape. This is an important methodological change. Indeed, many researchers have argued, and empirically documented, that sexual victimization is not unidimensional and limited to rape. Rather, it is multidimensional, covering a variety of types of sexual transgressions. In any event, consistent with the statutory reforms of this period, sexual assault is defined as:

> a wide range of victimizations, separate from rape or attempted rape. These crimes include attacks or attempted attacks generally involving unwanted sexual contact between the victim and offender. Sexual assaults may or may not involve force and include such things as grabbing or fondling. Sexual assault also includes verbal threats. (Bureau of Justice Statistics, 1997, p. 149)

Five types of sexual assault are operationalized in the NCVS: (1) sexual attack with serious assault, (2) sexual attack with minor assault, (3) sexual assault without injury, (4) unwanted sexual contact without force, and (5) verbal threats of sexual assault other than rape.

The respondent is asked the same series of questions as in the rape sequence of questions. The differences are in the respondent's descriptions of how the offender attacked, tried to attack, or threatened to attack the respondent. How sexual assault is operationalized is a bit more complex than how completed rape, attempted rape, or verbal threats of rape are operationalized. Therefore, more clarifications in the line of questioning are needed to ensure that a sexual assault is being measured and not a rape. For example, if the respondent indicates that the offender tried to attack her or him with unwanted sexual contact with force (e.g., grabbing, fondling), the interviewer is instructed to ask the respondent, "Do you mean forced or coerced sexual intercourse including attempts?" If the respondent says "yes," then the interviewer changes the "did the offender hit you" question to "yes" and proceeds accordingly to the "how were you attacked" question. Here, the respondent can describe a rape, attempted rape, sexual assault other than a rape or attempted rape, or anything else that happened.

BEYOND THE NCVS

The NCVS—the National Crime Victimization Survey—is important for two reasons. First, because it is collected by the federal government through the Bureau of Justice Statistics, the statistics that are published each year on completed/attempted rapes, sexual assaults, and other victimizations receive publicity. But to an unknowing public, these statistics are assumed to be accurate. As we have seen, this is a problematic conclusion. Second, although it is imperfect, considerable thought by many talented scholars has gone into the design of the NCVS. Most important, we have reviewed how interviewers must use carefully structured questions to decide if a victimization, such as rape or sexual assault, has occurred.

To us, the key strength of the NCVS is its incident report. Recall that Koss's Sexual Experiences Survey (SES) only used screen or cueing questions. This left her method open to Gilbert's (1997) critique that her behaviorally specific questions might have captured acts that would not actually cross the line that separates crime from bad behavior. But what if Koss had followed up her questions with a more specific incident report? Would not we have the best of both methods? That is, (1) Koss's behaviorally specific questions to make sure everyone who might have been raped or assaulted is prompted to say "yes," and (2) an incident report to address Gilbert's criticism that we need to know more specifically what really happened. As we will see, in designing our national study, this is precisely the lesson that we took from Koss's classic study, Gilbert's critique, the NCVS, and two important studies that we review next.

Measuring Sexual Victimization:
The Next Generation

During the 1990s, investigators built on the methodological insights from researchers such as Koss and her associates in the previous decade, from the Koss-Gilbert methodological debates, and from criticisms of the NCS and the redesigned NCVS. Several features characterized the studies undertaken by this "next generation" of investigators. Thus, they (1) broadened the scope of sexual victimization to include sexual coercion and unwanted physical contact, (2) included newly criminalized offenses such as stalking, and (3) used nationally representative samples of women. Perhaps most important, however, these investigators sought to measure sexual victimization by using behaviorally specific questions that were consciously grounded in the existing legal definition of rape (or other types of sexual victimization).

The next generation of investigators attempted to improve on Koss's work in two ways. First, some researchers employed questions that were more graphically explicit than those in the SES. The new series of questions not only included a description of the behavior in question but also provided a definition of what behaviors the act in question entailed. Second, some scholars in this "next generation" incorporated into their measures a strength that, as we noted, has marked the NCVS—an incident report. The incident report not only allows researchers to gather more details about a given victimization incident but also helps to classify the incident as to the type of sexual victimization, if any, the respondent has experienced.

Some of the methodological advancements we have identified were incorporated in two major national studies completed during the 1990s that examined sexual victimization among women, which we discuss in the next two sections.

The National Women's Study

According to Lynch (1996a, 1996b), the most frequently cited estimates of the incidence of rape in the United States are drawn from the NCS/NCVS and from the National Women's Study undertaken by Dean Kilpatrick and his colleagues (see Kilpatrick, Edmunds, & Seymour, 1992). The National Women's Study is known by the acronym NWS.

STUDY DESIGN

The National Women's Study is a three-year longitudinal study, conducted from 1990 to 1992, that sampled women 18 years of age and older. The NWS used a probability sample of 4,008 adult Americans, including a group of 2,000 women ages 18 to 34 who were oversampled. Kilpatrick and colleagues designed three waves of telephone interviews to collect information about the respondents' major mental health problems and about their alcohol/drug-related problems and consumption. In the first and second waves, they measured forcible rapes that had occurred (1) any time during the respondent's lifetime and (2) within the past 12 months, respectively. Professionally trained female interviewers were employed by the survey firm Schulman, Ronca, & Bucuvalas (SRBI) to administer the survey.

With respect to completed forcible rape, the first wave of interviews was unbounded, but the second wave was bounded by the previous interview. In the first interview, the respondents were asked about their lifetime forcible rape experiences. In the second interview, they were asked to report their forcible rape experiences for the year since their previous interview—that is, the 1-year period between Wave 1 and Wave 2. In both Wave 1 and Wave 2, those respondents who in the screen questions reported an incident, skipped into a sequence of questions about the characteristics of the rape incident(s) (e.g., whether they reported the incident to the police; their relationship to the attacker). Unlike in the NCVS, however, responses to these questions were *not* used to verify what happened but to classify the incident. The responses to the screen questions were used to estimate the extent of lifetime and annual rape, respectively (see Table 2.3). The third interview did not contain any questions about forcible rape or any other forms of sexual victimization.

Eighty-five percent of the women contacted participated in Wave 1. At Wave 2, 81% of the Wave 1 participants (n = 3,220) were located and participated in the study. The participation rate at Wave 2 was therefore 68.9% of the original sample.

MEASURING FORCIBLE RAPE

Kilpatrick and colleagues (1992, p. i) admit to using a "very conservative definition of rape—one which would be legally defined as forcible rape or criminal sexual assault in most states." They define rape as "an event that occurred without the woman's consent, involved the use of force or threat of force, and involved sexual penetration of the victim's vagina, mouth, or rectum" (p. i). Attempted rape was not covered by this definition; accordingly, the NWS measured and reports data only on completed rape.

Kilpatrick et al. (1992, p. 15) used four questions to operationalize their definition of rape, which according to them "provide clear answers for the first time to the critical elements of forcible rape: use of force or threat of force, lack of consent, and sexual penetration." These are contained in Table 2.3. As with Koss's SES instrument, each question is directly worded to describe a narrow, yet explicit, behavior. For example, in the NWS questionnaire (Question 48), the respondent is asked, "Has a man or a boy ever made you have sex by using force or threatening to harm you or someone close to you?" It is possible that some respondents might find this question to be ambiguous; if so, then measurement error might be introduced because these respondents might potentially overreport or underreport their sexual victimization experiences. To minimize the possibility that respondents would be confused about what kinds of experiences the question covers, Kilpatrick and colleagues use a follow-up statement to clarify the specific type of behavior they are asking the respondent about. Thus, in question 48, they follow up with a statement that defines what "sex" means: "Just so there is no mistake, by sex we mean putting a penis in your vagina." A similar follow-up statement containing an explicit definition of the behavior in question is also incorporated in the oral sex question (see Question 49 in Table 2.3).

Table 2.3 Questions in the National Women's Study Used to Elicit Experiences of Completed Rape[1]

Another type of stressful event that many women experience is unwanted sexual advances.[2] Women do not always report such experiences to police or discuss them with friends or family. The person making the advances isn't always a stranger, but can be a friend, boyfriend, or even a family member. Such experiences can occur anytime in a woman's life—even as a child. Regardless of how long ago it happened or who made the advances:

48.[3] Has a man or boy ever made you have sex by using force or threatening to harm you or someone close to you? Just so there is no mistake, by sex we mean putting a penis in your vagina.

49. Has anyone ever made you have oral sex by using force or threat of harm? Just so there is no mistake, by oral sex, we mean that a man or boy put his penis in your mouth or somebody[4] penetrated your vagina or anus with his mouth or tongue.

50. Has anyone ever made you have anal sex by force or threat of harm?[5]

51. Has anyone ever put fingers or objects in your vagina or anus against your will by using force or threat?

52.[6] During your lifetime, how many times (different occasions) have you been forced to have (sex/oral sex/anal sex) or been forcibly penetrated with fingers or objects? Please include any incidents that may have happened when you were a child.

53. Did this (any of these incidents) occur before you were 18 years old?

54. Did this incident (any of these incidents) occur within the past 12 months or since the last time you were interviewed?

SOURCES: Fisher and Cullen (2000); Kilpatrick, Edmunds, and Seymour (1992).

NOTES:

1. Unless noted, the wording of the questions came from the Appendix of the *Rape in America: A Report to the Nation* (Kilpatrick, Edmunds, & Seymour, 1992).
2. This sentence is taken from Lynch (1996b, p. 139).
3. Question numbers were taken from Lynch (1996b, appendix).
4. Lynch's (1996b) version reads ". . .or someone, male or female. . . ."
5. Lynch's (1996b) version reads "[J]ust so there is no mistake, by anal sex we mean that a man or boy put his penis in your anus."
6. Questions 52 through 54 come from Lynch (1996b).

Unlike the SES instrument, Kilpatrick and colleagues broaden the criterion of "threat of force" to include threats of harm not only to the respondent but also to "someone close to" the respondent (see Question 48 in Table 2.3). This wording is used explicitly only in the question measuring penile-vagina penetration and not in the questions measuring other types of penetration (i.e., oral, anal). Further, there is no explanation why this wording on "threats to someone close to you" is used to operationalize rape but is not mentioned in the definition of rape employed by the NWS researchers (see definition quoted previously).

According to the NWS, 13% of the women in the sample reported having experienced a completed forcible rape at least once during their lifetime (Kilpatrick et al., 1992, p. 2). Less than 1% (0.7%) of the women surveyed had experienced a completed rape within the past 12 months. Kilpatrick and associates (1992) compare their estimate of the number of women age 18 or older who were raped during a 12-month period—683,000—with the 1990 NCS's annual estimate of completed and attempted rapes for females age 12 and older—130,000. (The National Crime Survey data were used because its redesign into the NCVS had not yet been completed.) They claim that "the National Women's Study estimate was still 5.3 times larger than the NCS estimate" (p. 2).

This comparison must be interpreted with caution, or at least placed within an appropriate context. First, the NCS and the NWS have different definitions of completed rape. The NCS includes only penile-vaginal penetration, whereas the NWS includes more types of penetration. Second, the NCS's estimate includes completed and attempted rapes, whereas the NWS is limited to completed rapes. (Note, though, that the NCS does divide its rape counts into completed [n = 60,710] and attempted [n = 63,760]; 1990 figures cited here.) Third, the NWS includes females age 18 and older, whereas the NCS includes females age 12 and older. The NCS's results cannot be easily aggregated to match the sample of those 18 years and older because published reports on the NCS use the noncomparable age category of 16 to 19 years old. Note, however, that the NCS data tapes are publicly available, and thus comparable estimates by age could potentially be calculated from these data. Fourth, the NCS estimates cited in the *Rape in America* report include males and females; the NWS includes only females. Fifth, as Lynch (1996a, 1996b) points out, comparing estimates may be confounded because the NWS and the NCS use different procedures for bounding the victimization reference period. Last, the NWS has a 1-year reference period, whereas the NCS has a 6-month reference period.

METHODOLOGICAL LESSONS LEARNED

What methodological advances in measuring rape did the NWS introduce or emphasize? First, moving beyond the many case studies of college women (i.e., surveys of women attending one or two universities), the NWS used a nationally representative sample of adult women. As Koss (1993b, p. 1063) points out, the sample did exclude "several potentially high-risk groups for rape," for example, women living in college residences and women serving in the military. When the NWS was undertaken, however, it was the only national-level study of women in the general U.S. population other than the NCS. Related, Wave 2 of the NWS, which was used to compute the NWS's annual estimates of rape victimization, was bounded by the Wave 1 interview. Bounding has been shown to reduce measurement error associated with *telescoping*—that is, of respondents counting as victimization events that occurred outside the reference period that the survey covered (see Lehnen & Skogan, 1981, 1984). Because panel studies are rare in this area of research (again, the NCVS being the notable exception), this type of bounding is not found in the extant published literature.

Second, unlike many previous surveys, the investigators furnished the respondents with a clearly worded introduction to their rape questions, which contained several cues (1) as to the possibility that a sexual experience may have occurred even though it had not been disclosed to the police, family, and/or friends and (2) as to whom potential offenders might include (i.e., not "always a stranger, but can be a friend, boyfriend, or even a family member"). This introduction is meant to guard against respondents not reporting rape incidents to interviewers because they did not believe that victimizations unreported to others, or committed by people they knew, counted as rape.

Third, a special contribution of the NWS is the wording the researchers developed in the four questions used to measure completed rape. They attempted to employ wording that described the specific behavior in question in very graphic detail (e.g., "by oral sex, we mean that a man or a boy put his penis in your mouth or somebody penetrated your vagina or anus with his mouth or tongue"). These behaviorally specific questions were used to cue the respondent to the particular domain of behavior that was being measured. In this way, the researchers were attempting to minimize measurement error by making sure that respondents would understand what kinds of sexual experiences were covered by the questions being asked.

Despite these advantages, the NWS had three main limitations—measurement issues that later research would address: (1) the definition of rape does not include incidents when the victim was incapacitated, (2) it measured only completed forcible rape and not attempted rape or other forms of sexual victimization, and (3) it did not employ an incident report to "check" or validate whether respondents who answered "yes" to the rape questions should be counted as rape victims.

The National Violence Against Women Survey

The 1990s was a propitious time in which to pursue research on sexual violence against women. As pointed out in Chapter 1, the topic had been "discovered." This ensured that it would be an area of scholarly inquiry that was legitimate and that would be supported by funding agencies. This created the possibility for major studies—including ours. Another one of these large-scale projects was undertaken by Patricia Tjaden, along with her coauthor Nancy Thoennes. This was called the National Violence Against Women Survey. Its acronym is the NVAW Survey. We realize that the acronyms for the various surveys are accumulating; keeping them all straight can be a bit dizzying. As such, we will mention the surveys by their full name on occasion to remind you which study is which.

STUDY DESIGN

Building on Kilpatrick et al.'s National Women's Survey (NWS), Tjaden and Thoennes (1998a) conducted the National Violence Against Women (NVAW) Survey. In the introduction to the interview, the respondents were told that it was a survey on personal safety. The NVAW Survey includes questions about general fear of violence and about incidents of actual or threatened violence experienced during the respondent's lifetime and annually. It focuses in particular—this is a significant feature of the project—on different types of perpetrators. Indeed, 60 types of perpetrators were assessed (e.g., specific parent, spouse, specific ex-spouse, specific partner, cousin). Specific types of violence included sexual victimization (i.e., completed and attempted rape), physical victimization (i.e., slapping, getting beat up, using a gun on the victim), and stalking victimization.

The NVAW Survey is a nationally representative sample of 8,000 English-speaking and Spanish-speaking women 18 years of age and older who reside in households throughout the United States (Tjaden, 1996, p. 1). Using random-digit dialing within U.S. Census regions to draw the sample, eligible women in each household were identified (Tjaden & Thoennes, 1998a, p. 14). If, for example, more than one woman was eligible, a designated respondent was randomly selected using the "most recent birthday method" (Tjaden, 1996, p. 2). That is, the interviewer asked to speak to the female who last had a birthday in the household. The same firm that conducted Kilpatrick's National Women's Study—SRBI—did this survey as well. Using CATI, professionally trained female interviewers employed by SRBI pretested the survey.

The survey was administered from November 1995 to May 1996. The participation rate was 72% (Tjaden, 1996, pp. 3–4).

MEASURING RAPE

Tjaden and Thoennes (1998a, p. 13) defined rape as "an event that occurred without the victim's consent, that involved the use or threat of force to penetrate the victim's vagina or anus by penis, tongue, fingers, or objects, or the victim's mouth by penis." The definition included both attempted and completed rape. Table 2.4 shows how the NVAW Survey measured rape. Note that unlike the NWS, the NVAW Survey measures both completed rape and attempted rape.

The influence of Kilpatrick et al.'s NWS is evident in the questions used by Tjaden and Thoennes. First, both surveys begin the questioning about rape with an introduction for the respondents as to the nature of the questions that follow. Second, both studies use a lifetime reference frame of "regardless of how long ago it happened" to cue respondents. Third, the questions used in the NWS and the questions used in the NVAW Survey provide the respondent with a behaviorally specific definition. For example, Question F1 in Table 2.4 asks the respondent if "a man or boy ever made you have sex by using force or threatening to harm you or someone close to you?" Fourth, to minimize any respondent confusion regarding what behavior the question is asking

Table 2.4 Questions in the National Violence Against Women Study Used to Elicit Experiences of Completed Rape and Attempted Rape

F1. We are particularly interested in learning about violence women experience, either by strangers, friends, relatives, or even by husbands and partners. I'm going to ask you some questions about unwanted sexual experiences you may have had either as an adult or a child. You may find the questions disturbing, but it is important we ask them this way so that everyone is clear about what we mean. Remember the information you provide is confidential.

Regardless of how long ago it happened, has a man or boy ever made you have sex by using force or threatening to harm you or someone close to you? Just so there is no mistake, by sex we mean putting a penis in your vagina.

F2. Has anyone, male or female, ever made you have oral sex by using force or threat of force? Just so there is no mistake, by oral sex we mean that a man or boy put his penis in your mouth or someone, male or female, penetrated your vagina or anus with their mouth.

F3. Has anyone ever made you have anal sex by using force or threat of harm? Just so there is no mistake, by anal sex we mean that a man or boy put his penis in your anus.

F4. Has anyone, male or female, ever put fingers or objects in your vagina or anus against your will by using force or threats?

F5. Has anyone, male or female, ever attempted to make you have vaginal, oral, or anal sex against your will, but intercourse or penetration did not occur?

SOURCES: Fisher and Cullen (2000); Tjaden and Thoennes (1996).

NOTE: These questions were asked only of the female respondents.

about, the respondent is provided with a definition as to type of behavior in question. For example, Question F3 includes the phrase "by anal sex we mean that a man or boy put his penis in your anus" (see Tjaden, 1996, Questions F1–F6). According to Tjaden and Thoennes (1998a, p. 3), "These questions were designed to leave little doubt in the respondents' minds as to the type of information being sought."

By contrast, differences in the wording of the screening questions used in the NVAW Survey and the National Crime Victimization Survey (NCVS) are striking. As we have discussed—and similar to Koss—Tjaden and Thoennes's NVAW Survey uses five behaviorally defined screen questions to prompt respondents to report sexual experiences that meet the legal definition of rape used in many states. This approach thus relies on multiple questions, all narrowly worded, to ask about only one type of crime—rape. The NCVS, however, uses a more general approach in its screen questions. Thus, the screen questions employ general terms—such as asking respondents whether they have experienced "forced or unwanted sexual acts"—to capture a wide range of sexual victimizations, of which rape is but one type. The word *rape* is also used in the NCVS screen questions but not in the NVAW Survey. Finally, and importantly, the NCVS classifies incidents based on responses to the questions in the incident report and not on responses to the screen questions (see Bachman, 1998b). As we will discuss, the NVAW Survey *uses its behaviorally specific screen questions, not its perpetrator report,* to count whether a sexual experience was a completed rape or an attempted rape.

PERPETRATOR REPORT FOR RAPE

After the NVAW Survey interviewer asks the five questions presented in Table 2.4, she then asks the respondent questions concerning the type of perpetrator(s). Unlike the NCVS, which has the interviewers administer a separate incident-level report for the number of times the respondent indicates the incident happened, the NVAW Survey has the interviewers administer a "detailed sexual assault" report for each type of perpetrator (see Section J of the survey). Within this report, the respondent is asked on how many different occasions the specific perpetrator forced or tried to force the respondent to have sex or forcibly penetrate the respondent with his or her fingers or other object; the respondent is then asked when this incident happened. In the case of a single incident, the respondent is asked when this incident happened with respect to the number of years ago or in the past 12 months. If there is more than one incident, then the respondent is asked when was the first time this incident happened and when was the most recent time it happened. Once again, the response is with respect to the number of years ago or in the past 12 months (Tjaden, 1996, Questions J1–J2). Unlike Kilpatrick et al.'s NWS and the NCVS, the NVAW Survey is not bound by a previous interview because it is a cross-sectional design.

CLASSIFYING VICTIMIZATIONS

In Tjaden and Thoennes's NVAW Survey, the interviewers ask about four types of offenses—each with its own set of screen questions. For rape, the questions in Table 2.4 are used to determine whether the respondent experienced a completed rape or an attempted rape. The perpetrator report is used to determine when the rape occurred, not if a rape occurred. If a respondent answers "yes" to any of these questions, she is then counted as a rape victim. However, Tjaden and Thoennes do provide separate estimates for completed rape and attempted rape (see following discussion).

Thus, the NVAW Survey assumes that coherent sets of questions that cover a given domain of conduct (e.g., rape) and that these questions worded in a behaviorally specific way will yield accurate responses from women as to whether they have been sexually victimized. Again, this is similar to Koss's SES. In contrast, the NCVS assumes that the main purpose of such questions—which it calls "screen questions"—is to cue the respondent to recall that she had experienced some type of sexual victimization during the reference period. The NCVS then assumes that the set of questions in the incident report is needed to probe more carefully the detailed nature of the victimization experience ("what actually happened"). Accordingly, the NCVS uses responses from these second set of questions to classify victimizations.

COMPARISON OF RAPE RESULTS

Tjaden and Thoennes's results revealed that 17.6% of the surveyed women reported having experienced a completed (14.8%) or attempted rape (2.8%) during their lifetime. The NVAW Survey's estimate of completed rape is only slightly higher than the NWS's lifetime estimate of 13%. The NVAW Survey also found that 0.3% of the women reported experiencing a completed or attempted rape in the previous 12 months.

Tjaden and Thoennes (1998a) note that it is difficult to make direct comparisons between their estimates and the NCVS rape estimates. Bachman (1998b), however, attempted to address this issue by disaggregating the NCVS data to create rape estimates that would be more comparable to the NVAW Survey. Thus, she compares annual rape estimates for women 18 years and older who were raped by a lone offender. She reports that the NVAW Survey's rape estimate of 0.35 victims per 100 women is higher than the NCVS estimate of 0.16 victims per 100 women. She argues that "this difference underscores the very sensitive nature of estimation procedures and how slightly different methodological procedures can result in quite diverse estimates" (p. 16).

Making comparisons between Kilpatrick et al.'s NWS and Tjaden and Thoennes's NVAW Survey is also complicated. To be sure, these studies share many important features:

- Moving beyond the common reliance on college student samples, both used a nationally representative sample of women age 18 and older.

- They employed the same survey firm (SRBI), whose professionally trained interviewers used CATI.

- Both used a lead-in introduction to the screen questions to alert respondents that victimizations could involve incidents unreported to the police and committed by intimates.

- Their screen questions contained similar wording, and both are behaviorally specific about the types of experiences in question.

- Both used responses to their respective screen questions and time-frame questions to determine lifetime and annual estimates.

Despite these similarities, the NWS asked questions only about completed rape, not about attempted rape, whereas the NVAW Survey measured both completed rape and attempted rape. Of course, it might be possible to compare the NWS and the NVAW Survey figures for completed rapes. However, Tjaden and Thoennes (1998a) do not report annual estimates for completed and attempted rape separately. As a result, at this time, no comparison can be made to Kilpatrick et al.'s (1992) NWS annual estimate for completed rape.

STALKING

In the NVAW Survey, Tjaden and Thoennes also collected data on a form of victimization that has earned increasing public and legal attention: stalking. To date, only two national-level studies do so: the NVAW Survey and our investigation of college women (see Chapter 7 where we discuss our study's findings). Building their definition of stalking from the model antistalking codes for states developed by the National Institute of Justice, Tjaden and Thoennes (1998b, pp. 2–3) defined stalking as

> a course of conduct directed at a specific person that involves a repeated visual or physical proximity, nonconsensual communication, or verbal, written or implied threats, or a combination thereof, that would cause a reasonable person fear with repeated meeting on two or more occasions.

They clarify this definition by stating that "the NVAW Survey does not require stalkers to make a credible threat against the victim, but it does require victims to feel a high level of fear" (p. 3).

Space precludes a detailed review of how stalking is measured by Tjaden and Thoennes (1998b, p. 17). Still, we can note two central findings in the NVAW Survey:

- 8.1% of the women reported being stalked at some time in their life.
- Only 1% of the women reported being stalked in the previous 12 months.

Tjaden and Thoennes's (1998b) estimates of stalking, however, are dependent on what level of fear they use to count a respondent as a victim. Unlike other criminal offenses, legal statutes often assert that stalking is a crime only if it induces fear of being harmed in a reasonable person. The question that emerges is what it means legally to say that someone is "fearful" and, in turn, how this concept should be measured in victimization surveys. Tjaden and Thoennes made the decision to use a stringent criterion, counting as stalking victims only those women who said that stalking behavior had made them feel "very" frightened. However, if the standard is lowered to include women who said they felt "somewhat" or "a little" frightened, then the prevalence of stalking victimization in the NVAW sample rises markedly:

- The lifetime estimate increases from 8.1% to 12%.
- The estimate for the past 12 months jumps from 1% to 6%.

These results again reveal the challenge of measuring the victimization of women and how methodological decisions can affect the estimates that researchers produce.

The National College Women Sexual Victimization Study

Attentive readers now know a great deal about the measurement of sexual victimization! Indeed, in this chapter, readers have traced the precise steps that we took as we contemplated how best to design our own investigation on the topic of campus sexual victimization. We called this subsequent project the "National College Women Sexual Victimization Study." In line with other researchers, we developed an acronym as well: the NCWSV Study.

So, what did we learn from our methodological excursion? As readers might interpret from their own travels, we detected two methods for measuring rape and sexual aggression:

- First, Koss's SES, Kilpatrick's NWS, and Tjaden and Thoennes's NVAW Survey all used *behaviorally specific questions* both to cue respondents to disclose their sexual victimization and, if they did so, to classify victims as to the type of victimization experienced.

- Second, the NCVS used responses to questions in an *incident report* to classify incidents as to the type of crime, if any, that the victim experienced.

To reiterate, the strength of the behaviorally defined questions is that the respondent is provided with descriptive cues within a scenario framework. This makes it more likely that the respondent will recall an event and/or understand that the event might be a victimization. Using only behaviorally specific questions, however, assumes both that the respondent understands the experience she is being asked about and that these questions can cue accurate recall by the respondent (i.e., a rape question cues all rape victims to answer "yes"; an attempted rape question cues all attempted rape victims to answer "yes"; and so on). These assumptions are problematic, especially in the absence of follow-up questions to probe in detail what actually transpired in any given incident. Again, this is why critics, such as Neil Gilbert, were able to question the statistics that researchers, such as Mary Koss, have otherwise carefully produced.

By contrast, herein lies the strength of the NCVS and its use of an incident report. As discussed, the NCVS's measurement process includes screen questions about the criminal act followed by a series of short cues. Each victimization the respondent reports (answers "yes" to) is then followed up with a detailed incident report that contains multiple questions about what occurred during the incident. The responses to these questions are then used to classify the type of victimization that occurred. Of course, the NCVS's Achilles' heel is its screen questions; they are not sufficiently behaviorally specific.

It was at this point that we had an important insight. Why not take the best and avoid the worst of these two methodological approaches? And, indeed, this is precisely what we did! Thus:

- From Koss and similar researchers, we borrowed the idea to include in the design a series of behaviorally specific, graphically worded cueing or screen questions across a range of sexual victimizations.

- From the NCVS, we incorporated into the design the screen question–incident report method.

The result was a method that measures sexual victimization by cueing and screening potential victims with behaviorally specific questions and then classifies the type of victimization, if any, through a detailed incident report (Belknap, Fisher, & Cullen, 1999; Fisher, Cullen, & Turner, 1999; Fisher, Cullen, & Turner, 2000).

STUDY DESIGN

We designed the National College Women Sexual Victimization (NCWSV) Study to estimate the extent of different forms of sexual victimization among college women and to examine risk factors associated with such victimizations. We collected sexual victimization data from a random sample of female undergraduate and graduate college students during the 1996–1997 academic year. A total of 4,446 college women enrolled at 233 2-year and 4-year schools were selected using a two-stage probability sampling design (see Fisher et al., 1999, Chapter 2).

Approximately 2 weeks before a respondent was called, she was sent a cover letter that explained the nature of the study and its procedures (e.g., telephone call from a female interviewer, an 800 number and an e-mail address to contact for more information, voluntary participation, confidentiality). The cover letter was clear that the intent of the study was to examine the extent and nature of unwanted sexual victimizations. To administer the telephone survey, we contracted with SRBI—the same company used by Kilpatrick et al. in the NWS and by Tjaden and Thoennes in the NVAW Survey. SRBI used CATI and employed professionally trained female interviewers. The field period began in late February and ended in early May 1997. The response rate was 84.6%. Before undertaking the survey, the content and flow of the cover letter, the introduction to the survey, and the screen questions were discussed during two focus groups conducted at the University of Cincinnati. We also pretested the survey instruments in spring of 1996 with a random sample of 100 female students enrolled at the University of Cincinnati.

MEASURING SEXUAL VICTIMIZATION

Previous researchers had measured a limited range of sexual victimization (see, e.g., Kilpatrick et al., 1992; Koss et al., 1987; Muehlenhard & Linton, 1987; Tjaden & Thoennes, 1998a). By contrast, we measured 12 different forms of sexual victimization, including rape, sexual coercion, unwanted sexual contact, various threats, and stalking. Much of our concern is with attempted and completed rape, and thus we emphasize this issue below. Chapter 3 explores these issues in more detail. In later chapters, we present data and discuss relevant measurement issues on other types of sexual victimization.

Following the tradition of grounding our definition of rape in legal statutes, we defined rape to include unwanted penetration (completed and attempted) by force or threat of force. Penetration included penile-vaginal, mouth on genitals, mouth on someone else's genitals, penile-anal, digital-vaginal, digital-anal, object-vaginal, and object-anal.

As shown in Table 2.5, we used 12 behaviorally specific questions to screen for different types of sexual victimization. The numbers next to the items correspond to the question number on our survey instrument (just in case readers would like to find the original questions). All contain the same reference period—"since school began in the Fall of 1996." The reference period was approximately 7 months (6.91 months on average) This period is similar to the time frame of the NCVS, which interviews panel members every 6 months.

Table 2.5 Screen Questions in the National College Women Sexual Victimization Study Used to Elicit Possible Experiences of Rape and Other Forms of Sexual Victimization

Women may experience a wide range of unwanted sexual experiences in college. Women do not always report unwanted sexual experiences to the police or discuss them with family and friends. The person making the advances is not always a stranger, but can be a friend, boyfriend, fellow student, professor, teaching assistant, supervisor, coworker, somebody you meet off campus, or even a family member. The experience could occur anywhere: on- or off-campus, in your residence, in your place of employment, or in a public place. You could be awake, or you could be asleep, unconscious, drunk, or otherwise incapacitated. Please keep this in mind as you answer the questions.

Now, I'm going to ask you about different types of unwanted sexual experiences you may have experienced since school began in the Fall 1996. Because of the nature of unwanted sexual experiences, the language may seem graphic to you. However, this is the only way to assess accurately whether or not the women in this study have had such experiences. You only have to answer "yes" or "no."

7. Since school began in the Fall 1996, has anyone *made* you have *sexual intercourse* by using *force or threatening to harm* you or someone close to you? Just so there is no mistake, by intercourse I mean putting a penis in your vagina.

8. Since school began in the Fall 1996, has anyone *made* you have *oral sex by force or threat of harm*? By oral sex, I mean did someone's mouth or tongue make contact with your vagina or anus or did your mouth or tongue make contact with someone else's genitals or anus.

9. Since school began in the Fall 1996, has anyone *made* you have *anal sex by force or threat of harm*? By anal sex, I mean putting a penis in your anus or rectum.

10. Since school began in the Fall 1996, has anyone ever used *force or threat of harm to sexually penetrate you with a foreign object*? By this, I mean, for example, placing a bottle or finger in your vagina or anus.

12. Since school began in Fall 1996, has anyone *attempted but not succeeded* in making you take part in any of the unwanted sexual experiences that I have just

asked you about? *This would include threats that were not followed through.* For example, did anyone threaten or try but not succeed to have vaginal, oral, or anal sex with you or try unsuccessfully to penetrate your vagina or anus with a foreign object or finger?

14. Not counting the types of sexual contact already mentioned, have you experienced any *unwanted or uninvited touching of a sexual nature* since school began in the Fall 1996? This includes forced kissing, touching of private parts, grabbing, and fondling, even if it is over your clothes. Remember this could include anyone from strangers to people you know well. Have any incidents or *unwanted or uninvited touching of a sexual nature* happened to you since school began in the Fall 1996?

16. Since school began in Fall 1996, has anyone *attempted or threatened but not succeeded in unwanted or uninvited touching of a sexual nature?*

18. I have been asking you about unwanted sexual contact that involved force or threats of force against you or someone else. Sometimes unwanted sexual contact may be attempted using threats of nonphysical punishment, promises of *rewards* if you complied sexually, or simply continual *verbal pressure.* Since school began in Fall 1996, has anyone made or tried to make you have sexual intercourse or sexual contact when you did not want to by making *threats of nonphysical punishment* such as lowering a grade, being demoted or fired from a job, damaging your reputation, or being excluded from a group for failure to comply with requests for any type of sexual activity?

19. Since school began in the Fall 1996, has anyone made or tried to make you have sexual intercourse or sexual contact when you did not want to by *making promises of rewards* such as raising a grade, being hired or promoted, being given a ride or class notes, or getting help with course work from a fellow students if you complied sexually?

20. Since school began in the Fall 1996, has anyone made or tried to make you have sexual intercourse or sexual contact when you did not want to by simply being *overwhelmed by someone's continual pestering and verbal pressure*?

22. Not counting any incidents we have already discussed, have you experienced any other type of unwanted or uninvited sexual contact since school began in the Fall? Remember, this could include sexual experiences that may or may not have been reported to the police or other officials, which were with strangers or people you know, in variety of locations both on- and off-campus, and while you were awake, or when you were asleep, drunk, or otherwise incapacitated.

24. Since school begin in the Fall 1996 has anyone—from a stranger to an ex-boyfriend—*repeatedly* followed you, watched you, phoned, written, e-mailed, or communicated with you in other ways *in a way that seemed obsessive and made you afraid or concerned for your safety?* This includes waiting outside your class, residence, workplace, other buildings, or car.

SOURCE: Fisher and Cullen (2000).

NOTES: Each question was asked using a "yes-no" response set. After each series of questions or question (7, 8, 9, and 10; 12; 14; 16; 18, 19, and 20; 22) the following question was asked: "How many different incidents of [type of sexual victimization] happened to you since school began in the Fall 1996?"

After the stalking screen question (24) the following question was asked: "How many people have exhibited this type of behavior toward you since school begin in the Fall?

Numbers in this table correspond to the number of questions as they appeared in the original survey.

As in the NWS and the NVAW Survey, we included an introduction that explained the context of the study, cued respondents as to different situations and various potential perpetrators, and alerted them that graphic language would be used on the survey. This is provided in Table 2.5. Here are the other important features of the screen questions:

- The rape questions (Questions 7, 8, 9, 10, and 12) were similar, if not identical, to the ones used in the NWS (Kilpatrick et al., 1992) and the NVAW Survey (Tjaden & Thoennes, 1998a).
- Note how the completed rape questions (7, 8, 9, and 10) provided a graphic description of the behavior in question and a definition of what was meant by each term we used. Again, they are, like the other questions asked, all behaviorally specific.
- Attempted rape was screened by Question 12.
- Sexual coercion was screened by Questions 18, 19, and 20.
- Unwanted sexual contact was screened by Questions 14 and 16.
- Stalking was screened by Question 24.

When a respondent said "yes," that she had experienced the type of behavior asked about in the screen question, she was asked which different incidents of this type had happened to her (see Table 2.6). Similar to the NCVS, for every different incident, the interviewer completed an incident report.

MEASURING RAPE THROUGH THE INCIDENT REPORT

Modeled after the NCVS incident report, we also designed two incident reports: one for rape, sexual coercion, unwanted sexual contact, and threats, and one for stalking. In the first incident report, we obtained information (1) to determine exactly what type(s) of sexual victimization, if any, occurred based on types of physical and/or sexual contact and form of coercion, and to what degree (completed, attempted, or threatened); (2) to document information about the characteristics of the incident; and (3) to understand the reporting behaviors of the victim. The incident report for stalking differed, in part because stalking is a continuing event. It is discussed in Chapter 7.

To determine if the respondent had experienced a rape (either completed or attempted), we developed a series of questions. These are shown in Table 2.6. This process of categorizing what happened is complicated; it is easy at first glance to lose one's way in the details. This is why professionally trained interviewers are essential. Further, as with the NCVS, this detail was necessary to ensure that the criteria for an attempted or completed rape were met and to ensure that every student received the same interview. In short, these details are a systematic attempt to reduce measurement error. We will try to lead readers through the steps as clearly as possible.

Table 2.6 Incident Report Questions Measuring Rape and Attempted Rape in the National College Women Sexual Victimization Study

Initial Question	Response	Skip Question	Response	Skip Question	Response	Final Classification
R12. Was the sexual contact in this incident threatened, attempted, or completed (at least some sexual contact actually happened)?	Completed →	R13. Tell me which of the following actually occurred to you during this incident. Just say yes or no. Did you experience . . . .[1] **READ LIST AND MULTIPLE RECORD**	Any response from 1 through 8 in Footnote 1 →	R17. Was physical force actually used against you in this incident?[2] R18. Were you threatened with physical force in this incident?	Yes →	Completed rape
R12. Was the sexual contact in this incident threatened, attempted, or completed (at least some sexual contact actually happened)?	Attempted →	R15. What (other) type of unwanted sexual contact was ATTEMPTED?[3] **READ LIST AND MULTIPLE RECORD**	Any response from 1 through 8 in Footnote 1 →	R17. Was physical force actually used against you in this incident?[4] R18. Were you threatened with physical force in this incident?	Yes →	Attempted rape

SOURCE: Fisher and Cullen (2000).

NOTES:

1. The list included (1) penis in your vagina, (2) a mouth on your genitals, (3) your mouth on someone else's genitals, (4) penis in your anus or rectum, (5) finger in your vagina, (6) finger in your anus or rectum, (7) another object in your vagina, (8) another object in your anus or rectum, or (9) none of these.

2. If the respondent said "no" to R17, she is then asked R18.

3. The list included (1) penis in your vagina, (2) a mouth on your genitals, (3) your mouth on someone else's genitals, (4) penis in your anus or rectum, (5) finger in your vagina, (6) finger in your anus or rectum, (7) another object in your vagina, (8) another object in your anus or rectum, (9) touching, grabbing, or fondling of your breasts or genitals under your clothes, (10) touching, grabbing, or fondling of your breasts or genitals over your clothes, (11) kissing, licking, or sucking, (12) some other form of unwanted sexual contact, and (13) none of these.

4. If the respondent said "no" to R17, she is then asked R18.

First, the interviewer asked the respondent if the incident was threatened, attempted, or completed (see Question R12 in Table 2.6). Depending on the response, the interviewer then asked the respondent which sexual act(s) was completed, which act(s) was attempted, and/or which act(s) was threatened. We collected information on these three degrees of victimization because we believed that an incident could be a single victimization, but it could also involve a series of victimizations that led to the most serious type of victimization experienced.

A respondent could answer one of the three responses or all three responses because it was possible that a single incident resulted in more than one victimization, either of the same type or of a different type. For example, if a respondent reported that there was attempted vaginal-penile penetration with force and completed unwanted sexual contact (e.g., touching of her breasts or buttocks) with the threat of force, then there were two victimizations during this one incident: an attempted rape and completed sexual coercion. Another incident could have included the same type of victimization: a completed penile-vaginal penetration with force and an oral-genital penetration with force (both are completed rapes). Information was collected on all victimizations for that respondent arising from a single incident.

Because some incidents involved more than one type of victimization, counting each would have inflated our counts of the different types of victimization. To address this methodological concern, we classified each incident as to the most severe type of sexual victimization that the respondent experienced with that specific incident. Koss and associates (1987, p. 165) also used this "most severe" scoring procedure for respondents in her study. The NCVS uses this type of procedure, too. This is known as hierarchical coding or scoring.

As shown in Row 1 of Table 2.6, if the respondent indicated that the sexual contact was completed, she was then asked which type(s) of penetration was completed. The interviewer read her a list of different types of penetration (see Footnote 1 in Table 2.6). The respondent answered with a "yes" or "no" answer to one, some, or all the types of penetration.

The respondent was then asked two questions about the use of physical force or threatened use of physical force (see Questions R17 and R18 in Table 2.6). First, the interviewer asked her if physical force was used against her (see Question R17 in Table 2.6). If she said "yes," the incident was classified as a completed rape. If she said "no" to Question R17, the interviewer asked the respondent if she was threatened with physical force (see Question R18 in Table 2.6). If she said "yes," the incident was classified as a completed rape.

As shown in Row 2 of Table 2.6, an incident was classified as an attempted rape using the same series of questions that we discussed for a completed rape incident. The one difference is that the respondent indicated that the sexual contact included an attempted type(s) of penetration.

It would be premature to discuss the results of our study in detail. But we will disclose that main finding, which we will return to later. Thus, close to 2% (1.7%) of the college women in our sample experienced a completed rape since school had begun in fall of 1996. Slightly more than 1% (1.1%) of the sample experienced an attempted rape. The percentage of the respondents who experienced either a rape or an attempted rape was 2.5%. We explore these findings and their meaning in light of the existing controversy over rape on among college women in Chapter 3.

Revisiting the Koss-Gilbert Debate

As might be recalled from Chapter 1 and subsequent discussions, Neil Gilbert claimed that Mary Koss's use of behaviorally specific questions to measure rape would yield measurement inaccuracies. In the next chapter, we conclude that Koss's general portrait of rape on college campuses was fairly accurate. Here, however, we want to focus more narrowly on what a "yes" response on a behaviorally specific question means. Recall that because we follow up these questions with an incident report, we are uniquely able to assess whether a rape is, or is not, confirmed to have occurred.

ANSWERING "YES" TO A BEHAVIORALLY SPECIFIC RAPE QUESTION

As we have seen, studies such as Koss's college women, Kilpatrick's NWS, and Tjaden and Thoennes's NVAW Survey assume that a "yes" response to one of the behaviorally specific rape questions accurately measures whether a respondent has in fact been raped. In Table 2.7, we present results from our study that questions this approach. Our procedure is simple: first, we see how many respondents answered "yes" to the behaviorally specific screen questions; second, we check to see how many of these responses are confirmed in the incident report as being a rape.

Thus, in our study, the rape screen questions detected 314 incidents. However, only 25.2% were ultimately classified as a rape once respondents were probed further as to what occurred with questions in the incident report (see Table 2.7). In contrast, nearly half (49.4%) of the incidents that entered the incident report via the rape screen questions were classified as a type of sexual victimization other than a rape. Further, the fact that a respondent answered "yes" to a rape screen question does not necessarily mean that it can be determined that a victimization had, in fact, occurred. Slightly more than a fourth (25.5%) of the incidents cued by the screen questions could not subsequently be classified in the incident report. Here, 18.8% of these incidents could not be classified because the respondent refused to answer or said "don't know" to questions that would have allowed us to classify the incident (e.g., refused to answer the force questions but indicated that penetration took place). In 6.7% of the incidents, the respondent could not recall enough details to complete an incident report, or the incident was out of the reference period. Research studies that count incidents such as these as rapes thus risk including incidents in their victimization totals that may not qualify legally as rapes.

Table 2.7 Incident Classification in the National College Women Sexual Victimization Study

SOURCES: Fisher and Cullen (2000); Fisher, Cullen, and Turner (1999).

NOTES: The reported estimates do not include threats of rape.

1. In the stalking incident report, if the respondent indicated that the perpetrator made or attempted to make the respondent have unwanted sexual contact, she was then asked if she had mentioned this incident(s) when asked about unwanted sexual intercourse or contact earlier in the survey. If she said "no," the interviewer then administered a sexual victimization incident report for that incident(s).

2. We could not determine what happened because the respondent refused or said "don't know" to questions that would have allowed us to classify the incident.

Use of the incident report dramatically changed our rape estimate. If we had counted all 314 incidents that screened in to the incident report on our rape screen question, our victimization rate would have been 2 times higher than our rate calculated from the incident report—70.6 per 1,000 college women, compared with 35.3 per 1,000 college women.

ANSWERING "YES" TO A NON-RAPE SCREEN QUESTION

Gilbert might take solace in these results, but, alas, the situation becomes more complicated than he imagined! What neither Gilbert nor Koss anticipated is that answers to other screen questions—those not written to measure rape—might ultimately result in respondents' disclosing a rape incident. And this is what did occur. Thus, our method allowed respondents to screen into an incident report from any of our 12 screen (or cueing) questions (listed in Table 2.5). Regardless of the screen questions to which the respondent answered "yes," the subsequent, detailed incident report questions as to what "actually happened" allowed for the possibility that the incident could be classified as a rape if the respondent's answers met the required criteria.

As the results in Table 2.7 show, close to half (49.7%) of the incidents that we classified as a completed rape or an attempted rape screened in on our non-rape screen questions. A closer look at our findings reveal that all five non-rape screen questions yielded at least one incident that we classified as a rape. For example, the two non-rape screen questions that subsequently resulted in the highest number of classified rape incidents were the unwanted or uninvited touching question and the sexual coercion question (23.6% and 14.6% of the rape incidents, respectively). Again, a method that relied only on cueing questions and that did not include an incident report would have omitted these incidents from the count of rape incidents experienced by women in the sample.

These results again illuminate the challenges of measuring, during a telephone interview using a structured victimization survey, the nature of a sexual victimization that may have occurred. The value of our national study is that it allows us to unpackage the responses of the survey's participants in ways other prominent studies cannot. This transparency allows us to show precisely how our methodological choices produce the victimization statistics we later cite.

Comparing Two Studies

We have one final methodological issue to tackle. It is pretty interesting and returns us to issues discussed earlier. During the same time as the NCWSV Study, we were able to conduct yet another national-level study to examine the extent and nature of violence among college women. This was called the National Violence Against College Women

(NVACW) Study. The acts of violence that we collected data on included rape, sexual assault, robbery, aggravated assault, simple assault, and unwanted sexual contact. The response rate for this study was 91.6% (Fisher et al., 1999).

Here is what is important. This second study used virtually the same methods in conducting the survey as the NCWSV Study (e.g., the same sampling design, sent a cover letter to selected respondents, and had the same reference period and field period). But there was one critical exception. It was designed so that it measured victimization—including rape—in the *same way as the BJS's National Crime Victimization Survey*. Thus, in terms of measuring sexual victimization—specifically rape and sexual assault—we used all the violence screen questions contained in the NCVS. And in the incident report, we included those questions that were needed to determine the type of violent incident that the respondent had experienced (e.g., what happened, what was attempted, what was threatened, use of a weapon).

Readers might understand why this was important. This approach allowed us to conduct a measurement experiment: we could compare our two-step method of measuring victimization with the approach used by the National Crime Victimization Survey. Recall that we use behaviorally specific screen questions, whereas the NCVS does not. The analysis revealed that, indeed, methods matter, and specific to our focus, measurement matters.

A comparison of the two studies revealed that the estimate of rape in the NCWSV Study (the first project) is substantially higher than in the NVACW Study (the second project). For example, the rate of completed rapes per 1,000 female students was 9.5 times larger in the NCWSV Study than the NVACW Study—19.34 and 2.03, respectively. The incidence rate of attempted rape also revealed a similar pattern. The NCWSV Study had markedly higher estimates—8.8 times larger—than the NVACW Study estimates (15.97 compared with 1.81 attempted rapes per 1,000 female students) (Fisher & Cullen, 1999).

These results suggest, then, that even with a redesigned format, surveys using the National Crime Victimization Survey method to measure rape are likely to report far lower rates of victimization than surveys using behaviorally specific screen questions—even when these questions, as in the NCWSV Study (our first project) are also accompanied by an incident report similar to the NCVS. This finding thus confirms the initial wisdom of Mary Koss and others in trying to find innovative ways to measure rape and other forms of sexual victimization that went beyond the NCVS and other more traditional ways of painting a statistical portrait of sexual victimization against women in the United States.

Conclusion

Measuring sexual victimization is a challenging enterprise—the "biggest methodological challenge in survey research" (Smith, 1987, p. 185; see also Fisher &

Cullen, 2000). Although at times committed by strangers in public places, sexual victimization incidents, including rapes, are most often perpetrated by someone the victim knows, in a residence, and with one or more of the parties using alcohol, drugs, or both. Discerning how much force has been used, or the extent to which consent has not been given, is a daunting methodological task; objective behaviors may be open to diverse interpretations or "constructions of reality" by the people involved in an incident and by researchers seeking to measure what has occurred. This situation is complicated by the fact that many victims deny that their victimization has crossed the line to an attempted or completed rape, and that most do not report their victimization to the police, often saying that the incident was not "serious enough" to warrant such a step (see Chapter 6). Some researchers suggest that whether a victim defines an act as a rape or reports it to the police is irrelevant to whether a crime has transpired; others argue, however, that these very facts raise doubts about whether a sexual victimization has taken place (see, e.g., Gilbert, 1997; Koss, 1993a, 1996).

Some scholars' interest in measuring sexual victimization has been fueled, at least in part, by their political values. Without such value-laden interest, the progress in this area might have been slower, and our understanding of the extent of sexual victimization might have been commensurately limited. The risk, however, is that the politicization of the normally prosaic issue of how to measure crime/victimization pushes scholars into competing camps—one seeming to have a stake in finding as much sexual victimization as possible and the other seeming to have a stake in finding as little sexual victimization as possible. The ensuing "advocacy battles" may at times produce good scholarship, but they also risk generating more heat than light.

Thus, in this chapter, we have asked readers to move beyond the culture wars that have surrounded the study of sexual victimization—just as we, ourselves, have endeavored to do. The discussion has focused instead on the major methodological efforts to measure rape and other types of sexual victimization. We have tried to show both how measurement on this topic has evolved over time and the painstaking work that has gone into research studies. There is much to respect about and learn from these investigations.

Most important, we trust that readers are now equipped to understand the sexual victimization statistics that will be cited—including those based on our NCWSV Study—in the remainder of this book. Too often, readers are asked to consume such data with no real knowledge of how such numbers have been produced. This chapter, however, should serve as a methodological primer that makes understanding and critical analysis more possible. It is often said that there are "lies, damn lies, and statistics." But this is only true for those who lack a methodological lie detector test—who know too little to decipher which statistics reflect as opposed to which statistics distort empirical reality. Again, our goal has been to supply readers with the insight to know the difference and appreciate the strengths and weaknesses of these measurement strategies (see also Fisher & Cullen, 2000).

3

The Risk of Rape

Unsafe in The Ivory Tower?

Weekly happy hours advertising reduced-price beer and spirits, sporting event tailgate parties, post-exam celebrations coupled with illicit drug experimentation, and sexual promiscuity—not to mention Greek organization social mixers— have long been cornerstones of the collegiate experience. Students routinely enjoy these celebrated staples of collegiate life within the perceived idyllic safe haven of the "ivory tower" regardless of the size or makeup of student enrollment or its institutional affiliation. Enjoying the infamous college years to their fullest pleasure is among the most memorable years of one's life. But these youthful pleasures, part of students' everyday routines, may have a dark side. They may place college women at risk of being raped.

Commentators on opposite sides of the culture war do not dispute that female students are raped. As we have seen, however, they do disagree on whether the risk and ultimately the reality of rape constitute a "crisis." Critics argue that there is no "rape epidemic" on college campuses and that the effort to invent one is political correctness run amok. The alternative view is that the risk of rape is an integral and often unrecognized feature of college life. Calling attention to rape merely illuminates, rather than socially constructs, the objective crisis that exists.

In our view, a judicious discussion of these issues needs to move beyond the past culture war and use of terms such as *crisis* and *epidemic*. There is no agreed-upon standard for how much of a "bad thing" must exist for it to qualify as a crisis or epidemic. One side might see the glass half full, the other half empty. More subtly, seemingly small risks may have large consequences. In the case of virtually any serious, violent crime, the incidence of victimization in any one year may be low. But when a low prevalence rate for an offense is computed over a college career or across an entire student body, the significance of the problem can be striking. As we will show, this appears to be the case for the risk of attempted and completed rape. Further, the data reveal that many women are subjected to a range of other sexual victimizations (Chapter 4), experience repeat sexual victimization (Chapter 5), and are stalked (Chapter 7). Taken together, these realities mean that women experience a social "cost" of going to college not imposed on men.

In the pages ahead, we probe the risk of rape faced by college women. This analysis begins by exploring the extent to which women arrive at college as a rape victim. We then turn to the central issue: how many college women experience attempted and completed rape? This discussion revisits Koss's work and other studies based on her Sexual Experiences Survey. Given the limitations of the SES, we then highlight the findings of our national-level study introduced in the previous chapter. The role of drugs and alcohol in rape is reviewed. This issue is important because rapes can be facilitated by the use of drugs and alcohol, including to the point where victims are unable to consent to sexual intercourse. The extent of different forms of rape is examined. We conclude by revisiting the issue of the salience of rape on college campuses.

Coming to College as a Rape Victim

A substantial number of general population or community studies indicate that women with histories of childhood or adolescent sexual abuse are at an increased risk for subsequent sexual victimization during adulthood (see Breitenbecher, 2001; Logan, Walker, Jordan, & Leukefeld, 2006). More specifically, there is a growing body of research showing that female students with a history of prior sexual victimization are at risk of being victimized again (see Classen, Palesh, & Aggarwal, 2005). For example, Humphrey and White (2000), as well as Gidycz, Hanson, and Layman (1995), report that college women with histories of adolescent sexual victimization are at greatest risk for revictimization in college. Similar results were reported in the 1995 National College Health Risk Behavior Survey (Brener, McMadon, Warren, & Douglas, 1999). In this survey, 71% of college women who had forced sex were raped before the age of 18. Their results showed that adolescence is a particularly risky period for rape; of these college women, many were first forced to have sexual intercourse during the teenage years. Taken together, these findings reveal that female students do not enter campuses as blank slates. Rather, they arrive with past experience that may place them at an elevated risk of victimization—a reality we explore in more detail in Chapter 5.

Notably, such prior victimization is not only consequential but also is not a rare event. From the 1980s to the present, accumulating evidence from both large-scale and countless smaller studies revealed that a considerable number of college women are raped *before* entering college (Smith, White, & Holland, 2003). Recall the research of Mary Koss. According to Koss et al. (1987), just over one-quarter of college women were raped since age 14; at the time of her study, this was the age of legal sexual consent in Ohio and in many other states. Koss and her colleagues reported that since the age of 14, 8% of women in her study had been given alcohol or drugs by a man prior to having unwanted sexual intercourse (i.e., penile-vaginal intercourse). Nine percent reported having forced penile-vaginal intercourse, while 6% reported unwanted anal or oral intercourse or penetration with objects other than a penis.

In our National College Women Sexual Victimization Study, we asked respondents about victimization prior to when the school year began. To discern exposure to sexual victimization before entering college, we limited our analysis to the sample members who were freshmen. The data reveal that a substantial proportion of women have experienced rape before beginning their collegiate studies. Of the freshman respondents, 7.5% had been raped and 8.7% had experienced attempted rape prior to the start of their college tenure. All in all, 12% of the freshmen had experienced either a rape, attempted rape, or both prior to the start of their college tenure. Further, about one-third of these women had encountered unwanted sexual contacts.

These statistics are not necessarily precise. Prior sexual victimization was measured through behaviorally specific questions but a "yes" response was not followed up with an incident report. Still, while appropriate caution should be used in interpreting these findings, it is clear that sexual victimization, including rape, is not a rare event in the lives of young women headed to college. Again, the consequences of these prior experiences— as shown in other research and in our study—are disquieting (see Chapter 5).

Rape During the College Years: Koss Revisited

A plethora of studies has reported that women are vulnerable to rape across their life span—from childhood well into their golden years. Young women, however, are at high risk of being raped. Thus, Tjaden and Thoennes's (2006) National Violence Against Women Survey (NVAWS) discovered that the highest rates of rape are among young adult women. The National Crime Victimization Survey has consistently reported that women who are in their late teens to early 20s are the age cohort with the highest rape rates. They are almost four times more likely to be raped than all other female age groups (Rennison, 1999; see also Rand & Catalano, 2007). Given that 18 to 24 is the age range of the traditional college student, researchers have argued that this places female college students at a higher risk of being raped compared to any other time in their lives (Fisher et al., 2000). Mary Koss, of course, was among the first to make this claim.

SEXUAL EXPERIENCES SURVEY

In Chapter 1, we reviewed in detail Koss's Sexual Experiences Survey (SES) and the results of her national-level study (Koss et al., 1987). The study found that 296 women, 9.3% of the sample, had experienced an attempted or completed rape during the past 12 months. Of this number, 6.5% had been raped and 10.1% had experienced an attempted rape. Koss and her colleagues also presented the rate of attempted/completed rape victims per 1,000 female students: 166.3. Another statistic was the number of rape incidents per 1,000 students. This figure was higher because a single female victim could have experienced more than one incident. The 1-year incident rate was 278.0 per 1,000 female students—167.2 for attempted rape and 110.8 for completed rape.

Statistics can all seem to jumble together. But when seen in simpler terms, the notion of a rape crisis on the nation's college campuses did not seem farfetched:

- About 1 in 10 female students had been an attempted/completed rape victim in the past 12 months.

- Nearly 93 in every 1,000 students on a college campus was a rape victim. In a college with 10,000 coeds, this would mean that nearly 930 new female rape victims would be walking the campus each year.

Again, Koss's SES was criticized for measurement features that inflated the amount of rape victimization reported by female respondents. Further research would be needed to confirm these results. One avenue of research was to use her SES to measure victimization on campuses across the nation, typically in studies conducted by separate researchers within individual colleges. We will turn to this line of inquiry next. The takeaway point of this upcoming review is that investigations using the SES, modified versions of the SES, and similar measurement scales reach a similar conclusion: sexual victimizations, including completed and attempted rape, are not rare events among college women.

STUDIES USING THE SES

Koss's Sexual Experiences Survey (SES) or modified versions of the SES have been used extensively by subsequent researchers over the past 25 years. The SES has been administered to females in a variety of college settings with different samples of women and using different reference periods (e.g., during one's lifetime or ever; during a specific number of months, say 6 months). A sampling of the rape results from these studies follows.

- Ten percent of females enrolled in an introductory psychology course at a large, Midwestern university had experienced rape and/or attempted rape at a 6-month follow-up (Gidycz et al., 1995).

- Selected from a broad range of large and small social science courses at Ohio University, 19.3% of the female students reported having been raped and 10.5% reported experiencing attempted rape since enrolling at the university (Schwartz & Pitts, 1995).

- Of the 151 female introductory psychology students at the University of Kansas, 28.1% reported they had ever been raped (Hickman & Muehlenhard, 1997).

- As part of a sexual victimization prevention evaluation at two large universities in the Southeast and Midwest, during the 2-month follow-up period, 23% of the participants experienced rape victimization. Almost 30% of the women in the control group reported being raped during the follow-up period, compared with only 12% of the women in the intervention group (Marx, Calhoun, Wilson, & Meyerson, 2001).

- A convenience sample of 190 college women recruited from sororities and the general psychology participant pool at one large public southern university reported that 12.7% of these women were raped during a 5.5-month period (Combs-Lane & Smith, 2002).

- Of the 339 women from a medium-sized, public Midwestern university, recruited through flyers and class announcements, 7.7% reported experiences meeting the criteria for rape during the 30-week follow-up period (Messman-Moore & Brown, 2006).

- Four hundred and six female students enrolled in an introductory psychology course at Miami University participated in a study of risk perceptions and acquaintance rape. Of these women, 21.9% reported having experienced rape since they turned 18 years old (Crawford, Wright, & Birchmeier, 2008).

RESULTS FROM CANADA

DeKeseredy and Schwartz (1998) designed the first Canadian National Survey to estimate the extent of rape in male–female dating relationships. They administered a slightly modified version of the SES to measure the incidence and prevalence of attempted rape and completed rape that women had experienced with male dating partners. Using a national representative sample of 1,835 community college and university women enrolled in 44 schools, their results showed the following:

- Some 22.1% of the females reported attempted rape and 24.4% reported having been raped since leaving high school.

- During the past 12 months prior to the administration of the survey, 10.5% of the women experienced attempted rape.

- During the same 12-month time period, slightly more, 11.4%, of women were raped.

RESULTS FROM CAMPUS STUDIES USING OTHER VICTIMIZATION MEASURES

A small number of studies have opted not to use the SES to measure whether females have experienced rape. Similar to studies using the SES, these studies provide useful information that highlights the incidence of rape among college women.

- Fiebert and Tucci's (1998) sexual assault scale was used to estimate the extent of "serious" sexual assault among 674 female students enrolled in 12 southern postsecondary institutions in eight states. A total of 10.8% of the female students reported a serious sexual victimization within the most recent 6 months (Mustaine & Tewksbury, 2002).

- The College Sexual Assault questionnaire was administered to 5,446 female undergraduates enrolled at one of two large, public schools in the Midwest and the Southeast. Nearly 9% (8.5%) of the women reported they had experienced forcible rape and 3.4% had experienced an attempted forcible rape since entering college (Krebs, Linquist, Warner, Fisher, & Martin, 2007).

- The CORE Institute at Southern Illinois University reported that in 2005, 2.9% of their random sample of over 33,000 undergraduates at 53 colleges reported experiencing unwanted sexual intercourse in or around campus within in the past year. This estimate is slightly lower than the 3.3% in 2004, 3.5% in 2003, and 3.4% in 2002 who reported having unwanted sexual intercourse (Core Institute, 2009).

- Results from the American College Health Association–National College Health Association's Spring 2008 National College Health Assessment survey revealed that within the past school year, 1.9% of college women had experienced sexual penetration against their will and 3.7% had experienced attempted sexual penetration against their will (American College Health Association, 2008a).

The National College Women Sexual Victimization Study

Again, as just seen, research in the Koss tradition consistently concludes that rape is a meaningful problem on the nation's college campuses—and in Canada as well. The SES, however, is open to the criticism that the questions used to measure attempted and completed rape are imprecise and thus may yield inflated estimates of this form of sexual assault. As noted in Chapter 2, a central impetus for our undertaking the National College Women Sexual Victimization Study (recall the acronym: NCWSV Study) was to address the critics' methodological challenges to Koss's results. Although we borrowed the idea of using behaviorally specific questions from Koss (and others), we followed up any "yes" response to these questions with an incident report. This second step allowed us to confirm what had occurred and then to categorize each incident as a rape or as some other sexual victimization. The approach of using an incident report to determine the precise nature of an incident was, as might be remembered, taken from the methodology used by the National Crime Victimization Survey.

THE EXTENT OF RAPE: IS THERE A CRISIS?

What Did We Find? Table 3.1 reports the extent of rape found in the NCWSV Study. As shown, 2.8% of the sample had experienced either a completed or an attempted rape. The figure for rape was 1.7% and for attempted rape was 1.1%.

Recall that victims in the NCWSV Study are counted by a hierarchical scoring method; that is, they are classified by their most serious victimization. Thus, a respondent who experienced a completed and an attempted rape would be counted only as a completed rape victim. However, we can relax this scoring method and count as attempted rape victim respondents who also had reported to have experienced a completed rape. When this is done, the attempted rape figure increases to 1.3%.

The overall figures also are obscured somewhat by the inclusion of graduate students in the calculations. As it turned out, they had very low victimization levels: 0.8% for completed rape and zero for attempted rape. When they are omitted from the analysis, the overall rape victimization rate for undergraduates rises to over 3%: 1.8% were completed rape victims and 1.3% were attempted rape victims.

Table 3.1 also reports the incidence rate per 1,000 female students. Because women can experience more than one incident, this figure is higher than the number of victims per 1,000 female students. Thus, of the 123 victims, 22.8% experienced more than one rape. In any event, the rate of incidents for completed and attempted rape was 35.3 per 1,000 female students.

Table 3.1 Extent of Rape in the National College Women Sexual Victimization Study

Type of Victimization Incident	Number of Victims in Sample	Percentage of Sample	Rate per 1,000 Female Students	Number of Incidents	Rate per 1,000 Female Students
Completed Rape	74	1.7	16.6	86	19.3
Attempted Rape	49	1.1	11.0	71	16.0
Total	123	2.8	27.7	157	35.3

SOURCE: Fisher, Cullen, and Turner (1999).

What Are We to Make of These Results? Critics of the notion that there is a rape "crisis" or "epidemic" on college campuses might rightly note that the vast majority of female students will not experience a completed or attempted rape in any given academic year. Only 1 in 36 female students (2.8%) will be involved in a rape-related incident. But a closer, more nuanced inspection of the data yields a less sanguinary conclusion. Two considerations are particularly relevant.

First, the respondents in the NCWSV Study were surveyed during the academic year and asked to report their victimization since the start of the academic year. The average reference period—that is, between the school's year start and when the survey was completed—was 6.91 months. Extrapolating these results for an entire 12-month period is problematic because it assumes, for example, that the risk of victimization is stable across the school year and across the summer months. However, if the 2.8 victimization figure is calculated for a 1-year period, the data suggest that nearly 5% (4.9%) of college women are victimized in any given calendar year. And what if this risk of victimization is projected over a college career, which now lasts an average of 5 years? The percentage of completed or attempted rape among women in higher education might climb to between one-fifth and one-quarter.

Admittedly, these projections are speculative and await longitudinal studies that follow women throughout their college careers. The point, however, is that what initially seems to be a low victimization rate—2.8%—underestimated the annual rate of rape victimization and does not capture the full risk women will experience across their years in college.

Second, let us rely just on our estimates from the 6.91-month reference period. Remember, these figures are based on detailed questions aimed at excluding any incident that did not meet the legal criteria for a forcible rape. In many ways, the NCWSV Study uses a conservative methodology in that over half of the women who screened into the incident report on the behaviorally specific questions were not counted as rape victims. The results we report, when computed over a year, are about half of what Koss and her colleagues found using the SES. Again, no survey is free of measurement error, and it is conceivable that our methods inflated rape estimates. But the explicit purpose of the two-step measurement process we employed was to guard against this very occurrence.

So, let us now consider the incident rate reported in Table 3.1. From a policy perspective, college administrators might be disturbed to learn that for every 1,000 women attending their institutions, there may well be 35 incidents of rape in a given academic year. For a campus with 10,000 women, this would mean that the number of completed and attempted rapes could exceed 350. Even more broadly, when projected over the nation's female student population—now totaling over 10 million attending 2-year and 4-year institutions—these figures suggest that rape victimization is a potential problem of large proportions and of public policy interest.

The intent here is not to use data to create a false sense of crisis. But the findings of the NCWSV Study confirm the central point of Koss's earlier research: *college women experience rape at levels that should concern campus officials and citizens generally.* For a variety of reasons, which we explore later, it remains a type of crime for which victims receive little redress. Whether we wish to use terms such as *crisis* and *epidemic* is beside the point. The sexual victimization of college women is not a mere social construction but an objective reality to be understood and confronted. To the extent that our findings are accurate, this view is based not on ideology but on science.

THE CONTEXT OF RAPE

In later chapters, we return to other details surrounding rape and other types of sexual victimization. For now, however, we will review what we know about the context in which rapes occur.

Do Victims Know Their Offenders? A key finding of Koss and other researchers is that college women typically know their assailants—a reason that the terms *date rape* or *acquaintance rape* were put forward (see, e.g., Crowell & Burgess, 1996). Consistent with the existing literature, in the NCWSV Study, most victims knew the person who victimized them. In fact, for both completed and attempted rapes, about 9 in 10 offenders were known to the victim. There were a few rapes (5.5% of completed incidents, 2.8% of attempted incidents) that involved multiple assailants, but the numbers are too few to draw any meaningful conclusions. In any event, for incidents committed by one

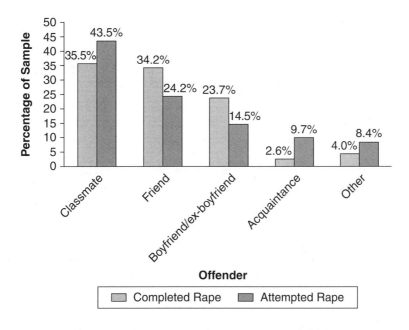

Figure 3.1   Victim–Offender Relationship for Rapes Committed by Single Offenders
SOURCE: Fisher, Cullen, and Turner (1999).

offender, only 6.2% of completed rapes and 10.1% of attempted rapes were committed by a stranger. In all other instances, the victim "knew or had seen before" the offender.

When probing the precise nature of the relationship between victims and single-offenders, three relationship categories predominate: classmate, friend, and boyfriend/ex-boyfriend (see Figure 3.1). In the case of completed rape, 93.4% of the offenders fell into one of these cases. For attempted rape incidents, the figure was 82.2%, with another 9.7% of incidents involving acquaintances. College professors were not identified as committing any rapes.

Notably, most victims in the sample were *not* victimized while on a date with the offender. For rape, only 12.8% of the incidents occurred on a date; the comparable statistic for attempted rape was 35.0%. Further, in none of these cases was the victim still romantically involved with the offender when she completed the survey. These findings suggest two conclusions that should be investigated further. First, the rape incidents may have occurred mainly among individuals who were not in a relationship but knew one another more casually—or not well at all. Second, it is likely that the victimization was a factor that contributed to the ending of any relationship that may have existed.

It appears that the use of alcohol and or drugs by victims before a victimization incident is not uncommon. For rape, victims had used alcohol and/or drugs before the incident in about half the incidents (54.6%). For attempted rape, the percentage was slightly less—in 43.6% of the incidents. It is noteworthy that the percentage of offenders using alcohol, drugs, both, or "something else" was even more pronounced. For rape and attempted rape, in only 26.2% and 32.4% of the incidents, respectively, did the respondents report that the offender was not using some mind-altering substance.

We cannot determine from these data if alcohol and/or drugs were causally related to being sexually victimized. We do not know if substances make women more vulnerable to victimization or make men more likely to sexually assault. It is possible, for example, that the findings simply indicate that when college men and women socialize, alcohol and drugs are present in that environment. Alternatively, however, we cannot dismiss the possibility that alcohol and drugs may affect judgment and conduct in victimization incidents.

Where and When Do Rapes Occur? The majority of the victimizations occurred off campus: 66.3% of completed rapes and 54.9% of attempted rapes. This finding, however, can be somewhat misleading, as an examination of the completed rape incidents shows. Again, one-third of completed rapes happened on campus. Even so, another 10 rapes occurred "in an off-campus student housing area." Thirteen took place in or around the victims' "living quarters." Further, one rape was in a fraternity house, two in "the off-campus business district," and three "at a party." In contrast, the victims stated that 20 incidents—35.1%—occurred "away from campus," such as while a victim was on vacation or at her parents' home. It also was reported that only 13 rapes—5.8% of the incidents—occurred during an academic break.

These statistics suggest that while two-thirds of rapes do not occur specifically on campus, a clear majority of rapes take place either on campus or in the course of attending college (such as having a residence) or are integral to college life (going to parties, seeing classmates/friends in off-campus housing). Thus, to the extent that, as a result of going to college, students' lives spill over into related social domains, the distinction between on-campus and off-campus sexual assaults becomes less meaningful. From a policy perspective, these findings mean that campus authorities may legitimately be concerned with not only rape and other types of sexual victimization within the geographical boundaries of their campus, but also with what may occur to their students who live and recreate near the campus.

It appears as well that the rapes and attempted rapes that the victims experienced occurred almost exclusively in or close to their own or someone else's living quarters. These data suggest that virtually all of the on-campus rapes in our sample did not occur in a public place but a more private location. A similar pattern—although not as clear-cut—was obtained for off-campus rapes. We cannot categorize the specific location of all rapes that occurred—such as when victimization is reported to have occurred "on another college or university campus" or while a respondent was "away from campus." Still, of the remaining 34 rape incidents, 22 occurred either in a living quarters area (n = 11), in an off-campus student housing area (n = 10), or at a fraternity (n = 1); three other incidents took place "at a party."

Relatedly, a substantial majority of all types of sexual victimization occurred in the evening hours (after 6 p.m.). For both rape and attempted rape, a majority of the victimizations took place after midnight.

What Is the Takeaway Point? Reviewing fairly detailed statistics is important because they allow us to gain insight into the features of sexual victimization incidents. But, of course, it can become a challenge to keep all the numbers straight and coherently arranged in one's mind. So, at this point, it is useful to draw the key conclusion—the takeaway point—from the National College Women Sexual Victimization Study regarding the context of rape.

- It appears that most rape incidents involve single offenders who assault women they know in private living areas, late at night, and often with alcohol and/or drugs present.

Is College a Risk Factor?

Implicit in the discussion thus far is that being in college—not just of college age—exposes women to elevated risks of rape. Unfortunately, evidence on this issue is limited and contradictory.

Thus, the National Crime Victimization Survey reported that between 1995 and 2002, male and female college students, 18 to 24 years old, experienced rates of rape/sexual assault that were statistically comparable (Baum & Klaus, 2005; see also Hart, 2003). The rate of rape/sexual assault for college students during this time period was, on average, 3.8 per 1,000 for persons ages 18 to 24. The rate of rape/sexual assault for non–college students was, on average, 4.1 per 1,000 persons ages 18 to 24. A closer look at rates for females only draws a similar conclusion. The average annual rape/sexual assault rate for female college students was 6.0 per 1,000 persons ages 18 to 24. For female nonstudents of the same age group, the annual average rape/sexual assault rate was 7.9 per 1,000 persons. For the NCVS annual estimates, female college students were thus slightly less likely than nonstudents to be rape/sexual assault victims.

Given the limitations of the NCVS in measuring rape (see Chapter 2), these results must be viewed with some caution. More relevant, Kilpatrick and associates' national-level study reveals a different conclusion (Kilpatrick, Resnick, Ruggiero, Conoscenti, & McCauley, 2007). They report that the projected annual percentage of college women raped (5.2%) was more than five times higher than the comparable victimization statistic for women from the general public (0.9%). A large gap persisted between college women and the general public regardless of the means used to undertake the rape. Comparisons can be made within three categories:

- Rapes in which the offender used force or threat of force or the victim sustained an injury during the assault (1.6% versus 0.5%).

- Rapes in which the offender used alcohol or drugs to render a woman unable to resist a rape (1.5% versus 0.2%).

- Rapes in which the victim voluntarily used drugs or alcohol and was unable to control her behavior or know what she was doing (2.1% versus 0.3%).

Although Kilpatrick et al.'s findings are striking in terms of suggesting that college attendance is risky, clearly, continued research on this issue is needed.

Forms of Rape

Kilpatrick et al.'s study, which we discuss in more detail later, also called attention to the role alcohol and/or drugs may play in fostering women's sexual victimization. Note in particular how rapes accomplished through force were less common than rapes facilitated by an intoxicating substance. In this regard, a growing number of researchers, as well as prosecutors, have begun to distinguish between different forms of rape. The distinction that is made between the forms of rape is primarily based on the means by which the assailant attempted or achieved unwanted sexual intercourse with the victim. The key distinction is between rapes that involve the use of force (i.e., *forcible rapes*) and those that are made possible when a victim's use of drugs or alcohol renders her unable to exercise consent to a sexual act (i.e., *alcohol-* or *drug-induced rape*). In some cases, explicit efforts can be made by perpetrators to purposely incapacitate a potential victim. These are referred to as *incapacitated rapes*.

This section lays a conceptual foundation for empirical data that is presented later in the chapter. We begin by discussing what different forms of rape have in common and then proceed to how they differ. Table 3.2 presents a handy summary of the issues to be discussed.

Table 3.2   Similarities and Differences Between Two Forms of Rape: Forcible Rape and Alcohol- or Drug-Induced Rape

Characteristic	Form of Rape		
		Alcohol- or Drug-Induced Rape	
	Forcible Rape	Incapacitated Rape	Alcohol- or Drug-Facilitated Rape
Similar Characteristics			
Lack of Consent by Victim to Engage in Sexual Intercourse	✓	✓	✓
Type of Penetration (only one type is necessary and sufficient)			
Attempted or Completed Vaginal Penetration of Victim	✓	✓	✓
Attempted or Completed Anal Penetration of Victim	✓	✓	✓
Fellatio Performed by Victim	✓	✓	✓
Cunnilingus Performed on Victim	✓	✓	✓
Distinctive Characteristics			
Use of Force			
Physical Force by Assailant	✓		
Threat of Physical Force by Assailant	✓		
Consumption of Alcohol or Drug			
Intoxicated by Voluntary Use by Victim		✓	
Deliberately Administered to the Victim by the Assailant			✓
Surreptitiously Administered to the Victim by the Assailant			✓
Deceptively Administered to the Victim by the Assailant			✓

WHAT RAPES HAVE IN COMMON

Legal statutes in many states define rape as unwanted sexual intercourse that occurs as the result of force, threat of force, or the inability of the victim to consent. Rape involves specific forms of attempted or completed sexual intercourse—that is, penetration of an opening of the body. Thus, from a legal perspective, the act of rape has an essential characteristic that distinguishes it from a consensual sexual act: the inability of the victim to consent to the sexual intercourse. The rape victim's lack of consent can result in one of two situations:

- Due to the perpetrator's use of force—for example, physical aggression, such as punching or holding down, or threatened use of force.
- The victim is mentally unable to provide consent.

Lack of Consent to Sexual Intercourse. In the eye of the law, the key element that distinguishes consensual sexual intercourse from rape is a person's ability or inability to provide consent to sexual intercourse (see Scalzo, 2007). This holds true regardless of the form of rape—whether forcible or alcohol- or drug-induced. As a result, researchers have had to ground their measurement of rape in legal definitions. As noted in Chapter 1, Koss is a prominent example. In developing the questions used to measure rape on the SES, she included the phrase "when you didn't want to." Similarly, in our NCWSV Study, the directions to the behaviorally specific screen questions emphasized "unwanted sexual experiences," and the rape items themselves used the phrase "made you have sexual intercourse by using force or threat of harm" (Fisher et al., 2000).

States also define the *age of consent.* Regardless of whether an act is consensual, sexual consent with a person under this age is legally referred to as statutory rape. The age of sexual consent ranges from 14 years old in one state, Hawaii, to 18 years old in 13 states, including the most populous ones, such as California, Florida, Illinois, and Ohio (Rymel, 2004).

Types of Penetration. Most states have abandoned the traditional, yet rigid, definition of rape as the forced vaginal penetration of a woman by a male assailant's penis (Spohn & Horney, 1992). After the rape law reform movement during the late 1970s and in the 1980s, the definition of rape was expanded. Prior to this reform effort, rape was commonly defined as carnal knowledge—vaginal intercourse between a male and female.

After the movement in many states, legislators passed laws that were gender neutral; perpetrators and assailants could be either or both genders. Further, anal, fellatio (i.e., oral sex performed on a male's penis), and cunnilingus (i.e., using the lips, mouth or tongue to stimulate female's genitals) between individuals were included as types of penetration that constituted sexual acts that defined rape. Body parts other than a penis (e.g., a digit such as finger or toe, mouth, or tongue) and object or instrument (e.g., a dildo, bottle, broom handle) were also included as means of penetration.

Though state rape statutes vary as to the types of penetration that constitute rape, researchers commonly define penetration of a female as the attempted or completed insertion of a penis, digit, mouth or tongue, object, or instrument into any of her genital, anal, or oral openings. Either actually completing penetration or attempting to penetrate any bodily opening without that person's consent or being able to consent to the act is considered rape among researchers. According to our NCWSV Study, rape incidents committed against college women most frequently involve finger–vaginal penetration (31.2%), penile-vaginal penetration (29.2%), and fellatio (21.7%) (Fisher et al., 1999).

HOW RAPES DIFFER

Despite commonalities, forcible rape and alcohol/drug-induced rape possess characteristics that differentiate them (see Table 3.2). The key factor is whether consent is overcome through physical force or through the use of intoxicating substances. Further, by taking into account the means through which such substances are ingested, alcohol- or drug-induced rape can be distinguished into (1) alcohol- or drug-facilitated rape and (2) incapacitated rape.

Forcible Rape. In most studies, a forcible rape involves the assailant using physical force or coercion or threatening to use physical force or coercion (e.g., threat of bodily harm) to achieve sexual intercourse. In the minds of many individuals, forcible rape is the "typical" rape, one involving some kind of physical force. This type of rape is an image widely depicted in the media as commonly occurring. This *aggravated rape* is portrayed as involving a stereotypical stranger who lurks in the shadows of the parking garage or jumps out from behind a bush with a weapon. He then rips off a woman's clothing, drags her to the ground and rapes her. Note that critical components of this widely shared societal perception of forcible rape are that it involves force and a stranger. In Chapter 1, where Susan Estrich's work is discussed, we noted that this kind of assault is called a *real rape.*

As we now know, the typical forcible rape scenario involves a woman who is assaulted not by a stranger but by someone she knows. This assailant uses physical coercion, which the woman tries to resist through forceful tactics (Sorenson, Stein, Siegel, Golding, & Burman, 1987). For college women, perpetrators use weapons only in a minority of cases. Most often, the offender holds her down or twists her arm as she tries to resist through physically struggling or verbal objection. In fact, results from our NCWSV Study reveal that in 84% of the incidents no weapon was employed. The victim reported a weapon actually being used in only two incidents (Fisher et al., 1999).

Alcohol- or Drug-Induced Rape. To make the remainder of the discussion simpler to follow, we will refer to this category by the acronym AD-induced rape. This conduct is sometimes referred to as alcohol- or drug-enabled rape (Krebs et al., 2007). As noted, AD-induced rape involves the victim being temporarily unable to consent to sexual intercourse due to the influence of a drug—narcotic, anesthetic, or other substance such as alcohol. The threat of force is not used to overcome a lack of consent. Rather, the woman is temporarily physically or mentally incapable of consenting to engage in sexual intercourse either because she has become intoxicated due to recreational or voluntary use of substances or due to the surreptitious or deceptive administration of a substance by an assailant.

In the first situation, the victim voluntarily consumes enough alcohol, drugs, or a combination that causes her to be physically or cognitively impaired. The victim can be using these substances for recreational or experimental purposes. She may consume so much of these substances or combine them in a way so as to become intoxicated to the point of being physically helpless or mentally incapable of resisting the advances of sexual intercourse. As shown in Table 3.2, this form of rape is referred to as *incapacitated rape* (see Kilpatrick et al., 2007; Krebs et al., 2007).

In the second situation, the assailant deliberately slips an intoxicating substance to the victim, say in an unsuspected beverage, which causes her to be physically or cognitively impaired. The assailant can administer an intoxicating substance surreptitiously or deceptively to the victim. This form of rape is referred to as *alcohol- or-drug facilitated rape* (see the right-hand column in Table 3.2) (Kilpatrick et al., 2007; Krebs et al., 2007).

In both types of rape—incapacitated or facilitated—the victim is passed out or, if awake, is too drunk or high to fully know what she is doing or to be in control of her current physical or cognitive state. Depending on the type of substance, either type of situation can limit the victim's decision-making ability, decrease her ability to identify a dangerous situation or to resist the perpetrator, cause unconsciousness, impair the victim's memory, or even cause death. Consent, in short, will be lacking.

We should note that there are also other factors that may render a person unable to form consent. These include being unconscious, asleep, and mentally or physically disabled.

Types of Drugs Used in AD-Induced Rape. Alcohol and drug use is a hallmark of the college experience; it also characterizes a large proportion of the sexual victimizations. The 2005 CORE Alcohol and Drug Survey data found that 83% of college students reported having unwanted sexual intercourse while under the influence of alcohol or drugs (Dowdall, 2007).

Alcohol is the substance that victims most often report using prior to being raped; it is also the most widely studied (Abbey, Zawacki, Buck, Clinton, & McAuslan, 2004; Logan et al., 2006). Much research has reported a high positive association between alcohol consumption, especially intoxication, and the risk of rape and other types of sexual victimization (Dowdall, 2007; Fisher et al., 2000; Testa, VanZile-Tamsen, Livingston, & Buddie, 2006). Researchers have estimated that half the rapes of female college students involve the use of alcohol or other drugs by the perpetrator, victim, or both (Abbey et al., 1994, Abbey et al., 2004; Testa, 2002, 2004). As reported above, this pattern was found in our NCWSV Study (Fisher et al., 2000). Victims and assailants consume alcohol prior to the incident, during the incident, or sometimes at both times. In these situations, women may voluntarily consume enough alcohol to be intoxicated to the point that their ability to consent to sexual intercourse is severely compromised and impaired.

Party situations where alcoholic or nonalcoholic beverages are part of the social scene are an "ideal" environment for a potential rapist to add a drug to someone's drink and have her consume it without her knowledge or consent. There are a variety of drugs that a would-be offender can give to a rape victim to make her unconscious or to diminish her level of resistance to a sexual assault. These types of drugs, which render women unable to provide consent, are commonly referred to as *date-rape drugs.*

The idea of using a drug to incapacitate a woman in order to rape her is not novel. What is novel, however, is the sheer range of drugs that are available to offenders. The Society of Forensic Toxicologists developed a list of all drugs that have been used or could be used to facilitate a rape (see Negrusz, Juhascik, & Gaensslen, 2005). The roster of both prescription and over-the-counter drugs available to would-be rapists is lengthy.

Rohypnol™ (flunitrazepam) is probably the best-known example of a date-rape drug due to highly publicized media reports about its perceived widespread or increasing use among college rapists. Only a small dose of the pill form of "roofies" or the "forget-me drug" mixed with a beverage and ingested is needed to produce anterograde amnesia. Because of the drug's amnesic effects, a rape victim may be unable to remember anything after taking the drug—including recalling that the assault ever took place or the identity of her assailant (Zorza, 2001). This drug, however, does not appear to be used extensively in sexual assaults (Fisher et al., 1999; Kilpatrick et al., 2007). Two limiting factors are that Rohypnol is illegal in the United States and is made in a pill that turns any liquid it is mixed with blue, thus alerting a drinker to its presence and thus discouraging consumption.

A second well-known rape-facilitating drug is GHB (gamma hydroxybutyric acid). More commonly known also as "liquid ecstasy" and "easy lay," GHB comes in the form of a clear or syrupy liquid or white powder. Its plastic, salty taste and even mild odor can be somewhat masked by adding the drug to a sweet liqueur or fruit juice. Because GHB inhibits neurotransmitters from being released in the brain, it can cause confusion, intense sleepiness, unconsciousness, dizziness, and memory loss. Under these conditions, a would-be offender can more easily commit rape with no consent on the part of the victim, little threat of her resisting, and almost no risk of his detection.

Other more general drugs such as sedatives, tranquillizers, pain killers (e.g., Oxycontin, Percocet) or narcotics such as antianxiety medications (e.g., Xanax) have been reported to been used in facilitated/incapacitated rapes.

The Role of Drugs and Alcohol

The discussion of the conceptual differences between types of rape set the stage for the presentation of studies on rapes induced through the use of drugs and alcohol. The traditional focus of studies on the use of physical force to accomplish a sexual victimization has diverted attention away from this other means of achieving rape. In probing this neglected form of victimization, we start our discussion with Mary Koss's study. We then move on to review the findings of a major study of alcohol use, which included a measure of rape, and a study by Kilpatrick et al. specifically designed to assess how much rape might be induced through alcohol and drugs.

KOSS REVISITED—AGAIN

A study is a "classic" not simply because it is the first but also because it lays a foundation for much of the scholarship that is to follow. Koss and colleagues' study using the Sexual Experiences Survey is the kind of foundational investigation that warrants being revisited. In this instance, Koss and her colleagues (1987) were among the first researchers to provide information about the extent of alcohol- or drug-induced rape. Thus, as part of the SES, she included this item:

- Have you ever had sexual intercourse when you didn't want to because a man gave you alcohol or drugs?

This decision was wise because it allowed Koss to measure a form of rape that was heretofore ignored empirically. The difficulty was that the wording opened this item up to criticism. The wording of the item has a potential response bias; it could induce a "yes" answer from women who had been raped and those who had not. In the first instance, rapes could have occurred because female students were intoxicated to the degree that consent was impossible and a man then "made" her have intercourse. In the second instance, a woman could have simply drunk too much, exercised poor judgment, and had sex when, once sober, wished she had not. This is Roiphe's (1993) "morning after"; a bad night but not a rape. Given that the question likely measured both kinds of events, reliable estimates of rape are not possible.

This does not mean, however, that Koss was not on to something very important or that her data are not, in the least, suggestive. In fact, the findings indicate that alcohol and drugs are intimately implicated in unwanted sexual acts and likely in victimizations that qualify as rape:

- Over 7% of college women annually experience alcohol- or drug-induced rape.
- The use of alcohol and drugs was more common in attempted (4.49%) than completed (2.86%) rapes.
- The annual victimization rate for this type of rape was 124 per 1,000 college women; 74 per 1,000 women annually experienced attempted rapes, and 50 per 1,000 women experienced completed rapes.

HARVARD'S COLLEGE ALCOHOL STUDY

Henry Wechsler of the Harvard School of Public Health led the College Alcohol Study (CAS) funded by the Robert Wood Johnson Foundation (see "College Alcohol Study," 2009). Wechsler and his colleagues pooled the samples from three of the CAS studies—1997, 1999, and 2001—to generate the largest national sample of college women (see Mohler-Kuo, Dowdall, Koss, & Wechsler, 2004). This included nearly 24,000 women enrolled at 119 four-year schools.

Wechsler and his colleagues asked the female students three questions on rape that conform to the legal definition of rape in many states (Mohler-Kuo et al., 2004). Variations of questions have been used in other studies by Kilpatrick et al. (2007), Koss et al. (1987), and Tjaden and Thoennes (2000). Specifically, their survey items asked about whether the respondents had sexual intercourse against their wishes while physically forced or threatened with harm, or had sexual intercourse when they were intoxicated to the point of being unable to consent. The reference period was "since the beginning of each school year"—a time span averaging about 7 months. Three relevant conclusions should be noted:

- First, 1.9% of college women in the sample had been forcibly raped.

- Second, less than 1% (0.4%) were raped when someone threatened them with harm.

- Third, the reference period for this study (about 7 months) matched that of our NCWSV Study. Notably, the College Alcohol Study estimate of forcible rape is comparable to that reported by Fisher and her colleagues (recall that 1.7% experienced completed rape).

Wechsler and his colleagues also attempted to measure how much rape was AD-induced (Mohler-Kuo et al., 2004). Unfortunately, their measure of such rapes is not explicit about the source of intoxication, either voluntary use or due to someone's dispensing a drug or alcohol to them without the victim's knowledge. Regardless, they asked women if they had experienced sexual intercourse when they were so intoxicated that they were unable to consent. Across the 7-month reference period, their findings were striking:

- Beyond forcible rapes, they discovered that across the 3-year period, on average, 3.4% of women reported having sexual intercourse when they were so intoxicated that they were incapable of consent.

- These rape estimates were quite stable across the 3 years of the study: 3.6% in 1997, 3.4% in 1999, and 3.2% in 2000.

Again, this study was mainly a college student alcohol survey. Undoubtedly, Wechsler and his colleagues could have used more sophisticated measures of the different forms of rape. Nonetheless, the findings reinforce Koss's and others' suspicions that rape on college campuses is not only undertaken through brute force but opportunistically when women are intoxicated and deceptively when women are drugged.

KILPATRICK ET AL.'S NATIONAL STUDY OF DRUG-FACILITATED, INCAPACITATED, AND FORCIBLE RAPE

Almost 20 years after Koss's first study, Kilpatrick and his associates (2007) carried out a national-level study to estimate the extent of alcohol- or drug-induced rape. Building on the past alcohol-consumption and rape research by two leading researchers, Maria Testa and Antonia Abbey, Kilpatrick et al. measured two distinct variants of alcohol- or drug-induced (AD-induced) rape: (1) alcohol- or drug-facilitated rape and (2) incapacitated rape. Recall that in alcohol- or drug-facilitated rapes, the perpetrator deliberately gives the victim drugs without her permission or attempts to get her drunk. In both of these situations, the assailant then commits an unwanted sexual act against his victim involving oral, anal, or vaginal penetration. The victim may be passed out or awake, but she is too drunk or high to know what she is doing or to control her behavior. An incapacitated rape is when unwanted oral, anal, or vaginal penetration occurs after the victim voluntarily consumes alcohol or drugs. Again, sexual penetration occurs when the victim's intoxicated state renders her mentally or physically unable to exercise consent.

As in Fisher et al.'s studies of the victimization of college women, Kilpatrick and his colleagues recruited their college women sample using the American Student List, the largest and most used list of college students in the United States. The college women sample consisted of 2,000 college women enrolled in 253 four-year schools located in 47 different states. As expected, they were young (on average, 20 years old, ranging from 18 to 67). Almost all the women had never been married (96%) and came from higher-income families reporting income greater than $40,000 (72%). Three-fourths of them were white, non-Hispanic, with the remaining women in the sample being Black, non-Hispanic (11%), Hispanic (6%), Asian American (6%), and Native American (1%).

Kilpatrick and his colleagues used forcible rape-screening questions similar to those developed in the National Violence Against Women Survey (see Tjaden & Thoennes, 2006) and Kilpatrick and colleagues' *Rape in America: A Report to the Nation* (1992). For example, three items used behaviorally specific wording to ask women if a man or boy ever made them have sex—vaginal, oral, or anal—by using force or threatening to harm them or someone close to them. A fourth question asked about fingers or objects penetrating their vagina or anus against their will or with force or threatening harm. In addition to forcible rape questions, they also included two questions about AD-induced rape.

The first question asked about self-induced intoxication by the victim; that is, incapacitated rape. This question described having sex when respondent did not want to after having drunk so much alcohol that she was very high, inebriated, or passed out. The second question asked about the perpetrator deliberately giving drugs, alcohol, or other intoxicants to the victim; that is, drug-facilitated rape. This question described having sex when she did not want to after someone gave her or she had taken enough drugs to make her very high, intoxicated, or passed out. All women who answered "affirmative" to one or more of these rape screening questions were asked a series of questions about the rape characteristics. For example, questions were included about the characteristics of the events (e.g., use of physical force, threats), victim–offender relationship, occurrence of injury, involvement of drugs or alcohol, receipt of medical care, and reporting behavior to authorities. Notably, these questions were not asked about each incident as was done in the National College Women Sexual Victimization Study (see Fisher et al., 1999). Also of note is that responses to these questions were not used to classify what type or types of rape, if any, these women experienced; they were used to describe the characteristics of rapes.

What did the results from Kilpatrick et al. study reveal about the prevalence of rape among college women during the past 7 months (about the length of an academic term)? Four findings are most noteworthy:

- Nearly 3% of college women (2.95%) were raped.
- Almost 2% (1.9%) experienced any forcible rape.
- Just over 2% (2.1%) experienced either drug- or alcohol-facilitated rape or incapacitated rape.
- A larger percentage of college women, 1.2%, experienced incapacitated rape compared to the 0.95% who experienced drug- or alcohol-facilitated rape.

College life is an important social domain that provides lifelong experiences and memories for millions of students each year. As these results show, part of this experience involves college women experiencing forcible rape and/or alcohol- or drug-induced rape. Clearly, to understand more fully the risks faced by women in the routine social situations that define their college years, more research will be needed on how drug and alcohol consumption are integral to victimization—regardless of whether these substances are voluntarily consumed by the victim or administered unknowingly by the would-be offender or with his intent of getting the victim too drunk to be able to consent to his sexual advances.

Conclusion

Critics such as Neil Gilbert (1997) and Katie Roiphe (1993) correctly cautioned that the issue of rape on college campuses would be enmeshed in politics—in a culture war in which those on each side would choose a position before the data had arrived. One side would cry "rape epidemic" whereas the other would cry "take responsibility for bad decisions." Amid all the bluster, a number of scholars have continued to diligently try to demarcate the risks of rape faced by female college students.

No method of measuring the scope of rape is foolproof. Measuring a complex social event is a daunting challenge. Specific point estimates can be set forth—for example, 2.8% of women experience completed or attempted rape in the school year according to our NCWSV Study. In all honesty, however, we do not know what the true confidence interval is around these estimates. Nonetheless, when all extant research is taken into account, an unmistakable conclusion emerges: A small but meaningful percentage of women face the risk of rape on college campuses. When this risk is computed for all women on a single campus, the number of rapes produced is alarming. Again, small percentages of serious events calculated over a large base produce social problems of a high magnitude.

We also have learned that beyond measures of forcible rape, there may be a significant number of other sexual assaults perpetrated against women who have incapacitated themselves through alcohol or drugs or who have been drugged into a stupor by would-be rapists. The research in this area is still in its beginning stages; more studies using more rigorous measures of rape (e.g., incident reports) are needed. Still, there is sufficient evidence to be concerned that alcohol and drugs are often intimately implicated in making women attractive targets for sexual victimization.

At this point, we can thus conclude that colleges are not safe havens but places that might present important risks for sexual victimization, including rape. Despite years of "raised consciousness" and rape prevention programs, there is little evidence that the risk of rape is declining. It may be that given the lifestyles of college students—frequent contact with members of the opposite sex at night, in private settings, with intoxicating substances at hand—a steady rate of rapes will be produced that are not easily counteracted. Opportunities for sexual victimization are ubiquitous and enough assailants are present to take advantage of them. This is a sobering view, but perhaps a first step to understanding that the risk of rape will not soon vanish from our college and university campuses.

4

Beyond Rape

The Pervasiveness of Sexual Victimization

The criminal status of rape, coupled with grassroots efforts by campus safety and women's advocacy groups, have combined to keep rape prominent on the policy agendas of federal and state policymakers and of campus administrators. Indeed, rape on campus has been among the most extensively addressed issues by state-level and congressional statutes (Carter & Bath, 2007; Sloan & Shoemaker, 2007). A key requirement of the federal The Jeanne Clery Disclosure of Campus Security Policy and Campus Crime Statistics Act (20 USC § 1092(f)) (hereafter the Clery Act), for example, is that postsecondary institutions publish and distribute an annual report of seven major categories of crime statistics. Included in this crime reporting requirement is sex offenses. Consistent with the FBI's National Incident-Based Reporting System, sex offenses must be divided into and reported in two categories: (1) forcible offenses, including rape as defined as the carnal knowledge of a female forcibly and against her will, forcible sodomy, sexual assault with an object, and forcible fondling, and (2) nonforcible offenses such incest or statutory rape (Ward & Lee, 2005).

These deeply rooted scholarly and legislative interests in rape among college students often overshadow other types of sexual victimization experienced by female students during their college years. In a way, rape is the "tip of the iceberg"—the part of the problem that receives the most attention but that sits atop a larger foundation of victimization. Indeed, a growing body of research documents that, beyond rape, college women experience much unwanted and coerced sexual contact.

Our exploration of this issue involves three main discussions. First, we examine why most attention has been devoted to rape and, in turn, why it is now important to understand the diverse ways in which college women are sexually victimized. Some of these are fairly serious; others are limited. But taken as a whole, they impose a cost on many female students that detracts from the quality of their college experience—a burden not confronted by most of their male counterparts. Second, we furnish a conceptual framework for understanding types of sexual victimization other than rape. In this regard, we categorize the dimensions of sexual victimization as a means of constructing a simple, but hopefully illuminating, framework. Third, the remainder of the chapter presents an overview of what researchers know about the extent of different types of sexual victimization beyond rape—namely (1) sexual coercion, (2) unwanted sexual contact, and (3) noncontact sexual abuse. Recall from Chapter 2 that, in our National College Women Sexual Victimization (NCWSV) Study, we measured diverse types of victimization. Accordingly, where possible, we cite these national-level data to enrich the discussions that follow.

Moving Beyond the Study of Rape

Women experience a wide range of different types of sexual victimization that, although not legally rape, are not consensual and not wanted. These "non-rapes" are part of a broader constellation of different types of unwanted and coerced sexual contact and abuses that many women, especially young college women, experience. They are often neglected, we suspect, because of the belief that unwanted sex compelled in the absence of force, threat of force, or incapacitation, is either not important or not that "serious." Unlike the construct of rape, these experiences lack any name in the nation's lexicon that intuitively captures their distinctive nature. As Basile (1999, p. 1039) observes, they exist in a "grey area"—not legally qualifying as a rape but not acts that can be dismissed as inconsequential.

Non-rapes are sexual victimizations that do not meet the legal criteria for completed or attempted rape. A variety of different types of victimization fall under this conceptual umbrella. Some types of sexual victimization, which would be included in the category of *sexual coercion,* involve sexual intercourse or penetration obtained by verbal coercion, such as continual arguments or misuse of authority. Other types of sexual victimization involve *unwanted sexual contact* that does not involve penetration of the body. This would include the perpetrator intentionally touching the victim's body in a sexual manner, such as fondling breasts or genitals, touching the thighs or neck, kissing lips or other body parts, or rubbing against a person's body. The perpetrator can seek sexual contact through a variety of forms of verbal coercion, misuse of authority, or threatened or actual use of force. *Noncontact sexual abuses* are nonpenetrative or nontouching acts. Examples include the perpetrator making sexist comments, jeering or taunting, or asking questions about one's sex life. Unwanted exposure to pornography, indecent exposure, exhibition, and voyeurism are also examples of noncontact sexual abuses (see Basile & Saltzman, 2002).

There are four main reasons that it is important to focus on sexual victimization other than rape. First, a substantial, if not alarming, proportion of college women experience non-rape victimization. This does not appear to be a new occurrence. Recall the research by Kirkpatrick and Kanin (1957), who first measured "male sexual aggression on a university campus" in the 1950s. In their investigation, 27% of the college women reported themselves offended at least once during the school year by a level of "erotic intimacy" that did not involve forceful attempts at "sex intercourse." Of the 1,022 offensive erotic intimacy episodes that college women reported happening during the academic year, 73% involved "necking and petting above the waist" and 19% involved "petting below the waist."

Most recent studies of non-rape sexual victimization suggest that little has changed since the 1950s with respect to the extent of these types of victimizations committed against college women. In their study during the 1980s, Koss and her colleagues reported that a large proportion of college women had been sexually victimized at least once during the past year. About 40% of their sample had experienced at least one non-rape experience during the previous year. Fifty-four percent of the incidents involved unwanted touching—fondling, kissing, or petting but not intercourse—and 22% of the incidents involved sexual intercourse that was coerced but not forced though the perpetrator's threat or physical action.

Results from two studies during the 1990s parallel these earlier findings. First, White, Smith, and Humphrey (2001) conducted a 4-year longitudinal study in the early 1990s on a single campus (see also White & Smith, 2001). Their analysis revealed that 46% of women experienced at least one non-rape—coerced sexual intercourse or unwanted touching—during their four college years. This is five times higher than the 9% of college women who reported having been raped at least once during their college years. Second, our National College Women Sexual Victimization Study found that 15% of college women in the sample were sexually victimized, with the vast majority of these women, 13%, experiencing at least one non-rape during the academic year. Two-thirds of the sexual incidents involved unwanted sexual touching with or without the perpetrator threatening or using force. One-fifth of the incidents involved coerced sexual intercourse without threat or use of physical force.

Second, there is mounting evidence that the proportion of women who experience non-rape sexual victimizations far exceeds the proportion who experience rape (e.g., Abbey et al., 2004; Fisher et al., 2000; Koss et al., 1987). Take, for example, the results of a study by the American College Health Association, which used a large probability sample of college students from over hundreds of postsecondary institutions nationally. This research reported that from 2000 to 2008, 2% of college women were raped, on average, each year. Twice as many college women, 4%, during this time experienced an attempted rape. Most striking, during this 9-year period, a considerably larger proportion of college women, 11% annually, experienced sexually touching against their will. An annual average of 4% of college women were verbally threatened for sex against their will (American College Health Association, 2000a, 2000b, 2001a, 2001b, 2002a, 2002b, 2003a, 2003b, 2004a, 2004b, 2005a, 2005b, 2006a, 2006b, 2007a, 2007b, 2008a, 2008b).

White and her research team's work is similarly instructive (Smith et al., 2003; White et al., 2001). Figure 4.1 shows that the sample of women on the campus studied were far more likely to experience a non-rape than rape victimization. Thus, on average annually, 21.5% of these college women experienced a non-rape victimization compared to the 7.1% who were raped. This finding also was true year by year. During each collegiate year from first to fourth, a much larger proportion of women experienced at least one non-rape victimization than experienced a rape (see Figure 4.1). For example, during the first year of college, 29% of women reported experiencing a non-rape, whereas 11% reported being raped. The difference between those who experienced a non-rape and those who were raped across each year of college is always 15 percentage points or higher. The fourth year of college, in fact, shows the largest difference between these two groups of victimized college women. There is a 21 percentage point difference between women who experienced a non-rape (24%) and a rape (3%).

Our National College Women Sexual Victimization (NCWSV) Study is further relevant. We found that within an academic year, 2.8% of college women reported being raped at least once. More college women, 3.7%, were coerced (but not by the

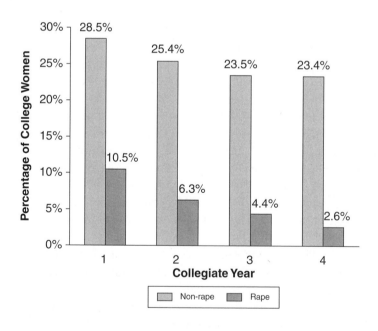

Figure 4.1 The Percentage of Women Victimized During Each Collegiate Year by Rape and Non-rape Victimization

SOURCE: Adapted from White and Smith (2001).

perpetrator's threatened or use of force) into having intercourse at least once during an academic year. An even much larger proportion of the national sample, 11%, experienced at least one incident of unwanted sexual contact during the school year. Noncontact sexual abuses, such as someone "flashing" his penis at her or having sexually tinged catcalls or sexually charged sounds or remarks directed at her, were experienced by the largest proportion of college women. Seventy-seven percent of the respondents experienced at least one form of noncontact sexual abuse during the school term.

Third, non-rape and rape victimization may have unique characteristics and correlates, which can only be discerned through careful investigation. In a study of a community sample of women, Testa and Derman (1999) revealed that the tactics used by perpetrators to obtain sexual contact is different in rape and other types of sexual victimization, in particular sexual coercion. Our NCWSV Study discovered that students' lifestyles and routines differentially affected the risk of college women experiencing rape and non-rape (Fisher & Cullen, 1999a). These findings suggest that whether they are researchers, policymakers, or campus officials, those who seek to unravel what places college women at risk will need to focus on the similar and unique risk factors associated with rape and different types of non-rape sexual victimization.

Fourth, for the allocation of prevention and intervention resources on campuses, it is important for campus administrators to understand the extent to which students are experiencing diverse types of sexual victimization, other than rape. This knowledge is needed to formulate a more informed campus policy and programmatic response that supplements the Clery Act crime statistics. Note that the Clery Act's sole focus is on a limited number of types of sexual offenses as defined by the Federal Bureau of Investigation. An exclusive focus on these offenses risks turning a blind eye to other forms of sexual victimization that are more commonly experienced and diminish the quality of college women's lives.

Categorizing Sexual Victimization

As we have seen from Chapter 3, the categorizing of a sexual victimization as a rape depends on the presence of penetration or intercourse, the use or threatened use of force by the perpetrator, and the lack of consent by the victim. Not all sexual victimizations are characterized by all of these of three dimensions—intercourse or penetration, threat of force or use of force, and lack of consent. However, this is not to say that those who experience unwanted sexual touching—for example, fondling of genitals or breasts—have not been sexually victimized. It is only to say that they have not been raped.

Non-rape sexual victimizations involve the assailant having unwanted physical contact with the victim. These contacts or acts are characterized by varying degrees of coercion, but they are not characterized by threats or use of actual physical force. Similar to rape, they also can be either completed or attempted acts.

To understand more fully different types of sexual victimization, it is useful to think about these behaviors falling along three dimensions. These dimensions can be used to categorize an act as a particular type of sexual victimization—whether rape or some form of non-rape. The three dimensions that characterize sexual victimization are as follows:

- Type of contact
- Degree of coercion
- Degree of action

It is useful to present each dimension along a continuum that captures the range of the behaviors included in each dimension. By doing so, different types of sexual experiences can be identified and then measured as distinct types of sexual victimizations. It is important to distinguish different types of sexual victimization beyond rape in terms of both naming the unwanted sexual contact and describing its dimensions.

TYPE OF CONTACT

The first dimension of sexual victimization categorizes the type of sexual contact that the perpetrator engages in to obtain physical interaction with the victim. As shown in Figure 4.2, the type of contact varies along a contact continuum. This continuum ranges from the perpetrator (1) having no sexual contact with any part of the victim's body to (2) using sexual advances to intentionally touch any part of the victim's body to (3) penetrating or engaging in intercourse with the victim's vagina, anus, or mouth. Having physical contact with any part of the victim's body can happen either underneath or on top of her clothing.

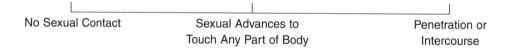

Figure 4.2   Continuum of Type of Contact

On one end of the continuum shown in Figure 4.2, the perpetrator has no sexual contact with any part of the victim's body. The perpetrator may direct a variety of behaviors or actions at the victim. Examples of no sexual contact include the perpetrator making general sexist remarks or comments to the victim. Also included are gendered behaviors such as undue attention (e.g., being too eager to please or help), body language (e.g., leering or standing to close), verbal advances (e.g., expressions of sexual attraction), or invitations for dates (Belknap & Erez, 2007). Other acts may involve no sexual contact yet be sexually abusive to the victim. These acts include the perpetrator exposing the victim to pornography or voyeurism (Basile & Saltzman, 2002).

In the middle of the type of contact continuum are sexual advances to intentionally physically touch any part of the victim's body. This would include physical advances such as kissing, touching, or rubbing with any part of the body, especially erogenous zones such as the head, lips, neck, hands, breasts, thighs, groin, or buttocks. Also included is the fondling of breasts, nipples, or a genital or sex organ (e.g., vagina, clitoris, vulva). Examples of sexual advances to physically touch someone's body would include a man intentionally touching a woman's breasts or buttocks or trying to kiss her lips or cheeks when she does not want him to do so.

On the farther end of the continuum is penetration or intercourse. This includes the insertion of the perpetrator's body part, such as his penis, mouth, tongue, digit (e.g., fingers), or an object (e.g., dildo, bottle) into any opening of the victim's body, including vagina, anus, and mouth. A man inserting his penis into the vagina or anus of a woman is an example of sexual intercourse or penetration. A woman performing oral sex on a man's penis (i.e., fellatio) or a man performing oral sex on a woman's vulva or clitoris (i.e., cunnilingus) are examples of sexual intercourse or penetration.

DEGREE OF COERCION

The second dimension, degree of coercion, refers to the characteristics of physical actions or tactics used by the perpetrator with the intent of having sexual contact with the victim. Various scholars have identified different levels or types of coercion to describe the diverse tactics through which the perpetrator uses coercion to obtain sexual contact with the victim—that is, to victimize her (Basile & Saltzman, 2002; Thompson, Basile, Hertz, & Sitterle, 2006). Finkelhor and Yllo (1985) were among the first researchers to conceptualize the meaning of sexual coercion. They identified four types of coercion: (1) social (e.g., institutional or cultural expectations as to the role of women in a relationship), (2) interpersonal (e.g., threatening behavior on the part of perpetrator), (3) threatened physical (e.g., threats to use physical force), and (4) physical (e.g., use of physical force).

Other researchers built on this theoretical foundation in an attempt to clarify and expand the conceptualization of the level of coercion. Thus, Hamby and Koss (2003) argue that in assessing different types of coerced sexual victimizations other than rape it is important to specify the type of force involved (see also Koss, 1996). For example, they use the term *psychological coercion* to include situations in which the perpetrator uses continual nagging, false promises, or similar strategies that "are not desirable but at the same time not crimes" (p. 244). Further, in his review of 120 studies of sexual victimization, Spitzberg (1999) identified five major categories of sexual coercion: (1) pressure and persistence, (2) deception, (3) threat, (4) physical restraint, and (5) physical force or injury.

The continuum shown in Figure 4.3 takes into account Finkelhor and Yllo's types of coercion, Hamby and Koss's degrees of coercion, and Spitzberg's five categories of sexual coercion. The continuum of degree of coercion has five discrete categories, ranging from the perpetrator engaging in psychological or emotional pressure to using physical force to obtain sexual contact with the victim. Across this continuum, the perpetrator is using varying degrees of intimidation or force. The perpetrator uses coercion to get the victim to engage in sexual contact in which she does not want to engage with the perpetrator. The victim's compliance is not voluntary, but rather it is the result of the perpetrator's level of coercion.

Figure 4.3   Continuum of Degree of Coercion

The first category on the degree of coercion continuum is psychological or emotional pressure. This category includes the assailant using verbal or emotional persuasion to obtain sexual contact with the victim's body. These persuasive tactics include continual requesting, nagging, pleading, urging, pressuring, pouting, or misusing authority to obtain sexual contact. Verbal aggression, not including threats of violence, could also be included, such as the perpetrator belittling or swearing at the victim. The perpetrator uses the power of persuasion to manipulate the woman into having sexual contact with him by eliciting feelings of guilt or obligation.

An example of verbal pressure is a boyfriend who pesters his girlfriend about having sexual contact—intimate touching, penetration, or intercourse—and continually mentions in virtually every communication with her that they should have more sex more often. She has repeatedly told him she is not interested, but he continues to verbally pressure her to have sexual contact with him. An example of emotional pressure could be a man making the victim feel sorry for him. She then has sex with him because of feelings of guilt or sympathy that he intentionally evoked.

The second category on this continuum, deception, includes the perpetrator communicating emotions, feelings, or promises that he does not really mean or intend to fulfill. These communications could include falsely professing some level of romantic emotion (e.g., love) to the victim, telling her lies, or making false promises. The perpetrator assures his victim that he will fulfill obligations once she gives into having sexual contact with him. Examples of deception include a professor telling a student he will not pass her in the course if she does not let him fondle her breasts and genitals. Another example is a classmate telling the victim that he will give her answers to the exam if she has oral sex with him.

The third category on the degree of coercion continuum, interpersonal threat, is another form of coercion used by a perpetrator to obtain sexual contact from his victim. Interpersonal threat involves the perpetrator threatening to terminate the relationship with the victim or to seek another person for sexual contact if the victim does not agree to have sexual contact with him. This type of coercion does not involve the perpetrator being physically violent toward the victim. Interpersonal threat entails the perpetrator threatening to carry through with unkind, callous, cruel, or mean actions directed at harming or terminating the relationship if the victim does not provide sexual contact to him. Also, the threat does not have to be communicated solely by word of mouth; it can be communicated via writing through a variety of mediums, such as a handwritten note, text messaging, an e-mail message, or a post on a social networking site such as Facebook.

Examples of an interpersonal threat include a man who tells his date or even a platonic friend that he will not drive her home unless she has intercourse with him. Another example is a man who pressures his girlfriend into having anal sex with him by telling her that, if she does not, he will end their relationship. He communicates his threat via text messaging to ensure his girlfriend receives the message.

Moving along the continuum toward physical force, the level of coercion shifts to include the perpetrator threatening to use, or using, physical means to obtain the victim's compliance to sexual contact. The fourth category on the level of force continuum is what Finkelhor and Yllo (1985) refer to as "threatened physical coercion," which specifically implies the use of physical force if sexual contact is not obtained. Threats of physical force involve the perpetrator threatening to use his body, such as his arms and hands, mouth, or feet, to inflict harm or pain on his victim or to threaten to use his strength to restrain her. He can also threaten to use a weapon, such as a knife or gun, so as to make her comply with his demands for sexual contact.

Examples of threatened physical coercion include a perpetrator threatening to hit, slap, or physically harm the victim if she does not have sexual contact with him. A husband who threatens to pull his wife's hair or to hit her if she does not perform oral sex on him is another example of threatened physical force.

The last category on the level of coercion continuum is physical force. Finkelhor and Yllo (1985) refer to physical force as physical coercion. As the term *physical force* suggests, the perpetrator actually uses physical force to obtain sexual contact with his victim. Physical force involves the perpetrator using his body, such as his arms and hands, mouth, or feet to inflict harm or pain on his victim or to use his strength to restrain her. He can also employ a weapon to force his victim to have sexual contact with him.

Examples of the use of physical force would include the perpetrator using his hands to slap the victim, holding her body down against her will, biting her, or pulling her hair in order to have sexual contact with her. Spitzberg (1999) uses a similar definition as that used by Finkelhor and Yllo. Spitzberg, however, distinguishes between physical restraint and physical force. Physical restraint is the perpetrator holding her arm down or her legs apart. Physical force is the perpetrator hitting or slapping his victim or using a weapon to get her to comply with his sexual demands.

It is important to understand and distinguish use of coercion from threatened use or use of physical force as one of the dimensions of a sexual victimization. It is also important when distinguishing pertinent characteristics of sexual victimization other than rape so to name or label the experience as a victimization and not merely as a "less serious" experience.

DEGREE OF ACTION

As shown in Figure 4.4, the third dimension of a sexual victimization is the degree of action. The continuum ranges from whether a perpetrator threatened to have sexual contact with the victim to attempted to but was unsuccessful in having sexual contact with the victim to successfully obtaining sexual contact.

A perpetrator can threaten to have sexual contact with a victim by verbally stating his intent in person or over the telephone. He also can threaten in writing that he will obtain sexual contact with the victim by sending her a text message or e-mail message.

If the perpetrator's action to obtain sexual contact with the victim was interrupted or thwarted, this could be considered an attempted sexual victimization. An example of an attempted sexual contact would be a perpetrator who reaches out to touch the breasts of a woman but she thwarts him before he does so.

A completed sexual contact would result if the perpetrator achieved sexual contact with the victim. A completed sexual contact includes actually having sexual contact with any part of the victim's body, such as her lips, neck, thighs, genitals, or buttocks. An example of a completed sexual contact would be when the perpetrator uses his fingers, hand, or penis to touch a woman's vaginal or anal areas.

Figure 4.4   Continuum of Degree of Action

A FRAMEWORK FOR CATEGORIZING SEXUAL VICTIMIZATION

The three dimensions of sexual victimization discussed thus far provide a framework for defining and naming different types of sexual victimization beyond rape; that is, non-rape victimizations. These different types of sexual victimization go beyond the legal, yet narrowly focused, view of sexual victimization as only including rape. The view of sexual victimization as defined as rape is limited. It only includes completed or attempted unwanted sexual intercourse or penetration that occurs as a result of the assailant using or threatening to use force or the victim's inability to consent.

There are many categories on each of the three continuums that can be used to distinguish rape from non-rape victimizations. Characteristics from each of the three continuums—type of contact, level of coercion, and degree of action—can be employed to categorize these experiences as distinct types of sexual victimizations beyond rape. The analysis to follow focuses on three main categories: (1) sexual coercion, (2) unwanted sexual contact, and (3) noncontact sexual abuses.

The next sections highlight what is known from the research about the extent of different types of sexual victimization other than rape that college women experience before and during their higher education tenure. The extent of a range of sexual victimizations, from sexual coercion to unwanted sexual contact to noncontact sexual abuses, are discussed below.

Sexual Coercion

Acts of intercourse or penetration are not always performed by the perpetrator with the threatened or the actual use of force. Sexual coercion is one such type of sexual victimization for which it is true that threats of force or force are not used by the perpetrator to obtain intercourse or penetration.

Sexual coercion is like rape on one dimension—type of contact. Like rape, sexual coercion is defined by vaginal, anal, or oral intercourse or penetration with the perpetrator's penis, mouth, tongue, digit (e.g., fingers), or with an object (e.g., dildo, bottle). Sexual coercion, like rape, is a matter of degree. Both rape and sexual coercion can be attempted or completed acts. Sexual coercion is unlike rape on the degree of coercion continuum. The type of contact that defines a sexual coercion is subsequent to the perpetrator's use of a variety of psychological or emotional tactics. Unlike with rape, the perpetrator does not engage in threats or use of force to obtain intercourse or penetration. In a sexual coercion, the perpetrator's purpose for using these tactics is to persuade or manipulate the victim into having sex she otherwise does not want to engage in.

In our NCWSV Study, we defined completed and attempted sexual coercion in the following way (Fisher et al., 2000, p. 8):

> Unwanted completed or attempted penetration with the threat of non-physical punishment, promise of reward, or pestering/verbal pressure. Penetration includes: penile-vaginal, mouth on your genitals, mouth on someone else's genitals, penile-anal, digital-vaginal, digital-anal, and object-anal.

TACTICS

Livingston, Buddie, Testa, and VanZile-Tamsen (2004) identified four types of tactics from women's descriptions of their verbal sexual coercion experiences that men use to obtain contact with the victim's body. These four tactics are (1) verbal persuasion, (2) persistence, (3) physical persuasion, and (4) gaining access.

They identified three types of verbal persuasion. First, negative sexual persuasion includes behaviors that were manipulative and emotionally hurtful to the victim, such as threats to end the relationship or go elsewhere for sex and belittling her or making her feel sorry for him. Second, positive sexual persuasion tactics were also used as a tactic by perpetrators to manipulate women into having sex. These tactics typically included the perpetrator sweet-talking or offering compliments to his victim, such as making promises to deceptively allure her into having sex. Third, neutral verbal persuasion was neither negative nor positive. Neutral verbal persuasion included the man continually nagging or pleading for sex without using emotionally charged statements. The man's intent is that his persistence will eventually wear the woman's resistance down and she will give in to having sex.

Persistence included the continual use of tactics to persuade the woman to comply with his sexual advances, such as sweet talk or sexual contact. Physical persuasion tactics involved sexual contact (e.g., kissing, sexual touching) or physical aggression (e.g., being held down). Gaining access strategies, such as isolating the woman or using false pretences to be alone with her, typically were employed by the perpetrator as a function of being in the relationship or by sexual precedence.

Using only those incidents involving verbal sexual coercion, Livingston et al. reported that verbal persuasion (81.6% of the incidents) and persistence (61.4%) were among the two most common tactics used by those who commit sexual coercion, followed by physical persuasion (48.2%) and gaining access (10.5%). In the incidents in which the perpetrator used verbal persuasion, negative verbal persuasion was most common (49.1% of the incidents), followed by positive verbal persuasion (19.3%) and neutral/nagging (18.4%). Nearly half of the women reported that the perpetrator used physical persuasion tactics in conjunction with the use of verbal tactics.

MEASUREMENT OF SEXUAL COERCION

Koss and her colleagues were among the first researchers to develop and incorporate the systematic measurement of sexual coercion into the measure of the extent of different types of sexual victimization that college women had experienced. They defined sexual coercion as experiences of "sexual intercourse subsequent to the use of menacing verbal pressure or the misuse of authority" (Koss et al., 1987, p. 166).

As noted in Chapter 2, within the Sexual Experiences Survey (SES), there are questions that distinguish the type of coercion experienced. In Table 4.1, the questions that Koss et al. used to measure the extent of sexual coercion among college women are presented again. The SES captures three different degrees of coercion: verbally coerced, misuse of authority, and threat or use of force.

Several researchers have used Koss's original questions to estimate the extent of sexual coercion (see Spitzberg, 1999; Thompson et al., 2006). Other researchers have modified these questions to take into account additional forms of sexually coercive tactics (see Jordan, Wilcox, & Pritchard, 2007; Thompson et al., 2006). One example of the modified version of the SES is by Broach and Petretic (2006). As shown in Table 4.1, their questions provide a description of three additional forms of coerced sexual intercourse to measure the degree of coercion used by the perpetrator. The first two forms, the victim's feeling of guilt or obligation to have intercourse and victim's feeling unable or useless to stop the perpetrator, are examples of psychological coercion. The third form, the perpetrator threatening to end the relationship, is an example of an interpersonal threat.

As also shown in Table 4.1, our NCWSV Study measured verbally coerced sex. In addition to measuring verbal coercion like the SES, this study included screen questions about two additional types of coercion that occur within a campus context: threats of nonphysical punishment and promises of reward. An example of nonphysical punishment includes a professor giving a student a bad grade for not having sexual

Table 4.1   Questions Used to Measure Sexual Coercion

Form of Coercion	Survey Question

Koss et al.: Sexual Experiences Survey (SES)

Have you ever . . .

Verbally Coerced	given in to sexual intercourse when you did not want to because you were overwhelmed by a man's continual arguments or pressure?
Misuse of Authority	had sexual intercourse when you didn't want to because a man used his position of authority (boss, teacher, camp counselor, supervisor) to make you?
Threatened or Used Force	had sexual intercourse when you didn't want to because a man threatened or used some degree of physical force (twisting your arm, holding you down, etc.) to make you?

Broach and Petretic: Modified Sexual Experiences Survey

Been in a situation where a man became so sexually aroused that you . . .

Guilty/Obligation	had sexual intercourse with him, even though you did not want to, because you felt responsible for "leading him on"?
Felt Unable to Physically/Useless to Try to Stop Him	would not be able to physically stop him/useless to try to stop him, so you had sexual intercourse with him, even though you did not want to?
Threatened to End Relationship	had sexual intercourse with a man when you didn't really want to because he threatened to end your relationship otherwise?

Fisher et al.: National College Women Sexual Victimization Study (NCWSV) (screen questions)

Since school began, has anyone made or tried to make you have sexual intercourse when you did not want to by . . .

Threats of Nonphysical Punishment	making threats of nonphysical punishment such as lowering a grade, being demoted or fired from a job, damaging your reputation or being excluded from a group for failure to comply with requests for any type of sexual activity?
Promises of Rewards	making promises of rewards such as raising a grade, being hired or promoted, being given a ride or class notes, or getting help with course work from a fellow student if you complied sexually?
Verbally Coerced	simply being overwhelmed by someone's continual pestering and verbal pressure?

SOURCES: Broach and Petretic (2006); Fisher, Cullen, and Turner (1999); Koss, Gidycz, and Wisniewski (1987).

intercourse with him. On the degree of coercion continuum, this could fall under inter-personal threat. Examples of a promise of rewards for having sexual intercourse with the perpetrator is a male student promising to give the answers to a test to his victim if she gives him oral sex or a teaching assistant giving the student a better grade for sex. On the degree of coercion continuum, these are examples of deception.

EXTENT OF SEXUAL COERCION

The extent that college women experience sexual coercion is a relatively new, but growing, field of study within the sexual victimization research. This escalating inter-est may well be fueled by research reporting that the college years are among the vul-nerable ones for experiencing sexual coercion. Thus, Abbey, McAuslan, Ross, and Zawacki (1999) report that of those women who had been sexually coerced, 61% reported that the "most serious" sexual coercion happened when they were between 18 and 21 years old, 14% reported that they were between 22 and 25 years old, and 7% reported they were between 26 and 28 years old. The first two age groups encompass the years when a large number of women are enrolled pursuing undergraduate and graduate college degrees.

Single-Campus Studies. Some of this emerging research has been conducted by researchers who undertook a survey on a single campus. Obviously, single-campus studies are limited in their generalizability. However, when taken together, they show common findings that lend credence to the assessment that their individual results are not idiosyncratic. In this case, it appears that the risk of sexual coercion is rela-tively high even over a short period of time and increases the longer a woman is a col-lege student.

This conclusion can be drawn from studies conducted on single campuses since 2000 that employ different reference periods.

- Over a 3-month period, Gidycz, Orchowski, King, and Rich (2008) reported that nearly 4% of women on a single campus were sexually coerced.

- Using a reference period of 8 months, Messman-Moore, Coates, Gaffey, and Johnson (2008) reported that almost 12% of women were sexually coerced into having intercourse.

- Within a 2-year time frame, Kalof (2000) found that 20% of college women were sexually coerced.

- Using a reference period of "since enrolling in college," Gross, Winslett, Roberts, and Gohm (2006) reported that 9.1% of the female students answered "yes" to having been physically unable, or that it was useless to try, to stop their male assailant from having sexual intercourse.

- White et al.'s data (2001) show that 30% of women experienced at least one form of sexual coercion over the course of an undergraduate career. Similar to other studies, this one found that more women were verbally coerced, 30%, compared to the 1.9% who were coerced by misuse of authority.

White et al.'s (2001) study is further relevant because as a longitudinal study, it was able to show that a sizable number of women are sexually coerced *each* of their four college years. These researchers followed two cohorts of freshmen at a single campus to examine their annual experiences with sexual coercion. Their results as to the proportion of women sexually coerced during each of their four college years are presented in Table 4.2. As can be seen, in their first year on campus, nearly 16% of the respondents reported being sexually coerced. Despite age and maturing, virtually the same proportion of the sample in their fourth year reported being victimized by sexual coercion. What is noteworthy about these results is that the proportion of sexually coerced college women does not change dramatically across college years. In fact, the results suggest that this proportion remains quite steady at about 15% annually.

Table 4.2   White, Smith, and Humphrey's Longitudinal Study of Sexual Coercion Against College Women

| | Year in College | | | |
Sexual Coercion	Year 1 Percentage (n)	Year 2 Percentage (n)	Year 3 Percentage (n)	Year 4 Percentage (n)
	15.9	15.2	14.9	14.5
	(222)	(179)	(142)	(108)

SOURCES: Adapted from White and Smith (2001); White, Smith, and Humphrey (2001).

NOTE: Percentages are based on total sample size that varied by year (Year 1, n = 1,378; Year 2, n = 1,178; Year 3, n = 954; and Year 4, n = 747).

National-Level Studies. Only three national-level studies have been published that report the extent of sexual coercion among women during their collegiate years. First, each year since 2000, the American College Health Association has been tracking the proportion of college women who have experienced a range of sexual victimizations, including sexual coercion. Between 2000 and 2007, the annual average of college women who experienced verbal threats for sex against their will has been 4%. There has been little year-to-year variation in this annual estimate across these 8 years. Every year, slightly more or less than 4% of college women are sexually coerced (American College Health Association, 2000a, 2000b, 2001a, 2001b, 2002a, 2002b, 2003a, 2003b, 2004a, 2004b, 2005a, 2005b, 2006a, 2006b, 2007a, 2007b, 2008a, 2008b).

Second, Koss and her colleagues (1987) found that within the past year, 11.5% of college women reported being sexually coerced into having intercourse. Eleven percent of women were verbally coerced. Much fewer, less than 1% of these women, were coerced through the misuse of authority.

Third, as noted above, our National College Women Sexual Victimization Study reported the extent of sexual coercion among college women during an academic year.

Recall that we used a two-step process: screen questions followed by an incident report to confirm what had occurred. This is perhaps one reason why the prevalence of sexual coercion is lower in the NCWSV Study than in investigations not employing a follow-up incident report. Even so, we found that over a 6.9-month reference period during the school year, 3.7% of college women experienced at least one completed or attempted sexual coercion.

Further, the use of the incident report allowed us to measure in the NCWSV Study what kind of coercion the perpetrator employed. Close to 4% of women experienced verbal coercion. Compared to other kinds of coercion, such as threatened with non-physical force experienced by 0.5% of women or promise of reward experienced by 0.2%, verbal coercion was by far the dominant form of sexual coercion used against college women.

This finding that verbal coercion was the most likely form of coercion mirrors the result by Koss et al. (1987). Of course, some commentators might argue that verbally coerced sexual intercourse is simply effective foreplay by males. But recall that the participants in the NCWSV Study were asked about being made to have sexual intercourse "when you did not want by simply being *overwhelmed* by someone's continual pestering and verbal pressure." It is when sexual advances reach this stage—unwanted and achieved through overwhelming verbal coercion—that a sexual victimization can be said to have occurred.

Unwanted Sexual Contact

Unwanted and coerced sexual contact includes the perpetrator intentionally using different coercive tactics to make sexual advances to touch any part of victim's body. This type of sexual contact is not penetrative but does involve physical touching. The perpetrator makes sexual advances to any part of the victim's body—lips, breasts, genitals, buttocks, or any erogenous zone—either over or underneath her clothing. Sexual contact includes such acts as kissing, groping or fondling, rubbing, petting, licking or sucking, or any other form of unwanted sexual contact perpetrated by the assailant.

The perpetrator engages in tactics along the continuum of coercion to obtain sexual contact with the victim's body. The degree of coercion used by the perpetrator ranges from using no force to using psychological or emotional coercion, deception, interpersonal threats, to using threats or force in his attempt to obtain sexual contact with the victim's body. The perpetrator's action to have contact with any of the victim's body can be an attempted or completed act.

MEASUREMENT OF UNWANTED SEXUAL CONTACT

There is no standard way of measuring unwanted sexual contact. However, to illuminate how this form of sexual victimization is assessed, we discuss two prominent measurement strategies. First, the most widely used measure of unwanted sexual contact is with items on the SES (Koss et al., 2007). As shown in Table 4.3, the three items from the SES that measure unwanted sexual contact describe the perpetrator's behavior in detail and his use of different forms of coercion to engage in "sex play." Recall that this does not include sexual penetration, which would qualify an act as a rape or sexual coercion. The three types of coercion represented in these SES items are (1) verbal coercion, (2) misuse of authority, and (3) threatened use of force or use of force. Verbal coercion is a form of emotional or psychological coercion. Under certain circumstances, misuse of authority can be an example of deception. Threatened use of force or use of force is the more severe form of physical coercion on the continuum of degree of coercion presented previously in Figure 4.3.

Table 4.3   Sexual Experiences Survey Items of Unwanted Sexual Contact

Form of Coercion or Force	Survey Question
Koss et al.: Sexual Experiences Survey (SES)	
Have you ever . . .	
Verbally Coerced	given in to sex play (fondling, kissing, or petting, but not intercourse) when you didn't want to because you were overwhelmed by a man's continual arguments and pressure?
Misuse of Authority	had sex play (fondling, kissing, or petting, but not intercourse) when you didn't want to because a man used his position of authority (boss, teacher, camp counselor, supervisor) to make you?
Threatened Use or Use of Physical Force	had sex play (fondling, kissing, or petting, but not intercourse) when you didn't want to because a man threatened or used some degree of physical force (twisting your arm, holding you down, etc.) to make you?
Fisher et al.: National College Women Sexual Victimization Study (NCWSV)(screen questions)	
Since school began, has anyone made or tried to make you have sexual contact when you did not want to by . . .	
Threats of Nonphysical Punishment	making threats of nonphysical punishment such as lowering a grade, being demoted or fired from a job, damaging your reputation or being excluded from a group for failure to comply with requests for any type of sexual activity?
Promises of Rewards	making promises of rewards such as raising a grade, being hired or promoted, being given a ride or class notes, or getting help with course work from a fellow student if you complied sexually?
Verbally Coerced	simply being overwhelmed by someone's continual pestering and verbal pressure?

SOURCES: Fisher, Cullen, and Turner (1999); Koss, Gidycz, and Wisniewski (1987).

Second, our NCWSV Study offers a related but different way of measuring this phenomenon. Recall, we used a two-stage measurement process with a series of screen questions and an incident report to confirm which type of unwanted sexual contact, if any, had occurred during the course of each incident. We included three behaviorally specific screen questions that describe the forms of coercive behaviors used by the perpetrator to obtain sexual contact. As shown in Table 4.3, similar to the Koss et al.'s SES, we incorporated a question about the use of verbal coercion. Two screen questions asked about other additional forms of coercion: threats of nonphysical punishment and promises of rewards. A threat of nonphysical punishment can be seen as an example of an interpersonal threat, whereas a promise of rewards is an example of deception.

Again, unlike the SES and most other investigations, the NCWSV Study measured rape, sexual coercion, and unwanted sexual contact through a two-step process. Thus, female students were categorized as experiencing unwanted sexual contact based on their responses to questions about type of physical contact and type of coercion in the incident report. They could be categorized in this way regardless of whether they screened into the incident report from the questions meant to capture unwanted sexual contact or from questions meant to capture other forms of sexual victimization (e.g., rape).

EXTENT OF UNWANTED SEXUAL CONTACT

The existing research shows that a large proportion of college women have experienced unwanted sexual contact. Single-campus and national-level studies are similarly revealing.

Single-Campus Studies. Recent single-campus studies have explored the extent of this type of sexual victimization. What is evident looking across these studies is that unwanted sexual contact is a persistent issue confronting college women. A substantial percentage of college women experience unwanted sexual contact during their college tenure. The percentage of women who experience unwanted sexual contact increased as the reference period lengthened—from 7.9% over 3 months (Gidycz et al., 2008) to 19.6% over about 6 months (Banyard, Ward, et al., 2007), to 29.8% among first-year and second-year undergraduate students during their time at the university (Flack et al., 2008). Gross et al. (2006) limited their research to those experiencing sexual contact through force or threat of force; 13.3% indicated being victimized.

Data from White and her colleagues' (2001) study of one campus over 4 years also reveals that a very large proportion of college women will experience unwanted sexual contact. Over 45% of the female students in the sample experienced at least one incident of unwanted sexual contact while in college. As seen in Table 4.4, there was a tendency for victimization to decline as the students' college careers progressed. Thus, the highest total victimization occurred in the first year of college, with 27.0% of the sample experiencing an unwanted sexual contact. Still, by year 4 in college, fully 22.1% of the female students were victimized by unwanted sexual contact.

Table 4.4 White, Smith, and Humphrey's Longitudinal Study of Unwanted Sexual Contact Against College Women

Type of Unwanted Sexual Contact	Year in College			
	Year 1 Percentage	Year 2 Percentage	Year 3 Percentage	Year 4 Percentage
Unwanted Sexual Contact Without Force	26.2	23.4	22.0	22.0
Unwanted Sexual Contact With Force	4.7	3.1	2.6	1.6
Total	27.0	23.9	22.3	22.1

SOURCES: Adapted From White and Smith (2001); White, Smith, and Humphrey (2001).

NOTE: Percentages are based on those who have at least one valid value across all 4 years of data (n = 1407).

National-Level Studies. National data are similarly revealing. As discussed above, the American College Health Association has been tracking sexual victimization over time. Between 2000 and 2008, it found that, on average annually, 12% of college women experienced sexual touching against their will. This statistic has remained relatively stable during this time, with the proportion of women sexually touched against their will ranging from a low of 10.6% to a high of 12.4% (American College Health Association, 2000a, 2000b, 2001a, 2001b, 2002a, 2002b, 2003a, 2003b, 2004a, 2004b, 2005a, 2005b, 2006a, 2006b, 2007a, 2007b, 2008a, 2008b).

Again, we consult the findings of Koss et al.'s (1987) classic studies. Their research revealed that 27.8% of the college women in their sample experienced unwanted sexual contact during the past year. Verbal coercion was the most prevalent form, but sexual contact also was accomplished in a minority of cases through threatened use or use of force (3.5%) and misuse of authority (1.6%).

Finally, we can report the findings from our NCWSV Study. We found that 10.9% of college women experienced at least one completed or attempted unwanted sexual contact incident since the start of the current academic year. This overall pattern included the following:

- Seven percent experienced verbally coerced contact.

- Slightly fewer, 5%, were threatened or physical force was used.

- Less than 1% of college women experienced an unwanted sexual contact through the perpetrator's promise of rewards (0.7%) or use of nonphysical punishment (0.5%).

Noncontact Sexual Abuse

Certain types of sexual victimization involve no sexual contact such as penetration or touching between the victim and offender (Basile & Saltzman, 2002). Such noncontact sexual victimization can be verbal or visual. The verbal type includes the perpetrator intentionally saying or making sounds that connote a condescending or abusive message to the victim. These encompass both words, such as sexist comments, and sounds, such as whistling or a catcall. The visual type includes acts such as the perpetrator exposing the victim to pornographic materials or to his sexual organs when she did not agree to see them, making obscene phone calls, or photographing the victim having sex or nude without her consent. Materials sent via texting or posted on the Internet would also qualify as examples of noncontact sexual abuse.

Noncontact sexual abuse can vary along the continuum of degree of coercion (see Figure 4.3). Thus, these acts vary on the continuum from verbal or emotional coercion to threats and actual use of force. For example, the perpetrator can continually nag the victim to look at pornographic material or he can forcefully restrain the victim's face so her eyes are directly in front of the pornographic material.

MEASUREMENT OF NONCONTACT SEXUAL ABUSE

As noted, the sexual victimization of women can take many forms. Previous research suggests that beyond victimization involving force or threats of force, females are subjected to a range of sexually harassing comments including, for example, sexist remarks, catcalls, insults, and unwelcomed statements tinged with sexual innuendo or sexually explicit content. Though not plentiful, some evidence that the supposed civility of the ivory tower life on college campuses does not insulate female students from such verbal sexual victimization (Fitzgerald et al., 1988; Hill & Silva, 2005; Lott, Reilly, & Howard, 1982; Paludi & Paludi, 2003). In our NCWSV Study, we wished to provide a complete portrait of the sexual victimization that college women experience. Therefore, we included five questions that attempted to assess harassing verbal comments. Although they are not typically found in research studies, we also incorporated five questions that assessed the "visual" victimization of women. Thus, we focused on instances in which the respondents were involuntarily exposed to sexually related content and instances in which their sexual privacy was violated. These verbal and visual questions are presented in Tables 4.5 and 4.6.

For verbal and visual victimization, we did not follow a screen question with an incident report. After undertaking a pretest of the survey instrument, it seemed likely that some of these victimizations would be so numerous that the study's interviewers would have to complete thousands of incident reports—an unrealistic task. As a result, we instead asked only whether a victimization had occurred. If the respondent answered "yes," then the person was asked "how many times has this happened to you" both on campus and off campus. We recognize that this approach—though not unlike that employed in past research—is less precise than using a methodology that uses an incident report to confirm that a victimization indicated on a screen question has actually taken place. Even so, the results reported here are suggestive of the extent to which different types of verbal and visual victimization are experienced by college women. Finally, we should reemphasize that the bounding period for this survey was approximately 6.9 months. As noted previously, extrapolating from just over 6-month figures to year-long figures is difficult. Nevertheless, the extent of sexual victimization reported here—which is particularly high for verbal victimization—does suggest that only a minority of women on college campuses escape some type of sexual victimization.

EXTENT OF NONCONTACT VERBAL ABUSE

As the results from the our NCWSV Study in Table 4.5 show, verbal sexual abuse appears to be a common experience for female college students. Over three-fourths, 76%, of the women in the study reported having experienced at least one type of non-contact verbal abuse during the school year. On average, these victimized women experienced eight incidents of noncontact verbal abuse.

Table 4.5   The Extent of Noncontact Verbal Abuse Among College Women During an Academic Year

Type of Verbal Abuse	National College Women Sexual Victimization Study	
	Percentage Within an Academic Year	Mean of Victimizations per Victim
General sexist remarks in front of you	54.3	13.0
Catcalls, whistles about your looks, or noises with sexual overtones	48.2	13.9
Obscene telephone calls or messages	21.9	5.0
Asked questions about sex or romantic life when clearly none of their business	19.0	5.6
False rumors about sex life with them or others	9.7	2.7
Total Experienced at Least One Type of Verbal Abuse	75.6	8.0

SOURCE: Fisher, Cullen, and Turner (1999).

Table 4.6 The Extent of Noncontact Visual Abuse Among College Women During an Academic Year

Type of Visual Abuse	National College Women Sexual Victimization Study	
	Percentage Within an Academic Year	Mean of Victimizations per Victim
Exposed to pornographic pictures or materials when you did not agree to see them	6.1	3.2
Someone exposed his sexual organs to you when you did not agree to see them	4.8	2.7
Observed while undressing, nude, or in sex act without your consent	2.4	2.9
Showed other people or played for others photographs, videotapes, or audiotapes having sex or in a nude or seminude state without your consent	0.3	1.2
Photographed, videotaped, or audio-taped you having sex or in a nude or seminude state without your consent	0.2	1.1
Total Experienced at Least One Type of Visual Abuse	11.4	2.2

SOURCE: Fisher, Cullen, and Turner (1999).

During the course of the academic school year, more than half the women, 54%, had experienced "general sexist remarks" voiced in their presence, while almost half, 48%, reported hearing "catcalls, whistles about your looks, or noises with sexual overtones" while on campus. Moreover, the number of victimizations per victim for these two offenses was startling: 13.0 and 13.9, respectively. These findings suggest that these students experience a flow of sexually tinged remarks and sounds.

About one in five women also stated that they had received "obscene telephone calls or messages." The mean number of victimization incidents per victim was five. Almost one in five women reported that they had been "asked questions about your sex or romantic life" when such inquiries were clearly none of someone's business. The mean for number of times college women experienced this type of noncontact sexual abuse was six. Finally, almost 1 in 10 women said that "false rumors" had been spread about their sex lives and this happened on average three times during the school year.

It is not clear, however, how much of this sexual verbal victimization related to being a college student and how much was simply a burden that young women in society generally experience. When we examined the data by whether the victimizations occurred on and off campus, there was variation across the five types of verbal victimizations; even so, in general they split about evenly—half taking place on campus, half off campus. Thus, while it cannot be stated that verbal sexual victimization is unique to college campuses, the results do suggest that campuses do not insulate college-aged females from sexism, lewd remarks, obscene phone calls, and unwanted inquires into and rumors about their sex lives.

EXTENT OF NONCONTACT VISUAL ABUSE

Table 4.6 reports the results from the NCWSV Study for five forms of noncontact visual abuse. As can be readily seen, visual victimization occurs far less often than verbal victimizations. Just over 11% of college women experienced noncontact visual abuse compared to the 76% who reported being verbally abused. These victims experienced, on average, 2.2 incidents of noncontact visual abuse. This is far less than the average number of noncontact verbal abuse incidents (mean = 8).

Even so, it is instructive that 6.1% of the college women reported that they had been shown pornographic materials that they did not wish to see. On average, this type of noncontact visual abuse happened 3.2 times to victims. Almost 5% of college women indicated that, during the academic year, someone had exposed his sexual organs to them when they did not give their consent. These abuses happened, on average, 2.7 times during the school year. Further, 2.4% stated that, also without their consent, someone had tried to observe them while "undressing, nude, or in a sex act," and on average this happened about three times during the academic year.

The other two forms of victimization were very rare—less than 1%—but were not nonexistent. Notably, 15 women in the sample reported that, without their consent, someone had shared "photographs, videotapes, or audiotapes" of them "having sex or in a nude or seminude state." Further, eight women indicated that they had been photographed or taped "having sex or in a nude or seminude state" without their consent.

NONCONTACT ABUSE IN STUDENTS' EVERYDAY LIVES

On one level, of course, noncontact sexual abuses seem relatively minor. In a social domain in which younger men and women students often attempt to interact or initiate intimate relationships, one might anticipate that some sexually tinged remarks will be made. But given the incidence of these abuses, the results from our NCWSV Study suggest that the verbal abuse of women goes beyond playful exchanges, harmless off-color humor, and unintentional affronts. Instead, many female respondents reported repeatedly having to cope with having their gender—especially their role as sexual objects—made salient against their consent. Further, in an era in which political correctness supposedly has chilled what can be said in the ivory tower, these results did not support the conclusion that college campuses provide a safe haven from verbal abuse.

In contrast, noncontact visual abuse did not appear to be ubiquitous in the lives of female students. Even so, considering that the results were only for a short time of the students' lives, the prevalence of involuntary exposure both to pornographic materials and to sexual organs is not inconsequential. Finally, it does not appear that the nonconsensual videotaping of women having sex or in the nude is a problem of any magnitude. Although a rare event, however, it is instructive that there were seven cases in which women were involuntarily taped on campus (and eight other cases in which taped material, voluntarily obtained, was without permission shown to others). These are serious violations of the victims' privacy, and, if publicized, a single incident can have a scandalous effect on the individuals involved and on a university's reputation. Further, the NCWSV Study was conducted before cell phone and related technology made recording and disseminating materials far easier, especially to a worldwide audience. As a result, this is an area of victimization that warrants further inquiry and updating.

Conclusion

Scholars' traditional focus on rape is understandable. After all, rape is a serious crime; acquaintance rape on college campuses and elsewhere was long hidden from view; and the consequences of being raped are potentially substantial for the victim. Even so, as a growing number of researchers have realized, the focus on rape should not obscure the extent to which college women face other forms of sexual victimization. These include the use of sexual coercion for purposes of intercourse, being groped or physically touched when the attention is uninvited, and having men express sexist remarks, whistle, make obscene comments in person or over the telephone, or involuntarily expose women to degrading sexual images.

We can anticipate that some critics will respond that our analysis is just an exercise in political correctness. Men, after all, "will be men"; it is just nature taking its course. In the pursuit of sexual gratification, young men will be persistent, clumsy, inarticulate, and crude; and some might commit criminal acts. For Katie Roiphe, the author of *The Morning After* (discussed in Chapter 1), women simply have to get a backbone and "deal with it." Roiphe admits to having her "bad nights." The solution is not to whine and assume a victim's role but to take responsibility and show self-efficacy. More broadly, claims Roiphe, this concern with supposed sexual victimization deprives sexual relations of essential human qualities:

> People pressure and manipulate and cajole each other into all sorts of things all the time.... No human interactions are free from pressure, and the idea that sex is, or can be, makes it what Sontag calls a "special case," vulnerable to inconsistent expectations of double standard. . . . these feminists are endorsing their own

utopian vision of sexual relations: sex without struggle, sex without power, sex without persuasion, sex without pursuit. (1993, pp. 79–80)

In the end, according to Roiphe, the attempt to place a protective veil over women robs them of their human agency and of their obligation to meet life as it presents itself. Under the supposed protection of feminists, college students are reduced to passive victims, who live in a world in which they feel "pinched, leered at, assaulted daily by sexual advances, encroached upon, kept down, bruised by harsh reality" (1993, p. 172).

Of course, when any new problem is discovered—in this case, sexual victimization—there is the risk of hyperbole, of trying to illuminate the problem's seriousness so that it will no longer remain hidden and ignored. So Roiphe has a point—but only to a degree. The sexual victimization reported in this chapter is not a mere fantasy but rather an empirical reality. Study after study—whether conducted 20 years ago or 2 years ago, whether conducted on a single campus or across the nation, whether asking one set of questions or another—all reach the same general conclusion: college women often reside in a sexualized environment where their bodies and personal space are violated in unwanted and potentially damaging ways.

In Roiphe's world, females are to manifest individual human agency but are expected to be passive about the gender relations as they find them. Their role is to cope with, but not try to change, this world—as the feminists she criticizes have argued should be done. More than this, the men in Roiphe's world lack human agency or responsibility. Implicitly, her argument suggests that beyond "real rape," males are free to use any form of coercion short of physical force to gratify their sexual desires. They are free to leer and whistle and grope and make sexist remarks. It is just men being men, or at least some men being who they are. This perspective, however, robs men of their human agency, of their responsibility to monitor their own behavior and to avoid ethical lapses. It offers male students a ready-made excuse for their sexual misconduct: "I was only being a guy." It is this thinking that can be transformed into "rape myths"—the techniques of neutralization that weaken normative restraint and permit potential assailants to traverse moral boundaries.

More broadly, Roiphe's attempt to correct what she sees as feminist excess ignores the fact that women on college campuses must endure sexual victimization that rarely touches men. This is a form of social inequality that imposes an unfair cost on female students not borne by their male counterparts. Roiphe's attempt to normalize this inequality only reinforces feminists' claims that patriarchy is hegemonic. In such a social context, male sexual aggression is given normative status, and it is up to women to cope with the "natural order of things." Efforts to complain about—or even to study—women's sexual victimization are in turn dismissed as political correctness run amok.

In the end, political debate is not the issue. Rather, what matter are the lives of college women that, each day, are affected in small and sometimes large ways by the sexual victimization they endure. This hidden cost of being a female student should not be dismissed as making a mountain out of a molehill. Rather, further research should be undertaken to confirm the conclusions of existing studies and to map out the ways in which diverse types of sexual victimization potentially diminish the quality of life experienced by college women.

5

It Happened Again

Sexual Revictimization

Following a victimization, it might be expected that victims would become more vigilant and take precautionary steps to ensure that they remained safe from crime. If that were so, revictimization would be a rare event and, in any case, victims would experience reduced risk of experiencing subsequent criminal events. As it turns out, however, this commonsense deduction proves to be misleading. Especially in the 1990s, research was undertaken that demonstrated that revictimization—sometimes also called repeat victimization—was commonplace (Farrell, 1992; Farrell, Phillips, & Pease, 1995). As Skogan observed, "the most important criminological insight of the decade has been the discovery in a very systematic fashion of repeat multiple victimization" (cited in Brady, 1996, p. 3). Beyond its substantive significance, this finding had important implications for crime policy and prevention. As Skogan (1990, pp. 269–270) yet again commented, "Repetitive victimizations are important for policy purposes because they are predictable from past reported crime, they typically involve offenders who are immediately identifiable, intervention is possible, and they add disproportionately to the overall crime count" (see also Farrell, 1992; Farrell & Pease, 2006; Weisel, 2005).

The question that concerns us is whether *sexual* revictimization occurs among college women who have suffered an initial sexual victimization. Our data from the National College Women Sexual Victimization Study allow us to address this issue. In Chapters 3 and 4, we have already documented the extent of initial sexual victimization among respondents in the NCWSV Study. Here, we build on this research to investigate whether "it happens again" to those once victimized. Note that because our data are limited to an academic year, we focus in particular on relatively short-term revictimization. Nonetheless, as is conveyed later in this chapter, we find that sexual victimization occurs with relative frequency among female students.

To set the context for this analysis, we begin by examining the issue of revictimization generally. This discussion shows that crime revictimization is common, is concentrated, occurs within a short period of time, and often involves a repeat of the same type of crime. We then explore what is known about sexual revictimization. This material provides a prelude to exploring the extent, nature, and explanations of sexual revictimization among college women.

Before proceeding, we need to complete some conceptual housekeeping. Scholars in this area use a variety of terms to describe the experience of being victimized a second time—or more times thereafter. The difficulty is that the second victimization might (1) involve the same or a different type of victimization and (2) occur shortly after or years after the initial incident. We use the term *revictimization* as an umbrella to capture any subsequent victimization regardless of the time frame. We also use the term *repeat victimization* to refer to a special subcategory of incidents: those that involve victimization by the same type of behavior within a short period of time.

Crime Revictimization

EXTENT OF REVICTIMIZATION

Several national-level victimization surveys reveal that most households or individuals are not victimized annually. For example, the National Violence Against Women Study (NVAWS) showed that only 2.1% of the women and 3.5% of men were either raped or physically assaulted in the previous 12 months (Tjaden & Thoennes, 2000, 2006). In this same vein, average annual household rates for burglary reported by the 2002–2003 National Crime Victimization Survey (NVCS) was 3% (Catalano, 2004).

These data, however, are potentially misleading. They mask that fact that of those who were victimized, a substantial portion experienced more than one incident. Indeed, much research has reported that households and individuals are at risk of experiencing not just one but repeated incidents (see Daigle, Fisher, & Guthrie, 2007; Weisel, 2005). For example, in the 2003–2004 and 2004–2005 British Crime Surveys, 16% and 14% of the burglary victims, respectively, were victimized two or more times within the same year (Nicholas, Povey, Walker, & Kershaw, 2005). In the United States, the National Violence Against Women Study reported that women who were raped in the previous 12-month period averaged 2.9 rapes (Tjaden & Thoennes, 2006). Rates are even higher when the perpetrator is an intimate partner. On average, females averaged 4.5 rapes by the same intimate partner, and female physical assault victims averaged 6.9 assaults by the same partner since the age of 18. Men averaged slightly fewer, at 4.4 intimate partner physical assaults by the same partner (Tjaden & Thoennes, 2000). Nearly 60% of the assaulted youths in Lauritsen and Davis Quinet's (1995) research using the National Youth Survey were repeat victims. Similarly, 61% of the robbery victims were robbed twice or more.

CONCENTRATION OF REVICTIMIZATION

Not only do a substantial portion of crime victims experience more than one incident, but a growing body of research shows that repeat targets also experience a disproportionate amount of all crime victimizations. For example, analyzing 10 years of British Crime Survey (BCS) data, Pease (1998) reported that 6% of the respondents experienced 68% of all of the property thefts. Studies of residential burglary, including the 1997 BCS results, also manifest this pattern, in which a small proportion of victims experience a large proportion of all victimization incidents (see Weisel, Clarke, & Stedman, 1999). A similar highly skewed distribution can also be seen in police data of residential breaking and entering in Australia (Budz, Pegnall, & Townsley, 2001).

Among young persons, this concentrated pattern is also evident. Barberet, Fisher, and Taylor (2004) examined victimization for university students in East Midlands, United Kingdom. They reported that 10% of the property victims experienced 56% of all property victimization incidents. Similar results were discovered by Lauritsen and Davis Quinet (1995) using data from the National Youth Survey. Their analysis revealed that 27% of the youths experienced 84% of all the larcenies whereas 13% experienced 82% of all acts of vandalism. Taken together, these results show that, regardless of the data used and the type of property crime examined, some victims experience a disproportionate amount of all property victimizations.

Similar concentration in victimization is found for personal victimizations. Thus, Pease's (1998) analysis of the BCS indicated that 3% of the respondents reported experiencing 78% of the personal crime victimization incidents. Work with college student samples conducted by Daigle, Fisher, and Cullen (2008) found similar results. To illustrate, less than 1% of the more than 4,000 college women surveyed in the National College Women Violent Victimization Study experienced more than one violent incident. However, this small group accounted for over 28% of all violent incidents (see also Barberet et al., 2004).

Other research has examined the distribution of repeat victimizations for younger persons. Lauritsen and Davis Quinet (1995) found that for assaults, 18% of the youths reported experiencing almost 90% of the assault victimizations. Slightly more than 14% of those surveyed reported experiencing 86% of the robbery incidents. Notably, although most young people included in the National Youth Survey do not report experiencing any assaults or robberies, a small proportion report experiencing almost all of the victimizations of these particular types of crimes.

This discussion on the likelihood and distribution of repeat victimization can generate two main conclusions. First, revictimization is a real phenomenon, with many households and individuals experiencing more than one crime incident within a relatively short period of time. Second, revictimization is concentrated. Although most individuals do not experience any crime victimization, a small portion of individuals and households account for a disproportionate share of all victimization experiences. It is revealing that these patterns are found (1) cross-culturally, (2) for victims of property as well as personal crimes, and (3) in studies using different sources of data and methodological approaches.

TIME COURSE OF REVICTIMIZATION

How soon does a revictimization happen? Two distinct patterns have begun to emerge from research on the time course of repeat property and personal crimes. First, if a second incident is going to occur, it is likely to take place relatively quickly after the first incident. Second, there is a period of heightened risk immediately following the occurrence of the prior incident that decreases over time.

Thus, with regard to residential burglary, repeats are most likely to occur within a month of the initial burglary episode. Analyzing police crime data in Canada, Polvi, Looman, Humphries, and Pease (1990) found that half of the second residential burglaries transpired within 7 days of the first burglary. Similarly, police data in cities within the United States show that the time immediately following an incident appears to hold the greatest risk for a repeat incident (Farrell, Sousa, & Weisel, 2002). For example, Robinson's (1998) examination of police call data in Tallahassee, Florida, revealed that 25% of the repeat burglary incidents occurred within a week and that slightly more than half occurred within a month.

Research further reveals that the risk of being victimized on a subsequent occasion decreases over time. That is, the relationship fits an exponential negative slope. In Canada, Polvi and her colleagues (1990, p. 10) reported that "a dwelling was 12.4 times more likely to be burgled a second time within a one-month period." After this first month, the risk of a repeat burglary diminished substantially, with it being 2.4 times more likely.

A similar pattern characterizes personal crimes, with the time course of repeat victimization manifesting a downward exponential fit. Thus, reporting results from national-level data on college women, Daigle and her colleagues (2008) show that over half (54%) of repeat simple assault incidents occurred within a month of the initial incident. Repeat domestic violence and racial attacks have also been shown to frequently recur in the time period immediately following a first episode (Farrell et al., 1995; Sampson & Phillips, 1992). To illustrate, one study found that 35% of households called the police for a second domestic violence event within 5 weeks of the first victimization (Farrell & Pease, 2006). In their study of racial attacks in London, Sampson and Phillips (1992) concluded that the risk of repeat racial attacks was most pronounced in the weeks immediately following the first attack, but that this risk diminished in around 14 to 17 weeks.

CRIME-SWITCH PATTERNS

After a crime victimization incident has occurred, what type of victimization is most likely to follow? Using data from the National Crime Survey (later the NCVS), Reiss (1980) developed an innovative strategy to address this question. He constructed crime-switch matrices that depicted both the number and percentage of personal and property victimization incidents that followed the original incident. One possibility is that the incident was followed by the same type of incident (e.g., an assault as the first incident and an assault as the second incident). This would show victim proneness for a given offense (see also Fienberg, 1980). The other possibility was that a different type of incident would transpire (e.g., an assault as the first incident and a rape as the second incident). This would indicate crime switching had occurred.

Overall, Reiss (1980) found that for victims, the most likely next type of crime victimization is the same type of crime. This proneness pattern was evident for people who experienced personal larceny, burglary, household larceny, and assault. For rape, however, crime switching appears to occur. For example, the most commonly occurring crimes that followed a rape were personal larcenies and assaults.

Sexual Revictimization

Our concern, of course, is with the sexual victimization of college women. Even if revictimization occurs with other property or personal crimes, it is possible that sexual victims escape future incidents. As we see below, the general research on sexual victimizations shows that this is not the case. If anything, sexual victims are more prone to revictimization.

EXTENT OF SEXUAL REVICTIMIZATION

Notably, victims of sexual victimization have the highest revictimization rate of any group apart from domestic violence, with one study indicating that these women are 35 times more likely to be sexually victimized than women with no history of sexual abuse (Canadian Urban Victimization Survey, 1988; National Board for Crime Prevention, 1994). A high risk of revictimization for those sexually abused in childhood, adolescence, and adulthood has been established in a multitude of studies across various populations—for example, college, clinical, military recruit, and community samples (for reviews, see Breitenbecher, 1999; Classen et al., 2005; Roodman & Clum, 2001). Indeed, a meta-analysis by Roodman and Clum (2001) found a moderate effect size (.59) for revictimization and noted that between 15% and 79% of women sexually abused in childhood were raped as adults.

The prevalence of revictimization is consistently high even in studies that use inclusive (as opposed to clinical) samples. An epidemiological study of 3,131 adults by

Sorenson et al. (1987) found that of the 447 participants who reported sexual abuse, 67% experienced more than one sexual assault. Randall and Haskell (1995) reported that in a community sample of women who had experienced child sexual abuse, 62.4% were revictimized.

REVICTIMIZATION ACROSS DEVELOPMENTAL PERIODS

Although research clearly establishes a correlation between a history of sexual abuse and risk of revictimization, this relationship changes over time and developmental life stages. An abundance of research focuses on the link between child sexual abuse (CSA) and revictimization in adulthood. The findings, in fact, are remarkably consistent (for a review, see Classen et al., 2005).

Among community samples, it has been estimated that CSA doubles or triples the risk of adult sexual victimization (Fleming, Mullen, Sibthorpe, & Bammer, 1999; Wyatt, Guthrie, & Notgrass, 1992). In an analysis of a nationally representative sample of adults, Desai, Arias, Thompson, and Basile (2002) found that women with CSA were 6 times more likely to be sexually victimized by a current intimate partner, were 11 times more likely if they experienced physical abuse in addition to CSA, and held an even greater risk for sexual victimization by a nonintimate partner. Russell (1986) determined that of women with CSA before the age of 14, a full 63% experienced rape or attempted rape as opposed to only 35% of the non-CSA sample—thus indicating a rate of victimization nearly twice that for women without a history of sexual abuse. In the National Violence Against Women Study, 18% of women raped before the age of 18 were also raped as adults, an estimate that does not include other types of sexual victimization or attempted rape (Tjaden & Thoennes, 2006).

Further, researchers have tied the severity of childhood sexual abuse to the risk of revictimization in adulthood. Coid et al. (2001) reported that whereas women who experienced unwanted intercourse were two to three times more likely to be sexually assaulted or raped after age 16, women who experienced sexual abuse other than intercourse were three to four times more likely to be sexually assaulted after age 16, even after controlling for demographic factors.

Other research has focused on the risks between CSA and (1) sexual victimization in adolescence and (2) revictimization in late adolescence or young adulthood. Humphrey and White (2000) examined the incoming freshman classes at two different universities and found that, prior to entering college, 13% of the women experienced rape before the age of 14. These women were 14 times more likely than other women to be raped within their first year at college. In a prospective, longitudinal study, Noll, Horowitz, Bonanno, Trickett, and Putnam (2003) studied CSA victims between the ages of 6 and 16 (mean age at baseline = 11 years) who reported sexual abuse at the age of 14 or younger. Participants were assessed three times over a 7-year period. Those with a history of CSA were twice as likely to be sexually assaulted or raped as their matched counterparts. Even across adjacent developmental periods, revictimization remains a significant risk for sexual assault victims.

Other studies lend further credence to this point. Thus, Boney-McCoy and Finkelhor (1995) studied a random sample of 2,000 youths between the ages of 10 and 16 and found that, within the past year, 7.6% were sexually victimized. Those with a prior history of CSA were 11.7 times more likely to experience a repeat victimization. The authors established that these results were not likely attributable to the repeated assaults of one perpetrator. Similarly, using a national probability sample of adolescent women in Grades 7 through 12 drawn from the National Longitudinal Study of Adolescent Health, Raghavan, Bogart, Elliott, Vestal, and Schuster (2004) reported that of the 7% of women raped at the first wave, 8% had experienced a repeat victimization by the second wave. Additionally, Small and Kerns (1993) found that in a sample of 1,149 adolescents, 20% reported an unwanted sexual experience within the past year (one-third of which involved rape), which was predicted by a history of sexual victimization.

Equally disheartening, and pertinent to our research with the NCWSV Study, revictimization among college women is also a common occurrence. Gidycz and her colleagues (1995) found that college women are at risk of experiencing more than a single sexual victimization during a single academic year. Their research showed that of those women who were sexually assaulted during the first quarter, 38% were sexually revictimized during the second quarter (see also Gidycz, Coble, Latham, & Layman, 1993). Other research by Gross et al. (2006) found similar results, with 37% of college women reporting experiencing more than one forced sexual incident since enrolling in college. Thus, it appears that revictimization can occur within the same developmental stage.

Sexual Revictimization Among College Women: The NCWSV Study

In the National College Women Sexual Victimization Study, we were able to record how many victimization incidents each respondent experienced during the academic year. For each incident, detailed questions were asked. This allowed us to explore whether most victims experienced only a single incident or were revictimized. If revictimization occurred, we were able to assess the nature of the incident and the time between incidents. Accordingly, we can now present data on the extent and nature of revictimization over a relatively short period of time. First, however, we briefly explore the impact on revictimization of women who entered college with a history of being victimized.

SEXUAL REVICTIMIZATION OVER TIME

As may be recalled from Chapter 4, a number of women come to college having been sexually victimized. When asked about victimization prior to the current school year, 15.1% reported experiencing a completed rape and/or an attempted rape. Of those college women who were victimized during the school year, 61.5% had experienced some previous type of sexual victimization. Our analyses show that this earlier victimization predicts current sexual victimization. In multivariate models designed to distinguish victims from nonvictims, those college women who reported having experienced a sexual victimization prior to the current school year were more likely than women without a previous history to be sexually victimized since school began in the fall of 1996. Being sexually victimized prior to college also increased the likelihood that a college woman would be stalked during college.

EXTENT OF SEXUAL REVICTIMIZATION

Table 5.1 shows the proportion of college women who were victimized, how many times they were victimized, and the proportion of incidents that happened to these women. This includes rape, sexual coercion, unwanted sexual contact, and threats (e.g., threat of rape, threat of contact with force or threat of force, threat of penetration without force, threat of contact without force). Several noteworthy findings, consistent with the previous research, can be gleaned from Table 5.1:

- Some 15.5% of women experienced at least one form of sexual victimization during the academic year. Of these women, 47.1% were revictimized.

- Victimization is concentrated. Thus, revictimized female students accounted for a disproportionate number and percentage of all sexual victimization incidents.

Table 5.1 Proportion of College Women and Incidents by Number of Times Sexually Victimized

Number of Times Sexually Victimized	Percentage Sexually Victimized (n = 4,466)	Percentage of Victims (n = 644)	Number of Incidents (n = 1,318)	Percentage of Incidents Experienced by Victims	Percentage of Recurrent Incidents
0	84.5 (3,757)				
1	8.2 (364)	52.9	364	27.6	
2 or more	7.3 (325)	47.1	954	72.4	47.7

SOURCE: Adapted from Daigle, Fisher, and Cullen (2008).

- Specifically, almost three-fourths (72.4%) of the sexual victimization incidents were experienced by 7.3% of the recurrent victims.

- Finally, 47.7% of all sexual victimization incidents were recurrent incidents, indicating that almost half of sexual victimizations that college women experienced were not a single incident.

Table 5.2 elaborates this analysis by breaking down the data by type of sexual victimization. First, across types of sexual victimization, revictimization was common, ranging from about 22 to 25%. The percentage of repeat incidents was also striking. For example, 22% of rapes were repeat rape incidents. Similarly, just over 25% of sexual coercions and unwanted sexual contacts with and without force, respectively, were repeat incidents. Even more of the threats, 32%, were repeat incidents.

Second, within *each* type of sexual victimization, a disproportionately small percentage of the victims experienced a large proportion of the incidents. For example, 23% of the repeated rape victims experienced close to 40% of the rapes. Just over 25% of the victims of unwanted sexual contact without force experienced 44.3% of these incidents. A quarter of the repeat threat victims experienced 47.5% of the threats.

TIME COURSE OF SEXUAL REVICTIMIZATION

We were able to compute the time between victimization incidents for our sample (see Figure 5.1). For each pair of repeated type of victimization, the difference in the number of months between the most recent incident and the next most recent incident was calculated. For example, if the most recent rape occurred in January and the rape before this one happened in November, then the number of months between the two incidents is 2. The number of months between paired repeat incidents that happened in the same month was zero.

Notably, there is an elevated risk of sexual revictimization over a short period of time. In particular, this elevated risk is greatest within the same month. For example, 48% of rape revictimization happened within the same month, as did 36% of the sexual coercions, 32% of the threats, and 28% of the unwanted sexual contacts with force. The only exception to the increased risk of being victimized a second time within the same month was for unwanted sexual contact without force. The risk of unwanted sexual contact without force happening a second time was highest a month after the first incident. Thirty-nine percent of these incidents occurred in the following month, which is greater than the 25% that occurred within the same month.

The risk of sexual revictimization, with the exception of rape, steadily declined over the passage of time. Take, for example, unwanted sexual contact with force. Over the 6 months following an initial incident, the percentage of unwanted sexual contacts declined monthly: 28%, 23%, 20%, 10%, 10%, 7%, and 2%. This pattern suggests that the risk of a second sexual victimization decreased after the passage of 1 month.

Table 5.2 Rates of Repeat Sexual Victimization in NCWSV Study

Type of Sexual Victimization	Percentage of Victims (n)	Number of Incidents	Percentage of Incidents	Percentage of Repeat Victims (n)	Number of Repeat Incidents	Percentage of Repeat Incidents	Percentage of Incidents Experienced by Repeat Victims
Sexual							
Rape	2.8 (123)	157	11.9	22.8 (28)	34	21.7	39.5
Sexual Coercion	3.7 (164)	221	16.8	23.2 (38)	57	25.8	43.0
Unwanted Sexual Contact With Force	5.0 (221)	296	22.5	22.6 (50)	75	25.3	42.2
Unwanted Sexual Contact Without Force	7.2 (318)	427	32.4	25.5 (81)	109	25.5	44.3
Threats	3.4 (152)	217	16.5	25.0 (38)	69	31.8	47.5
Total	15.5 (691)	1,318	100.0	47.3 (327)	627	47.6	72.4

SOURCE: Daigle, Fisher, and Cullen (2008).

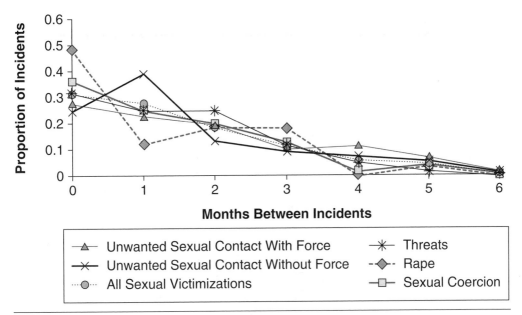

Figure 5.1   Time Course of Repeat Sexual Victimization

SOURCE: Adapted from Daigle, Fisher, and Cullen (2008).

The pattern for rape is slightly different given the relatively small number of repeat rapes that happened within 1 (n = 4), 2 (n = 6), 3 (n = 6), and 5 (n = 1) months of each other, while 16 repeat rapes happened within the same month.

CRIME-SWITCH PATTERNS

To examine whether victims are likely to experience the same or a different type of victimization in consecutive incidents, we constructed a crime-switch pattern matrix. For each victim of two or more incidents, we examined her sequentially paired incidents as to the type of victimization that comprised the preceding-following incident pair (e.g., a rape followed by a rape; a sexual coercion followed by a rape). A matrix was constructed to reflect the total number of each type of victimization pairs that had occurred.

There is a statistically significant relationship between the type of victimization that occurs in the preceding incident and the type of victimization that occurs in the following incident. Regardless of type of sexual victimization, victims were most likely to have experienced the same type of victimization in consecutive incidents as opposed to another type of sexual victimization. Thus:

- Almost 30% of all rapes were followed by a rape.

- Half of the sexual coercions were followed by a sexual coercion.

- Almost half of the sexual contacts with force, 43%, and over half of the sexual contacts without force, 52%, were followed by the same type of incident.

- Over one-third (36%) of threats were followed by a threat.

Why Does Sexual Revictimization Occur?

Thus far, we have examined the extent and nature of revictimization among college women. We have seen that revictimization is common and concentrated, occurs quickly after a first incident, and often involves a repeat of the same sexual victimization (see also Daigle et al., 2008; Daigle et al., 2007; Fisher, Daigle, & Cullen, in press). Beyond this empirical documentation, the broader question is why revictimization occurs. We address this question in two parts. First, we approach this issue theoretically, discussing two divergent explanations: risk heterogeneity and event dependence. Second, in the next section of the chapter, we return to our NCWSV Study and present empirical information on this issue.

RISK HETEROGENEITY: ROUTINES/LIFESTYLES MATTER

One explanation for victimization is that people take risks that expose them to potential offenders. Because people differ in their victimization risk, we use the term *heterogeneity* rather than *homogeneity*, which would indicate a uniformity of risk exposure. Risk heterogeneity can be due to an underlying personality orientation that may make them inattentive or even attracted to risky situations (e.g., lack of self-control, impulsivity, high risk-taking preferences). Most studies, including our NCWSV Study, have not measured these traits (for exceptions, see Schreck, 1999; Schreck, Stewart, & Fisher, 2006). Risk heterogeneity also may reflect the everyday routine activities or lifestyles that people follow. Some activities or lifestyles—such as going to bars or walking home alone at night—place people in situations where victimization is likely; others, such as watching television at home with one's family, do not. Accordingly, routines or lifestyles, which can be a function of both personality preferences and the social environment in which one is enmeshed, differentially expose people to risk.

This insight that daily routines and lifestyles contribute to risk heterogeneity was discovered independently in the late 1970s by two sets of scholars. Lawrence Cohen and Marcus Felson (1979) developed *routine activity* theory, whereas Michael Hindelang, Michael Gottfredson, and James Garofalo (1978) developed *lifestyle* theory. They advanced virtually identical explanations for understanding victimization. In brief, they contended that for a victimization to occur, a potential victim had to come into contact with a potential offender. From the offender's standpoint, this meant that being motivated to commit a crime was not enough; one still had to possess the *opportunity* to offend. From the victim's standpoint, the person presented offenders with the opportunity to victimize when he or she came into contact with them. And here is the key point: the extent to which potential victims came into contact with potential offenders—the extent to which they created opportunities for crime—depended on their everyday routine activities or lifestyles.

As it turned out, Cohen and Felson's routine activity approach proved to be the more popular version of this perspective (see also Felson, 2002). In large part, this was because they elaborated the concept of opportunity by dividing it into two components—a matter we return to very shortly. Now, Cohen and Felson largely took criminals for granted; they did not attempt to explain why some people wanted to break the law. They simply assumed that there are plenty of "motivated offenders"—to use their term—in American society. Their key insight was that the routine activities people engage in bring them together with motivated offenders in time and space. When that happens, a crime can occur; if not, there is no opportunity to offend and thus no crime takes place.

However, they added two further insights. When offenders and people coincide, two other features shape the nature of the opportunity. First, Cohen and Felson conceived of potential victims as "targets." A target could, of course, be a person, but it could also be property. Targets, they observed, differed in their attractiveness. For example, when a criminal is breaking into a house, a portable computer is a more attractive target than a refrigerator for the obvious reason that it can be easily transported. Second, Cohen and Felson argued that victimizations are less likely when an attractive target has "capable guardianship." This might involve a burglar alarm or barking dog in a house or being surrounded by friends or near a police officer while strolling on the streets late at night. In this framework, then, risk heterogeneity is highest when routines lead attractive targets without capable guardianship to converge in time and space with motivated offenders. Risk heterogeneity is diminished to the extent that people are well guarded, take steps to make themselves or their property less attractive targets, and stay away from offenders.

In earlier chapters, we have implicitly used routine activity theory to suggest why college campuses are places where sexual victimization might be prevalent (see also Cass, 2007; Daigle et al., 2008; Fisher et al., in press; Fisher, Cullen, et al., 2002; Fisher et al., 1998; Mustaine & Tewksbury, 1999, 2007; Schwartz & Pitts, 1995). For one thing, attractive targets—female students—come into contact frequently with potential motivated offenders—male students. They also frequently do so in the absence of capable guardianship—alone in a room late at night. Routine activity/lifestyle theory would thus predict high levels of victimization in this population. Again, this is an argument we have voiced previously, albeit not formally within the routine activity framework. We revisit this perspective, in some detail, when we explore sources of stalking in Chapter 7.

This perspective should also help explain two additional patterns of victimization. First, routine activity theory would explain why some students are more victimized than others. Thus, the theory would predict that sexual victimization is highest among students who engage in routines that expose them more often to motivated offenders in the absence of capable guardianship (e.g., going to parties, going alone in an intoxicated condition to a man's room, frequently dating). That is, routines or lifestyles are a source of risk heterogeneity. Second and pertinent to this chapter, risk heterogeneity in routine activities should explain not simply why a female student is victimized once but also why she is victimized subsequently. That is, routines should explain both the initial victimization and revictimization: regardless of the incident, victimization is more likely when exposing oneself to motivated offenders with no guardianship present.

EVENT DEPENDENCE: FIRST INCIDENTS MATTER

Event dependence, sometimes called *state dependence,* might explain why a revictimization does or does not occur. It also is a perspective that is not well developed because most research does not focus on how first and subsequent incident characteristics are potentially interrelated. Regardless, to get to the chief point, event-dependence theory argues that what transpired *during or shortly after* the first incident possibly shapes a victim's vulnerability to future victimization incidents. This might involve, for example, whether the victim resisted her assailant during the initial incident or subsequently reported the incident to authorities or to a friend. Such measures might reflect a capacity to confront a victimization directly and inspire more confidence in how to avoid becoming vulnerable in the future. Again, beyond the general insight that the state of an initial event might affect a later event, this approach is undertheorized. Even so, it is a possibility that should be considered in research on revictimization. In this regard, it is relevant that the construct of state dependence has been used in life-course research to explain stability in offending (Nagin & Paternoster, 1991). Here we are, in essence, exploring stability in victimization.

Findings From the NCWSV Study

In our NCWSV Study, we were able to explore these competing—or possibly complementary explanations—of victimization. Our data had two important features. First, we collected sexual victimization data on every incident that a respondent experienced. Second, in the incident report and survey instrument, we collected information that allowed us to measure key elements of routine activity theory and event dependence theory. We report our findings below, first examining sources of first-incident sexual victimization and then of sexual revictimizaton.

EXPLAINING SEXUAL VICTIMIZATION

Our analysis showed that routines or lifestyle did impact whether a woman was sexually victimized during the academic term. Those women who were in close proximity to motivated offenders and exposed to crime and who were suitable targets were more likely to be sexually victimized than women with less risky routines or lifestyles. Specifically, as seen in Table 5.3, we found that women who had a greater propensity for being in places that were exclusively male (e.g., fraternity parties, all-male residence or dorm, parties attended by male student-athletes) and in places with alcohol (e.g., bars, parties where alcohol was served) were more likely to be sexually victimized than other women. In addition, being in a committed relationship increased the likelihood of sexual victimization. Women who had a greater propensity for substance use—drinking enough alcohol to get drunk and smoking pot or hashish—were more likely to be sexually victimized. Lack of capable guardianship was also related to sexual victimization risk. As expected, women who lived alone were more likely to be sexually victimized than women who shared housing. Contrary to the expectations, women who carried self-protection were more likely to be sexually victimized than others. It is possible that women began carrying self-protection after being sexually victimized, which would account for the discrepancy.

EXPLAINING REVICTIMIZATON

Although routines and lifestyles were found to be predictive of being sexually victimized at least once, we were interested in determining what factors, if any, differentiated those women who were sexually victimized a single time from those who experienced more than one sexual victimization during the study period (approximately 7 months). We found that the same routines and lifestyle factors that place women at risk of being sexually victimized initially were the same factors that predicted risk of revictimization (for more details on this analysis, see

Table 5.3   Factors Shown to Increase the Likelihood of Experiencing Sexual Victimization in NCWSV Study

Proximity to Motivated Offenders and Exposure to Crime
　　Propensity to be in places exclusively male
　　In committed relationship
　　Propensity to be in places with alcohol

Target Suitability
　　Propensity for substance use

Capable Guardianship
　　Carry self-protection
　　Living alone

SOURCE: Adapted from Fisher, Daigle, and Cullen (in press).

Daigle et al., 2008; Fisher et al., in press). In other words, risky routines and lifestyles increase the risk of being sexually victimized a single time and subsequent times. Although the lack of difference between single and revictimized women at first may appear to be unimportant, it has clear implications for reducing the incidence of sexual victimization. If the factors that place a woman at risk of being victimized initially can be eliminated or their salience diminished, not only would fewer women be sexually victimized, but fewer women would be sexually revictimized as well. Reducing the extent of sexual revictimization could dramatically dimish the overall rates of sexual victimization, given that revictimized women experience a disproportionate amount of all sexual victimizations.

We also included five measures of event dependence to see what, if anything, that happens during the initial incident predicts revictimization. In doing so, we used measures of whether the victim used self-protective action at the first incident, whether the incident was reported to the police, whether the incident was disclosed to persons other than the police, whether the offender was an intimate, and whether the offender was a stranger.

We found that one event-dependence factor—use of self-protective action at the first incident—distinguished the two victim groups. Women who used some type of self-protective action during the initial sexual victimization incident were *less likely* to be revictimized than women who did not employ self-protective actions. Using the logic of event dependence, women who use self-protective action, particularly if it is successful in thwarting the attack, may *learn* that they are able to protect themselves and, as a result, believe that they are less vulnerable to future sexual victimizations. This perception may reduce future victimization risk. In addition, offenders may learn that they can successfully victimize a woman if she does not use self-protective action. He may see her as a vulnerable target in the future and subsequently revictimize her. Women who do not use self-protective action, however, may feel more vulnerable to attack and be less able or willing to employ self-protective actions in risky situations. Would-be offenders may specifically target such women.

Knowing that the use of self-protective action may reduce future victimization risk is integral in the development of risk-reduction programs. Women should be educated on how to identify and respond to risky situations to reduce both initial victimizations and revictimization. Past research on the ability of sexually victimized women to recognize risk and to express behavioral intentions of avoiding risky situations indicates that women with histories of sexual victimization are less apt to identify a situation as risky. They are more likely to have higher scores when evaluating the point at which they would leave a hypothetical acquaintance rape scenario (Messman-Moore & Brown, 2006). Revictimized women may stay in risky situations past the point at which they would be successfully able to prevent victimization, such as agreeing to go alone to a secluded place with an acquaintance. These women especially need education regarding risk cues and how and when to use self-protective actions.

Conclusion

It happens again—and sometimes again and again. As we have seen, revictimization is integral to any understanding of sexual victimization among college women. Of those initially victimized, a large minority, it appears, will be victimized again, if not repeatedly, and will account for a sizable proportion of all victimization incidents. Previous researchers in this area have observed that early victimization in life predicts later victimization as an adult. However, due to the designs of their research, most major studies have been unable to explore the extent to which victimization occurs during a more delimited time—in our study, within a single academic year. Our data from the NCWSV Study reveal that, in fact, revictimization is commonplace and occurs more often within a short period of time after an initial victimization incident.

Beyond the criminological importance of this substantive finding, the reality of revictimization holds inordinate importance for preventing future sexual victimization. Trying to derail initial victimizations—while a worthy effort to pursue—is difficult because many female students, simply by pursuing "normal" lifestyles for college women, place themselves at risk for sexual victimization. By contrast, once a student has been victimized, it might become possible to intervene in more specific ways to knife off the risk of subsequent victimization. Accordingly, it would seem incumbent upon researchers in this area to make revictimization a prime line of inquiry, to understand more fully both its sources and its prevention.

6

Victim Secrets

Acknowledging and Reporting Sexual Victimization

Consider these two scenarios.

Scenario 1: You are walking home alone and an assailant steps in front of you, pulls a gun, and demands your purse. You surrender it and, though scared, you feel fortunate only to have lost your property, which can, after all, be replaced. You clearly know what has happened to you; a *crime* has been committed. If you decide to call a police officer, you are confident that the officer will believe you and record your complaint. You do not mind telling your parents because, although embarrassed a bit (they had told you "never to walk home alone"), being robbed was not your fault.

Scenario 2: You meet a guy at a bar and go back to his room. You know him a bit but not well. You have seen him around and been in groups where everyone was talking; he seemed nice. After drinking some more, he comes on to you. You "fool around" a bit, but then he keeps pushing for more sexual contact. You say "please don't, I don't want to." But he seems unconvinced. It is as though he does not hear you. You push him away and say "stop it," but he continues to touch you all over and to try to undress you. Things are going so fast that they seem a blur; he suddenly penetrates you. What has happened? Is it a *crime*? A *rape*? Illegal yes, but serious enough to call the police? You have no bruises; maybe, you think, you did not say "no" strongly enough. If you call the police, you doubt they will believe you. You also do not want to contact campus officials or your parents because you are embarrassed that you "let this happen to you." You know that even if they do not say anything, your parents will wonder how you could have been drunk and in the room of a guy you "barely knew" who had picked you up at a bar. You can hear them want to say, "What did you think would happen?" But you also feel violated, taken advantage of. You tell a friend. Maybe she'll understand. Maybe she'll help you forget.

These contrasting scenarios are intended to illuminate key differences in the nature of traditional street crimes, such as robbery, and of sexual victimizations, such as acquaintance rape. In the first instance, the quality of the act is not questioned. It is clear that robbery is a crime. The good actor (the innocent victim) and the bad actor (the offender) are transparent. Nobody would question that the victim should report the *armed robbery* and that, if caught, the offender should be subjected to a criminal sanction.

In the second instance, however, the crime is more complicated. The boundaries between moral and immoral are fuzzier. What is legal, intimate, and pleasurable one moment is illegal, attacking, and violating the next. The offender may not think of himself as a rapist and, if confronted with this fact, would likely claim the victim's consent or, at worst, miscommunication. The victim is left to come to grips with what has just occurred. Thoughts of *rape* and *crime* may not come to mind amidst the sense of violation and degradation—not to mention intoxication. Feelings of self-doubt, if not self-blame, might rival feelings of having been victimized. Acknowledging what had just occurred and mustering the courage to call the police may not be possible. Seeking the support of a friend one can trust might seem like the best option.

In short, a special feature of an acquaintance sexual victimization is how victims interpret "what has happened" and respond. Recall Estrich's (1987) discussion of "real rape" in Chapter 1. In such cases where a stranger uses force to sexually assault a woman in a public setting, there is less ambiguity involved. The rape is clearly "real," not invented. But acquaintance rapes, by their very nature, tend to involve a victimization that is unexpected and is perpetrated by someone who is not initially seen as a criminal. Understanding and acknowledging that a rape or other sexual assault has transpired is no longer taken for granted but potentially problematic. Reporting an assailant to the police or to university officials may seem like an overreach or as unlikely to amount to much.

In fact, as discussed in this chapter, the proportion of victims acknowledging and reporting to the police rape or other types of sexual victimizations is low. As may be recalled from Chapter 1, this failure to acknowledge and report has been taken by critics as evidence that no victimization really occurred. For example, Gilbert (1991, 1995, 1997) has argued that if women, particularly college-educated women, do not think their experience was a rape, then it is likely that what occurred was something other than a rape—at least by legal standards. By contrast, other scholars have taken acknowledging and reporting sexual victimizations as a problem to be explained. Investigating these issues meaningfully depends on the use of sound methodology: establishing that a victimization has, in fact, occurred and then assessing whether it was acknowledged and reported. We have attempted to move toward this goal through the measurement strategy that we employed in our NCWSV Study. Thus, where appropriate, these data are consulted in the analysis that follows.

The first half of the chapter explores the acknowledgment of victimization—its extent, consequences, and empirical determinants. The chapter's second half examines the reporting of victimization—its extent, importance, reasons given for doing so or not doing so, and empirical determinants. We also disclose a finding that is not well known but has important implications: Although college women keep their victimization secret from police and campus officials, a number of persons who are sexually victimized, including rape victims, tell someone they know about the victimization.

Acknowledging Victimization

Research has shown that when rape victims are asked if they have been raped, they do not typically say "yes." These women are considered *unacknowledged rape victims*. By contrast, *acknowledged rape victims* are those who respond affirmatively when asked if they have been raped. As with many aspects of research on sexual victimization, Mary Koss provided early, important data on this issue. Our NCWSV Study attempted to extend this research. The findings from these two projects are discussed below.

KOSS'S SEXUAL EXPERIENCES SURVEY

One of the major findings from Koss's (1988b) national-level study of college women that used the Sexual Experiences Survey (SES) was that the majority of rape victims did not acknowledge being raped. In fact, 73% of college women who were raped were unacknowledged rape victims.

The method by which this finding was reached is important. Recall from Chapter 2 that in Koss's study, women were asked if they had experienced four different types of sexual victimization since the age of 14 through 10 behaviorally specific questions. The questions from the SES that measured completed rape were used to determine if a woman was indeed a rape victim. If any of these questions were responded to affirmatively (with a "yes"), then the woman was counted as a rape victim. Later in the survey, any woman who was victimized was subsequently asked: "Looking back on the experience, how would you describe the situation?" The women were given several responses from which they could choose: "I believe I was a victim of rape; I believe I was a victim of a crime other than rape; I believe I was a victim of serious miscommunication; I don't feel I was victimized." Women who responded that they believed they were a victim of rape were classified as acknowledged rape victims. Others were classified as unacknowledged rape victims.

Many other researchers have employed either the SES or strategies similar to Koss's to determine acknowledgment. Most of this work has used the question, "Have you ever been raped?" to examine acknowledgment among college women. Often, respondents who first answer "yes" to a behaviorally specific question describing a rape "since the age of 14" are then asked specifically if they "had *ever* been raped." These studies find that anywhere from one-third to about three-fourths of rape victims do not acknowledge that they have been raped (Bondurant, 2001; Botta & Pingree, 1997; Frazier & Seales, 1997; Kahn, Mathie, & Torgler, 1994; Layman, Gidycz, & Lynn, 1996; Pitts & Schwartz, 1993). The divergence in these findings may reflect methodological concerns. First, each study relies on a unique sample, with some using small samples from a single university and others (such as Koss's) using large, representative samples. Second, although the SES questions ask respondents about sexual victimizations since the age of 14, the question used to measure acknowledgment ("ever" been raped) is not limited to incidents occurring during that time period. It is possible, then, that women may have said they had been raped, but were referencing an incident not captured by the SES.

THE NCWSV STUDY

Our NCWSV Study measured acknowledgment in a different and, we believe, more precise way. As explained previously (see Chapter 2), our project used a two-step process that involved screen questions and then an incident report. The advantage to this methodology is that it allowed us in the incident report to ask a variety of detailed questions to clarify exactly what had happened.

In this regard, the incident report contained a measure of acknowledgment. Unlike in some previous studies, the question did not concern rapes over a number of years or ask if the person had ever been raped. Rather, for *each incident,* the respondent was asked the very specific question, "Do you consider this incident to be a rape?"

We were able to separate out those women categorized as having experienced a completed rape (i.e., who answered "yes" to one of the screen questions and in the incident report said that penetration was achieved through force or threat of force). We also separated out those categorized as experiencing an attempted rape. Finally, we were able to assess what proportion of rape incidents were defined as a rape. As shown in Figure 6.1, here is what we found:

- Almost half (46.5%) of completed rape incidents were acknowledged as rape.

- Attempted rape incidents were less likely to be acknowledged as rape—only 2.8%.

- Across both completed and attempted rape incidents, 26.8% were acknowledged as rape.

Notably, very few non-rape incidents were considered rapes by the women in the study: only 3.4%. Figure 6.2 indicates that of these non-rape incidents, sexual coercion incidents (8.1%) were most likely to be considered rape. Because sexual coercions by definition include penetration or the attempt at penetration, it is not surprising that they would be considered rape more frequently than the types of sexual victimizations that do not involve penetration. Very few sexual contact with force (2.7%), sexual contact without force (1.4%), and threat (3.7%) incidents were acknowledged as rape.

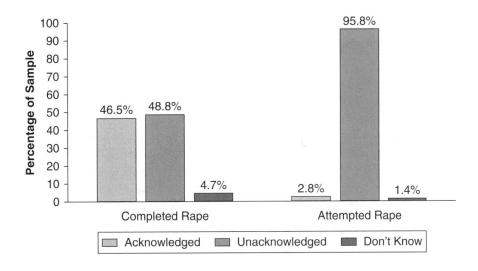

Figure 6.1   Acknowledgment of Rape Incidents in the NCWSV Study

SOURCE: Adapted from Fisher, Daigle, Cullen, and Turner (2003b).

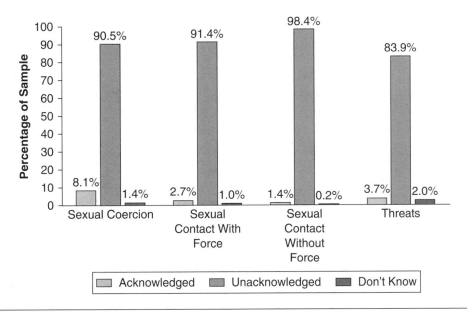

Figure 6.2   Acknowledgment of Sexual Victimization Incidents in the NCWSV Study

SOURCE: Adapted from Fisher, Daigle, Cullen, and Turner (2003b).

These latter findings are of some importance. The fact that very few incidents in the NCWSV Study that were not categorized by us as rape were acknowledged as rape is instructive. It adds credence to the measurement strategy employed in the NCWSV Study. If those incidents that were not classified as rapes were thought to be rapes by victims, then it would be questionable as to whether the NCWSV Study was actually measuring rape. Thus, the results support the two-stage measurement strategy that was employed.

Further, these findings suggest that female college students do not define any uncomfortable sexual act as a "rape." In contrast to what some critics might suggest, we found no evidence of political correctness run amok—of respondents applying the label of rape indiscriminately. Rather, victims are more discerning. The percentage acknowledging rape was pronounced—almost half (47.4%)—only for completed rapes. That is, acknowledgment is highest precisely where it should be found.

Finally, it is important that among incidents categorized as rape *using the same precise methodology*, about half were acknowledged and half were not. It seems unlikely that acts defined and not defined as rape by the respondents differed behaviorally. Rather, there seems to be ample grounds to conclude that even when the victimization is the same, it can be interpreted and acknowledged differently. Accordingly, exploring why this is the case seems worthwhile—an issue we revisit shortly.

What Do Unacknowledged Victims Call It?

If women do not think that they were raped, even when their experience meets a legal definition of rape, then the question arises, "How do unacknowledged victims define their rape?" The studies that measured rape acknowledgment through Koss's method that employed multiple response categories to the question can help address this question. Koss (1988b) found that the greatest percentage of completed rape victims said that they believed they were a victim of serious miscommunication. Almost half of the completed rape victims felt this way. Almost 15% stated that they were in fact a victim of a crime other than rape, and only 10.6% believed that they were not victimized.

More recent research shows a similar pattern: between 45% and 62.5% of unacknowledged victims labeled the assault a miscommunication (Layman et al., 1996; Littleton, Axson, Breitkopf, & Berenson, 2006). In the Littleton and colleagues study, 11% of unacknowledged victims labeled their experience a seduction, while 45% were not sure how to label it. Layman et al. (1996) reported that 15% of unacknowledged victims thought they were the victim of a crime other than rape. What these findings suggest is that there are great individual differences in the way in which college women view their rape experiences. It seems that most college women recognize that their experience was somehow "wrong," even if they do not label it a rape.

Consequences of Acknowledgment

Past research suggests that women who are raped often experience emotional, psychological, and social distress. To deal with the event, it has been suggested that acknowledgment may prove beneficial to women—that is, that women cannot sufficiently recover from sexual victimization if they do not define it and acknowledge that it happened (Gidycz & Koss, 1991). In this view, unacknowledged rape victims should fare worse in the long run psychologically because they have not started the recovery process by acknowledging or defining their rape.

This belief has underscored an area of research that set out to investigate how acknowledgment impacts recovery. Despite this interest, there is not a clear benefit that victims receive from acknowledging their rape or defining it as such. While some researchers find that acknowledgment improves psychological adjustment (Botta & Pingree, 1997), others report that labeling an act as a rape is associated with post-traumatic stress disorder (PTSD) symptomology (Layman et al., 1996) and more negative affect after the experience (Kahn et al., 2003). We probe this issue in more detail below.

BENEFICIAL EFFECTS

Although many believe that acknowledgment is a necessary step for victims to take in their healing process, only a few studies have shown a benefit. Botta and Pingree (1997) found that, among college women, acknowledged victims had better post-rape psychological adjustment than unacknowledged victims. In terms of coping, college women who are acknowledged rape victims show a greater adherence to a belief in a just world (Littleton et al., 2006).

HARMFUL EFFECTS

Contrary to these findings, acknowledged victims may view the stress of rape as overwhelming, feelings that outstrip their existing coping resources; hence, they may turn to avoidance coping strategies such as simply wishing that the situation would go away or be over or suppressing thoughts or emotions about the rape. Use of these types of coping strategies suggests that acknowledgment may not lead to a coping process in which the victim actively deals with the stress of being raped. Instead, by acknowledging the victimization, the victim then is forced to deal with her experience, possibly relying on coping strategies that may not produce immediate recovery. Supportive of this point, Kahn and colleagues (2003) report that acknowledgment is related to more severe negative emotional reactions to the rape. However, the study could not establish cause and effect definitively. Thus, acknowledgment may contribute to or possibly be a response to this emotional reaction—or both.

Beyond coping, Layman et al. (1996) and Littleton et al. (2006) report that acknowledged rape victims exhibit greater PTSD symptomology than unacknowledged victims. Importantly, though, this experience of PTSD symptoms could be related to the rape itself in that acknowledged rapes tended to be more forceful and victims tended to use resistance. It could be that the PTSD resulted from the rape, irrespective of acknowledgment. It is also noteworthy that unacknowledged rape victims experienced a greater number of PTSD symptoms than did nonvictims, suggesting that unacknowledged victims were indeed impacted by their rape.

FEW EFFECTS

Despite the research revealing that acknowledgment impacts adjustment—albeit negatively or positively—another body of research finds little difference between those women who do and do not acknowledge their rape. For example, defining an incident as a sexual abuse/assault does *not* predict negative outcomes such as body-shape concern, psychological distress, substance use, or school/academic withdrawal (Harned, 2004). Those who do and do not acknowledge show similar levels of psychological distress, belief in the benevolence of the world, and self-worth (Littleton et al., 2006).

Using longitudinal data of college women across 5 years, McMullin and White (2006) were able to examine the effects of acknowledgment among rape victims on a wide range of outcomes, including psychological well-being, sexual activity, alcohol use, and attitudes. They found that women who defined their incident as a rape were no different in terms of psychological well-being from those who did not. Acknowledgment had no impact on number of sexual partners, drinking behavior, or gender attitudes. These results show no long-term differences in the functioning of rape victims who did and did not label their experience a rape.

These findings have a potential implication for the measurement debate issue of whether unacknowledged rape victims are really rape victims at all. If it is true—as Gilbert, Roiphe, and others argue—that unacknowledged rape victims are truly not rape victims, then they should experience few negative outcomes or outcomes that rival acknowledged rape victims—who would be "real" victims. The fact that this is not the case suggests that these groups of women may not differ in their victimization experience.

In sum, considering the research on acknowledgment and outcomes collectively, it appears that it is the rape itself, not the labeling, that creates a host of problems in women. College women who do and do not acknowledge their incident as rape are more similar to each other than to nonvictims (McMullin & White, 2006). This is additional support that acknowledgment "cannot be considered a valid criterion for determining who has experienced sexual victimization" (Harned, 2004, p. 1090).

Factors Related to Acknowledgment

Research has explored the empirical factors that predict whether or not a rape will be acknowledged. These determinants include both factors that characterize the individual victim and factors that characterize the situation in which the victimization occurs. We cite a number of studies but also rely on the analyses we conducted on the NCWSV Study (see Fisher et al., 2003b).

INDIVIDUAL FACTORS

Individual characteristics such as rape scripts tied to "real rape," prior victimization experiences, and demographics influence whether a woman acknowledges being raped. Table 6.1 indicates those factors that have been found in the empirical literature, including the NCWSV Study, to be associated with rape acknowledgment.

Rape Scripts. Generally, scripts allow us to make sense of our world. We often have an idea about what constitutes normal behavior for particular events. When events occur

Table 6.1   Rape Acknowledgment by College Women

Acknowledgment is most likely when:

- Victim's rape script involves violence and a stranger as the perpetrator.
- Victim is high in rape myth acceptance.
- Victim's rape myth corresponds to own victimization.
- Victim has previously been sexually victimized.*
- Victim has friends who have been acquaintance-raped.
- Victim is an older college woman.*
- Victim does not know the perpetrator well.
- Romantic partner is not the perpetrator.
- Incident results in physical injury.*
- A weapon is present.*
- Victim uses resistance strategies during the incident.
- Victim uses forceful verbal resistance strategy.*
- Offender used or threatened to use physical force.*
- Victim has arms twisted or held down.
- Victim was hit or slapped.
- Penetration was completed.*
- Victim thought that what happened was sex.

SOURCE: Adapted from Fisher, Daigle, Cullen, and Turner (2003b).

NOTE: *Factor statistically significant in the NCWSV Study.

in our lives, we may compare our event to "organized cognitive schemas" (Kahn & Mathie, 2000, p. 383) that we have in order to cognitively process what has happened. A rape script, then, is what we may think a rape "looks like" or what a rape event would entail. When a woman experiences a sexual victimization, she may compare what transpired to whatever rape script she has. College women tend to have rape scripts that entail a rape that matches what is known as a "real rape." A "real rape" is a rape that results in an injury and that is perpetrated in a blitz-style attack, by a stranger who has a weapon, and in an unfamiliar place (Estrich, 1987; see also Williams, 1984). Among the reasons a woman may not label her rape as rape is that it does not match her rape script, which is likely to have characteristics of this stereotypical rape (Parrot, 1991).

As discussed in Chapter 3, college women are most likely to be raped by someone they know who does not use a weapon and does not cause serious physical injury. A blitz-style attack is unlikely to occur. Accordingly, a college woman's rape is usually quite different from a "real rape." When a woman thinks about what has happened to her and tries to make sense of it, she may reference her rape script and conclude that her victimization does not look or seem like a typical rape. Research on college women is supportive of this scenario. In one study, the rape scripts of unacknowledged rape victims were more violent and more likely to have a stranger as the offender than the scripts of acknowledged rape victims (Kahn et al., 1994). Other research shows that characteristics corresponding to a blitz rape script predicted acknowledgment (Bondurant, 2001).

Rape scripts are similar to rape myths, which are "prejudicial, stereotyped, or false beliefs about rape, rape victims, and rapists" (Burt, 1980, p. 217). Rape myths—such as "women ask for it," "only girls who sleep around get raped," and "rapists are insane and sex-starved"—may be used by both men and women to justify or deny sexual violence (Burt, 1980). They can also pertain to the characteristics of a rape. A rape myth might be that women receive cuts and bruises, if not worse, when they are raped. Men who adopt this myth, may examine their own sexually coercive behavior in this light; if what they do to a woman does not result in physical injury, then it is not rape. Taken together, rape scripts and rape myths narrowly define rape, blame victims for what happens to them, and affect how a rape is conceptualized by the victim (Peterson & Muehlenhard, 2004). Peterson and Muehlenhard proposed that the acceptance of rape myths interacts with the characteristics of a rape to predict acknowledgment. Specifically, if a woman has high rape-myth acceptance and her victimization is high in correspondence with the rape myth, then she will be unlikely to acknowledge her rape. They found two rape myths that did interact with victimization characteristics. First, participants were less likely to acknowledge rape when they accepted the rape myth that women who are sexually teasing deserve rape and believed their actions may have been viewed as sexually teasing. Second, those who believed that it is not rape unless a woman physically fights back and who did not physically resist were less likely to be acknowledged victims than others.

Prior and Vicarious Victimization. Unfortunately, college women who have been sexually victimized before entering college or during college are more likely to experience a subsequent sexual victimization during college (Daigle et al., 2008). As a result, they may react differentially to a newer sexual victimization. In terms of acknowledgment, prior sexual victimization increases the likelihood that a sexual victimization occurring during college will be defined as rape (Fisher et al., 2003b). This finding is salient because it suggests that experience with victimization may sensitize women to the precise illegal nature of their rape.

Many college women will also become aware of the victimization experiences of others, which may shape how they define their own experience should they too become a victim. This "vicarious victimization" may help a woman recognize and label a rape as a rape. Research by Botta and Pingree (1997) supports this link. In their study, college women who had a friend who experienced acquaintance rape were more likely to be acknowledged victims than women who were not vicariously victimized. A measure of vicarious victimization was included in our NCWSV Study, but it was not significantly related to rape acknowledgment.

Demographics. Demographic characteristics, such as age and race, have also been examined for the role they may play in rape acknowledgment. Although race does not appear to differentiate acknowledged and unacknowledged rape victims, age does. Older college women in the NCWSV Study were more likely than younger college women to acknowledge their incident as a rape. Other researchers have found similar results regarding the relationship between age and rape acknowledgment (Botta & Pingree, 1997; Kahn et al., 2003).

SITUATIONAL FACTORS

Victim–Offender Relationship. Based on the stereotype of what constitutes a "real rape," it has been hypothesized that women may be more likely to acknowledge a rape perpetrated by a stranger than by someone they know. Although the victim–offender relationship was not significant in research employing the NCWSV Study, some research on college women supports this hypothesis (Kahn et al., 2003). Koss's (1985) results suggest that incidents are most likely to be acknowledged when the victims do not know their perpetrators well and when romantic partners are not involved. She also found that women who had a higher level of intimacy with the perpetrator prior to the attack were less likely to label their experience a rape.

Seriousness of Incident. Characteristics of the incident that make it serious in nature—injury and the presence of a weapon—play a role in victim acknowledgment. Thus, studies find incidents that result in physical injury are more likely to be defined as rapes than those that do not produce physical injury (Bondurant, 2001; Fisher et al., 2003b). Similarly, the presence of a weapon prompts college women to view their experience as a rape (Bondurant, 2001; Fisher et al., 2003b). Notably, those incidents that are in line with a "real rape" are more often acknowledged than sexual victimizations that transpire without a weapon and that do not cause physical harm. In turn, this finding suggests that as discussed above, rape scripts may provide an interpretive framework used by victims to define what happened to them.

Substance Use. As previously discussed, sexual victimization of college women is often tied to alcohol and drug use on the part of the offender, the victim, or both. Such substance use has been investigated as a possible influence on rape acknowledgment. However, use of alcohol or drugs prior to the incident by the victim has not been found to be related to rape acknowledgment. Thus, drug use by either the victim or the offender in Koss's (1985) study did not differ across acknowledgment categories. Similarly, our NCWSV Study showed a nonsignificant effect of alcohol or drug use by the victim and/or the offender. It is perhaps the somewhat commonplace presence of alcohol and drugs in sexual victimization and rapes that negates any potential impact it would have on acknowledgment.

Resistance Strategies. What the victim does during the course of the incident may also impact how she defines the incident. Generally, women who use resistance strategies during the incident in hopes of stopping it may be more likely to view what happened to them as rape (Layman et al., 1996). Indeed, acknowledged rape victims are more likely to have used physical force and/or verbal strategies to resist than unacknowledged rape victims (Bondurant, 2001). Our NCWSV Study revealed that the only type of resistance strategy that increased the likelihood of rape acknowledgment was forceful verbal resistance. Finally, Ullman (1997) suggests that it is not the type of resistance but the amount and level of resistance that matters.

Offender's Behavior. Aspects of the offender's behavior during the course of the incident also are related to how a woman subsequently defines her sexual victimization. An offender's use of force and whether penetration occurred are both elements to consider. First, as shown in the NCWSV Study, when the offender used or threatened to use physical force during the incident, the woman was more likely to consider the incident a rape. Other research also supports the link between physical force and acknowledgment (Bondurant, 2001; Kahn et al., 1994). An offender's use of physical force for vaginal, anal, or oral intercourse was significantly related to acknowledgment among the university women in Botta and Pingree's (1997) study. The type of physical force used by the offender was also considered by Layman et al. (1996). They reported that being threatened with force, having her arms twisted or held down, and being hit or slapped during the rape increased the likelihood that a woman would be an acknowledged victim.

In addition to force, whether the offender attempted and/or completed penetration is related to acknowledgment. Incidents in which penetration was completed were more likely than other incidents to be acknowledged by women in our NCWSV Study. Using another approach to investigate the relationship between penetration and acknowledgment, Peterson and Muehlenhard (2004) considered whether the woman thought that what had transpired was in fact sex. They hypothesized that many people do not consider genital penetration by a finger or object to be sexual intercourse. If so, people who experience nongenital penetration, even without consent, may not believe that a rape has occurred. Supportive of this view, they found that college women who did not consider their experience to be sex were in fact less likely to label it as a rape, even though the act met the legal definition of rape.

A final element of acknowledgment to consider is how it may impact the choices a college woman makes after she is sexually victimized. Defining a rape incident as a rape or other types of sexual victimization as crimes may be an integral first step to engaging help that may or may not include the police.

Reporting Sexual Victimization to the Police

Despite the prevalence of sexual offenses committed against college women, the majority of women who are victimized do not report the incident to the police (Fisher, Daigle, Cullen, & Turner, 2003a). In fact, results from our NCWSV Study show that a very small proportion of victims contacted the police to disclose what they had experienced:

- Across victimizations, only 2.1% of victims reported to the police.
- Rapes were more likely than other forms of sexual victimization to be reported to the police.
- Still, fewer than 5% of rapes were reported.
- Only 1.4% of unwanted sexual contacts were reported.
- None of the sexual coercion incidents was reported to the police.

Victims, in short, kept their victimization secret from police officials.

Other research using national-level college samples has found similar results (Fisher et al., 1998; Koss et al., 1987; Sloan, Fisher, & Cullen, 1997). Koss (1989) reported that only 5% of the rape victims told the police. Fisher and colleagues (1999) also found high levels of nonreporting. The majority of rapes (86.7%) and sexual assaults (85.7%) and almost all unwanted sexual contacts (97.7%) were not disclosed to the police. Findings from the National Crime Victimization Survey (NCVS) also show that only 12% of rapes and sexual assaults of college students are reported to the police (Hart, 2003).

This latter finding is important. It shows that the discovery that the vast majority of sexual victimization goes unreported is not unique to studies on college campuses supposedly conducted by biased, politically correct researchers. Rather, the NCVS is administered by the U.S. Census Bureau on behalf of the Bureau of Justice Statistics. Accordingly, it appears that regardless of method or sample, college students keep their sexual victimization secret from police officials.

More recently, research has investigated the reporting behaviors of women who are the victims of drug- or alcohol-facilitated sexual assault. Notably, this body of research has found that incapacitated sexual assault victims were less likely to report their victimization to the police than victims of forced sexual assault (Krebs et al., 2007). In fact, in their national study of college women, Kilpatrick et al. (2007) found that 10% of college women who had experienced a drug- or alcohol-facilitated or incapacitated rape reported the incident to the police compared to 18% of victims of forcible rape.

This lack of reporting is not unique to sexual victimizations committed against college women. Studies of the general population show that about half of all violent victimizations are not reported to the police (Hart & Rennison, 2003). Studies of college students also reveal that a relatively low percentage (between 25% and 34%) of violent victimizations perpetrated against college students are reported to the police (Hart, 2003; Sloan et al., 1997).

Sexual victimization, however, remains one of the most underreported types of victimization. Specifically, in the National Crime Victimization Survey between 1992 and 2000, 63% of completed rapes, 65% of attempted rapes, and 74% of completed and attempted sexual assaults against females were not reported to the police (Rennison, 2002). When other forms of sexual victimization are also taken into account, reporting rates are even lower (Russell, 1982). In this broader context, college women's reluctance to report being sexually victimized to the police is not surprising.

The Importance of Reporting

Reporting sexual victimization receives special attention because the decision to report carries many consequences. Importantly, when a woman reports her victimization to the police, she is taking the first step in invoking the formal criminal justice system and activating the investigative process. Although not all investigations result in an offender's being apprehended, there is no chance of an assailant's arrest in the absence of a victim report. To the extent that arrest and criminal justice processes dissuade perpetrators from reoffending, nonreporting undermines specific deterrence (see Bachman, Paternoster, & Ward, 1992). As we have seen in Chapter 5, we also know that for college women, experiencing more than one sexual victimization is an unfortunate reality that many face (Daigle et al., 2008). Especially if a repeat victimization is committed by the same offender, it is possible that reporting would allow women to thwart this subsequent incident.

Reporting may also be important in that services that victims could utilize may not be provided if no one is made aware of the victimization. Importantly, research on rape and sexual assault victims using the National Crime Victimization Survey (NCVS) shows that women who report their victimization to the police are more likely than nonreporters to receive medical attention for their injuries (Rennison, 2002). Further, victims may benefit from services that the police can be helpful in coordinating. For example, many district attorneys' offices have victim advocates, who help victims navigate the criminal justice process as well as provide information regarding other services such as victim compensation (Frazier & Burnett, 1994). Unfortunately, victims may be left unaware of the availability of such services without first reporting their victimization to the police. Access to some benefits is explicitly tied to reporting. For example, monetary compensation through state victim-compensation programs cannot be given if a victim did not report the incident to the police. Finally, nonreporting may mean that campus officials remain unaware of a female student's victimization. This might knife off opportunities for these officials to furnish counseling and other support services.

Although reporting is important for a number of reasons, it is possible that victims do not view reporting positively. In fact, in the Campus Sexual Assault Study, of the victims of forced sexual assault who did report to law enforcement, less than half indicated they were satisfied with the way their reporting was handled (Krebs et al., 2007). Other women (17%) stated they actually regretted reporting.

Why Don't College Women Report Sexual Victimization?

Because most female students keep their victimization a secret from law enforcement officials, research has been undertaken to explore why nonreporting is so prevalent. Studies have tended to fall into one of two approaches (though we used both in our NCWSV Study). First, in a very straightforward manner, women are asked why they did not report their victimization. This approach has the advantage of probing victims' thinking. Mapping this cognitive landscape is potentially important because it may identify "thinking errors" that serve as barriers to reporting. If understood, attempts to encourage reporting may become more strategic and successful. The potential weakness of the asking-victims approach is that it is difficult to disentangle reasons that (1) were actually present at the time of the victimization that influenced the nonreporting decision from (2) mere justifications that victims might invent ex post facto to account for their failure to report. The second approach is to measure characteristics of the victims, offender, incident, and context so as to explore empirically the factors that most affect the decision to report or not report a victimization. The following sections of this chapter are devoted to each of these two approaches.

FINDINGS FROM THE NCWSV STUDY

In our NCWSV Study, women who were sexually victimized but did not report their victimization to the police were asked why they did not come forward. The victims were not asked an open-ended question but rather were read a list of possible reasons for not responding. Victims were asked to indicate all those that were "important reasons why it [the incident] was not reported to the police." They were instructed to choose all reasons that applied to their decision making. The list of reasons was developed using previous research on reporting crimes generally and from the research on sexual victimization that pointed to sources of nonreporting. The advantage of providing such a roster of answers is that, in a survey, it allows respondents to consider a range of possible factors that might have shaped their nonreporting decision. The disadvantage is that it might prompt the selection of reasons that would not independently come to mind to victims.

Table 6.2 provides the reasons, in rank order, the victims gave for not reporting completed rape; the responses for attempted rape are also included. It should be noted that the reasons given for not reporting sexual coercion and sexual contact were quite similar to those reported for rape.

Table 6.2   Most Common Reasons Why Rape Incidents Are Not Reported to the Police (Percentage Giving Answer Reported)

Reasons	Completed Rape	Attempted Rape
Not Seriousness Enough to Report	65.4	76.5
Did Not Want Other People to Know	46.9	32.4
Not Sure Crime or Harm Intended	44.4	39.7
Did Not Want Family to Know	44.4	32.4
Lack of Proof That Incident Happened	42.0	30.9
Afraid of Reprisal by Person (Offender)	39.5	25.0
Police Wouldn't Think It Was Serious Enough	27.2	33.8
Would Not Want to Be Bothered	25.9	13.2
Fear of Being Treated Hostilely by the Police	24.7	8.8
Did Not Know How to Report	13.6	7.4

SOURCE: Fisher, Cullen, and Turner (1999).

As can be seen, the most often-cited reason was that the victim did not think that the incident "was serious enough to report." Two-thirds of rape victims and three-fourths of attempted rape victims selected this answer. Further, for these two types of victimizations, 44.4% and 39.7% of the victims also said that it was not clear that a crime had been committed or that harm was intended. What is not clear, however, is *why* they gave these reasons. One interpretation is that many of the incidents were relatively minor and should not be classified as a rape. Another interpretation is that victims are not well educated about what constitutes a crime of rape—even when their victimization involves force and lack of consent. Further, although they may see the victimization incident as serious, turning in the offender—whom they may know—to the police is a major undertaking that would exact high costs on both the offender and them personally. We return to these issues in a following section.

In making the decision not to report an incident to the police, victims might best be seen as making a *rational choice*. Is it "worth it" to call in the police? Notably, the other responses in Table 6.2 reveal some of the potential costs to reporting identified by victims. It is noteworthy that in nearly half of the completed rape incidents, victims cited as their reason for not reporting that they did not want their family to know (44.4%) or other people to know (46.9%); the figures for attempted rape were about one-third of the victims. This lends credence to the view that concern over embarrassment prompts secrecy. Another common answer was that they lacked proof that the incident had happened. About one-fourth of the rape victims feared a negative reaction from the police—either they would be treated hostilely by the police and/or the police would not think the incident was serious enough. Further, two in five rape victims and one in four attempted rape victims stated that they were afraid of a reprisal by the person who had victimized them. Taken together, these various considerations comprise a meaningful disincentive for victims to notify police officials and initiate an inquiry into their victimization.

FINDINGS FROM OTHER STUDIES ON REPORTING

Other research has also examined reporting of sexual victimization among college women. Perhaps not surprisingly, the reasons given most commonly are quite similar to those given by the college women included in the NCWSV Study. Take, for example, a study by Thompson, Sitterle, Clay, and Kingree (2007), conducted at a large southeastern university. Of the college women who had been sexually victimized but who did not report, 79.9% indicated they did not think the incident was serious enough. Additional reasons given for nonreporting included not wanting the police involved or not wanting anyone to know. College women in this study also said they felt shame or embarrassment that precluded them from reporting. A unique finding is that over one-fourth of sexual assault victims thought that if they reported, the incident would be viewed as their fault.

Fear of embarrassment was also evident in Kilpatrick et al.'s (2007) national study. They found that over half of the college women did not report because they did not want family members or other people to know. Other prominent reasons for not disclosing the victimization were that the women believed that they lacked proof and feared reprisal by the offender or other people. These reasons were found for women who had been forcibly raped and for women who had experienced drug- or alcohol-facilitated or incapacitated rape.

Most of the research examining reporting among college women has focused on the underreporting of sexual victimization. There is a small body of research, however, that has examined the reasons that college women do not report other offenses either. Fisher and Cullen's (1999) national study of college women that examined victimization rates and reporting levels furnishes important findings. Their analysis revealed that robbery victims' most frequently stated rationale for not contacting authorities was that they did not think the incident was serious enough to report. Similarly, this reasoning was most commonly cited by those who experienced aggravated and simple assaults. Victims of these three types of violent crimes also said that they did not report because they lacked proof that the incident happened and because they did not think the police would think it was serious enough. Taken together, these findings provide an important comparative context. They show that a common reason that victims give for nonreporting violent crime is their belief that the incident is not "serious enough." This reasoning, in short, is not unique to female college student rape victims.

Results from the NCVS show that violent crime victims indicate that they did not report their victimization because they perceived the incident to be a private or personal matter or to not be important enough (Hart & Rennison, 2003). In the NCVS, the most common reason female victims of rape and sexual assault cite for not reporting is that the incident was a private matter (Bachman, 1998a). Victimized college students (both male and female) also said that they did not report to the police because other officials had been made aware of the incident (Hart & Rennison, 2003).

REASONS FOR REPORTING VICTIMIZATIONS

Researchers typically ask victims reasons for nonreporting, but some inquiries have been made to ask the opposite question: why do victims notify the police? Findings from the NCVS provide some understanding as to why college students in general (i.e., not just rape/sexual assault victims) report their victimizations to the police. Generally, victims of violent crime report to the police to prevent future violence or to stop the incident. Other common reasons include the desire to punish the offender and to protect others (Hart, 2003; Hart & Rennison, 2003). Similar reasons are given by college women who have been the victims of drug- or alcohol-facilitated or incapacitated rapes. The small proportion of women who did in fact report to the police in Kilpatrick et al.'s (2007) study noted that they did so to prevent crimes against others, to punish the offender, and because it was a crime. Victims of forcible rape most frequently contacted the police to prevent crimes against others and against themselves, because it was a crime, to get help after the incident, and for other unspecified reasons.

IMPLICATIONS

Three implications can be drawn from these findings on why most college women say that they do not report their sexual victimization. First, a good portion of the victims, approaching half in our NCWSV Study, simply wished to keep their victimization a secret—a private matter. They did not want their parents or other people to know what had happened to them. This suggests that possible embarrassment or desire for sexual privacy restrains the desire to disclose victimization to the police. Second, many of the women were not sure that a crime had been committed or, if it had, whether they would have proof it had transpired. This indicates an assessment that contacting the police would yield no legal intervention; it would be, in short, a waste of time.

Third and most salient, the judgment that the incident "was not serious enough" was most often cited as a reason for nonreporting. There is a risk that this finding will lend credence to the view that the sexual acts in question were trivial and thus did not amount to "real" crimes; they are, in short, a methodological artifact. Three considerations, however, argue against this conclusion. First, recall the study of college students who found that robbery victims also did not report their victimization because it was "not serious enough" (Fisher & Cullen, 1999). It is doubtful that critics would conclude that robbery victims were a methodological artifact created by politically correct researchers. Second, we need to probe more deeply into what *seriousness* means to victims. It appears that it involves suffering an injury and the presence of a weapon. Acquaintance rapes do not typically involve these features. Third, the female students did not say that their victimization was not serious but not serious *enough*. This standard suggests that reporting a sexual victimization to the police involves a cost—a loss of privacy, potential embarrassment, having to "deal with" one's parents, rejection by friends of the perpetrator one accuses, the necessity to perhaps leave the campus and drop out of college, and having to testify at a college disciplinary hearing or court case. In this context, the harm experienced—especially in the absence of visible physical injury—may not seem serious enough to pursue an assailant legally.

Factors That Influence Reporting

The second approach to understanding sources of victim reporting choices relies on empirical (usually multivariate) studies of factors that might shape the disclosure of a victimization. Research on why some incidents of sexual victimization are reported to the police while others are not has centered on examining characteristics of the incident, offender, victims, and context. These are presented in Table 6.3 and then are examined in more detail in the sections to follow.

INCIDENT CHARACTERISTICS

As previously noted, one of the most common reasons cited by college women for not reporting sexual victimization to the police is that the incident was not serious enough to warrant such a disclosure. Accordingly, those incidents that are more serious in nature in terms of the harm that results are more likely than other, less serious, incidents to be reported to the police. Results from the NCWSV Study show that two factors especially are related to reporting sexual victimization for college women. First, those incidents in which the offender has a weapon are more likely to come to the attention of the police than incidents in which there is no weapon. Second, incidents that are considered to be rape are more likely to be reported than those incidents not considered rape.

Table 6.3   Factors Shown to Increase Likelihood of Reporting Sexual Victimization to the Police by College Women

Incident Characteristics

  Weapon Present*

  Acknowledgment*

  Physical Injury

  Perceived Fear of Death or Injury

Offender Characteristics

  Perpetrated by Stranger*

  Offender and Victim of Different Races/Ethnicities*

Victim Characteristics

  African American non-Hispanic Victim*

  Memory of Incident

Contextual Characteristics

  Occured on Campus Property*

  Alcohol Part of Assault

  Too High or Drunk to Control Their Behavior

SOURCE: Adapted from Fisher, Daigle, Cullen, and Turner (2003a).

NOTE: *Factor statistically significant in the NCWSV Study.

Kilpatrick et al. (2007) also found that when college women who were raped experienced a physical injury, they were more likely to report to the police. In addition, they found that rapes involving physical force were reported more often than other rapes. Acknowledged rapes were similarly more likely to be reported than incidents not identified by the victim as rape. Another element of crime seriousness examined was whether the victim experienced a perceived fear of death or injury during the assault. When this perception occurred, the incident was more likely to be reported.

The fact that the seriousness of a victimization impacts reporting is in accordance with rape myths and the "real rape." Again, the real rape is one in which a rape transpires in a blitz-style attack in a public, deserted location. The real rape is committed by a stranger and results in physical injury. Because rapes that coincide with this scenario are deemed to be legitimate or real, they are more likely to be reported by victims.

OFFENDER CHARACTERISTICS

Research shows (1) that when a college woman is sexually victimized, the likely perpetrator is someone she knows and (2) that college women infrequently report their victimization to the police. When taken together, these points suggest that the victim-offender relationship may contribute to a woman's decision to disclose her victimization to the police. Not surprisingly, in our NCWSV Study, those incidents perpetrated by a stranger were more likely to be reported. Women may be reluctant to come forward when they know the person they potentially would be "getting in trouble." This reluctance may also be driven by the fear that incidents perpetrated by a stranger are more "believable" and hence more likely to be proven.

Another factor that may influence the victim's decision to report is whether the offender is of a different race. The NCWSV Study examined whether this factor did indeed impact the decision to report. When the offender and victim were of different races or ethnicities, college women who were sexually victimized were more likely to report.

VICTIM CHARACTERISTICS

Although characteristics of the incident and offender influence a college woman's decision to report to the police, there are also individual factors that play a role in this crucial decision. Victim demographic characteristics as well as her recall of the incident are important influences.

Race. Reporting of victimizations has been thought to be tied, at least in part, to the race of the victim. The findings are mixed in relation to race and sexual victimization reporting generally. Some research has shown that white women are more likely to report (Hart & Rennison, 2003). Others have shown that being African American increases the likelihood of reporting rape (Feldman-Summers & Ashworth, 1981). For college women, race also seems to be tied to reporting. In fact, incidents perpetrated against African American non-Hispanic college women in the NCWSV Study were more likely to be reported to the police than incidents in which the victim was Caucasian.

Memory of Incident. How well the victim can recall specifics about the victimization itself also contributes to her decision to report to the police. In their study of college women, Kilpatrick and colleagues (2007) found that college women who said they remembered the incident extremely well (22%) were more likely to report than those who remembered very well (6.7%). It appears, then, that confidence in their ability to provide an accurate and thorough depiction of what occurred influences college women's reporting decisions. This bivariate relationship may not be found, however, in multivariate models that control for other factors.

CONTEXTUAL CHARACTERISTICS

The context in which sexual victimizations occur, such as where they happen and what else is occurring, potentially shapes victim decisions. Research suggests that where a college woman is sexually victimized and whether alcohol or drugs are involved affect reporting to the police.

Location of Incident. Based on the ideas put forth about what constitutes a real rape, reporting may be tied to where a victimization occurs. A real rape is one that is perpetrated by a stranger in an unfamiliar place and causes substantial physical injury (Estrich, 1987). Accordingly, incidents that occur outside of a person's living quarters should come to the attention of the police more frequently. Supportive of this relationship, those incidents in the NCWSV Study that occurred on campus (e.g., classroom, another person's dorm room, fraternity) were more likely to be reported to the police.

Alcohol and/or Drug Use. As discussed previously, alcohol and drugs often play a role in the victimization of college students, whether through use by the offender, the victim, or both parties. When alcohol and drugs are involved in sexual victimizations, it is possible that college women may be less likely to report to the police. In the NCWSV Study, however, alcohol and drug use were not found to be related to reporting. By contrast, when alcohol use was a part of the assault, Kilpatrick et al. (2007) found that college women were less likely to report being raped. Similarly, women who were too drunk or high to control their behavior were less likely to report the incident than those who perceived themselves to be more in control (Kilpatrick et al., 2007). This lower likelihood of reporting could be tied to self-blame and the feeling that they were more culpable for their experience if they consumed alcohol or drugs.

Reporting to Other People: Telling Friends

Most college women do not choose to report their sexual victimization to police agencies. This is not to say, however, that women remain silent about their experiences. Indeed, a majority of college women are likely to tell others outside of the formal criminal justice system. Below, we examine whom they tell and the potential consequences of doing so.

WHOM DO VICTIMS TELL?

In our NCWSV Study, college women were asked if they had told anyone else other than or in addition to the police about each incident they experienced since school began that academic year. For those women who indicated that they had told someone, they were then asked to whom they disclosed the incident.

Again, less than 5% of the incidents were reported to the police. As seen in Table 6.4, in almost 70% of all sexual victimization incidents, someone other than the police was told about the incident. In about two-thirds of rape and attempted rape incidents, victims disclosed the incident to someone besides the police. Similar or higher

Table 6.4   Reported Incident to Someone Besides the Police

Reporting Decision	Percentage	n
Victims Told Someone Other Than the Police	69.9	919
Whom They Told		
Friend	87.9	808
Family Member	10.0	92
Husband, Boyfriend, or Partner	8.3	76
Other Nonspecified Person	3.3	30
Employer, Boss, Supervisor	1.7	16
Counseling Service	1.0	9

SOURCE: Fisher, Daigle, Cullen, and Turner (2003a).

percentages of victims of sexual coercion (62.9%) and sexual contact (74.1%) told others. Notably, as seen in Table 6.4, victims most often disclosed the incident to a friend; thus, 87.9% of incidents disclosed to someone were to a friend. Other persons told about the incident were intimates, parents, and family members, but these totals were all under 10%. It is instructive that victims rarely contacted university officials, residence hall advisors, or help services.

These results regarding college women's reporting are similar to what other researchers have found when examining reporting among college students and general samples. Their investigations reveal that, overall, the majority of persons who were sexually victimized told a friend (Dunn, Vail-Smith, & Knight, 1999; Golding, Siegel, Sorenson, Burnam, & Stein, 1989). Friends, relatives, and other intimate partners are also often chosen as confidantes (Ahrens, Campbell, Ternier-Thames, Wasco, & Sefl, 2007; Feldman-Summers & Ashworth, 1981; George, Winfield, & Blazer, 1992).

We should note that in the NCWSV Study, we also explored what factors increased the likelihood that a female student would disclose her victimization to others (not including, of course, the police). Five factors heightened this type of reporting:

- The incident involved sexual contact and not just a threat.
- The victim was injured.
- The perpetrator was known by the victim.
- The victim was using drugs and/or alcohol before the incident.
- The perpetrator was using drugs and/or alcohol before the incident.

The finding regarding the perpetrator is illuminating. Whereas it appears that stranger incidents are more likely to be reported to the police, victimizations by acquaintances are disclosed to friends one knows.

CONSEQUENCES OF TELLING OTHERS

The reason college women confide in their friends may seem intuitive—they are seeking support. Victims reach out to others to gain general support rather than specific advice. In fact, victims turn to the supports they deem most helpful (Biaggio, Brownell, & Watts, 1991; Golding et al., 1989). Despite the fact that victims may be seeking support, research shows that victims of rape and other types of sexual victimizations may not always be responded to positively. Instead, disclosing may actually result in victim blaming. Other victims may experience an overall unhelpful or negative response. Using samples of adult (Ahrens et al., 2007; Golding et al., 1989) and adolescent (Ageton, 1983) female samples, researchers have found that a meaningful minority (up to 39%) of victims report receiving such responses. Studies of college women who said that at least one woman had disclosed a date or acquaintance rape to them reveal that their responses were not always positive. In fact, some respondents acknowledged that they reacted in ways such as blaming the victim and questioning the legitimacy of the experience and the victim's actions (Dunn et al., 1999). These overtly negative responses that are unsupportive can be harmful. Indeed, negative responses can be destructive to the psychological adjustment of rape victims (Ullman, 1999).

Social supports may also influence a victim's decision to report to the police. What do friends, family members, and others tell these women about reporting? Unfortunately, some research shows that college women are seldom advised to report their victimization to the police (Pitts & Schwartz, 1993). In cases of drug- or alcohol-facilitated rape or incapacitated rape, only 40.7% of the college women who did tell someone received encouragement to report. Importantly, just slightly over half of the women who experienced forcible rapes were encouraged to report to the police after they confided in someone (Kilpatrick et al., 2007). The lack of receiving a strong push to report is critical given that other researchers have found that, when a victim is assisted with seeking help or when someone else decides to report, she is quite likely to contact the police herself (Burgess & Holmstrom, 1975).

At least one study has examined the circumstances under which college students are likely to encourage victims to report to the police by using vignettes that depicted the victim as being either a male or female and as either having consumed alcohol or not. Females and students over the age of 21 were more likely than males and younger students to encourage reporting across various crime types. When the victim was described as not having been drinking, the respondents were most likely to suggest that the victim notify the police. When the type of victimization was a sexual assault, subjects were more likely to suggest calling the police when the offender was a stranger than when he was described as being her boyfriend. Males under 21 were significantly less likely to advise calling the police when the victim of sexual assault was drunk in the scenario. Gender and drinking also interacted. Females were less likely to suggest disclosing to the police when the victim had been drinking and was victimized by her boyfriend (Ruback, Menard, Outlaw, & Shaffer, 1999). The findings from this study suggest that college students be taught that perpetrators of sexual assault can be an intimate partner and that alcohol use does not negate the criminality of sexual assault. If students perceive victimizations involving alcohol and intimate partners as "real," then college women who are sexually victimized may receive advice to report and, consequently, be more prone to reporting.

Despite the fact that an overwhelming majority of college women do tell at least one person about their sexual victimization experience, there are some women who remain silent. Although not a main focus of research in the past, the reasons behind this silence have been investigated. At least two key factors have been identified. Being under the influence of alcohol or drugs appears to reduce the likelihood that a woman will tell someone she has been victimized (Pitts & Schwartz, 1993). For some women, self-blame may prevent them from telling others in that they may perceive themselves to be at least partly responsible for their own victimization (Koss, 1985; Pitts & Schwartz, 1993).

Conclusion

More than 2 decades ago, Koss's classic study illuminated that most female students do not acknowledge as rape incidents that legally qualify as this crime and do not report their victimization to the police. More contemporary research suggests that little has changed. On today's campuses, only a minority of victims acknowledge that they have been raped and report sexual victimizations to the police officials.

In a sense, this means that victims live with two "secrets." First, the lack of acknowledgment might be called a *self-secret*. Something untoward, possibly very disquieting, has happened to them, but they are limited in how to interpret the event. Unless the victimization approaches a "real rape," they lack the script to define their sexual victimization as a crime that crosses the legal boundary into the category of rape. Second, by not reporting incidents to the police, female students keep their victimization secret from law enforcement officials and all those who would, in turn, "find out"—parents, friends at school, the public in general.

It is tempting to suggest that the lack of acknowledgment and reporting means that the incidents that female students experience are not victimizations but trivial events—male foreplay that goes a bit too far or sexual acts that a woman regrets once the haze of intoxication has passed the morning after. But dismissal of the victimization women experience is too cavalier. Especially in our NCWSV Study, a methodologically conservative approach was used to categorize someone as a rape victim (i.e., unless questions in the incident report were answered appropriately, the incident was not counted as rape). Further, it is instructive that almost half of completed rape victims did acknowledge their victimization as a rape and about 70% told someone, usually a friend, about the incident.

Although we did not study the issue in the NCWSV Study, it is not clear that sharing secrets about a rape or other sexual assault will always result in the receipt of social support and in heightened psychological well-being. Far more research needs to be conducted on the factors that shape whether acknowledgment and/or reporting produces beneficial or negative effects. But we can observe that acknowledgment and reporting prevent a disquieting secret from fading away and make this incident something that must be addressed—either within the confines of one's own mind (with acknowledgment) or in a very public, prolonged way (reporting to the police). The cost of unraveling secrets is that they may inspire reactions—from self-blame to blame from others—that are difficult to surmount. We are not counseling secrecy, of course, but it is important to consider that disclosing a rape or sexual victimization to oneself or to others is a step that, if not supported by others in a healthy way, can have adverse consequences.

7

Being Pursued

The Stalking of Female Students

U ntil the 1990s, relatively little attention was paid to stalking. During this period, however, various "claimsmakers" succeeded in defining stalking as a social problem—so much so that the word *stalking* became part of the public's lexicon (Lowney & Best, 1995). Thus, several educational and victim service organizations, such as the National Victim Center and Survivors of Stalking, heightened the public's awareness of the problem of stalking (see Monaghan, 1998). The media prominently publicized stalking cases involving Hollywood stars, public officials, and fatal outcomes. Perhaps most noteworthy, legislatures across the nation moved to criminalize stalking behavior (Marks, 1997; McAnaney, Curliss, & Abeyta-Price, 1993).

The first antistalking law was passed in 1990 in California in response both to the murder of Rebecca Schaeffer, a young actress who was shot to death in 1989 by an obsessed fan who had stalked her for 2 years, and to the murders of five women in Orange County who had been stalked by former boyfriends or spouses (McAnaney et al., 1993). These cases galvanized national and state attention as to the seriousness of stalking. Legislatures subsequently initiated a torrent of antistalking statutes (McAnaney et al., 1993). By the end of the 1990s, all 50 states and the District of Columbia had implemented antistalking laws (Marks, 1997). Although legal scholars addressed the constitutionality of state antistalking statutes and numerous constitutional challenges to these statutes were waged, generally the courts have upheld the laws (U.S. Department of Justice, 1996).

In addition to state-level interest in antistalking statutes, a substantial investment in the passage of antistalking legislation occurred at the federal level. In fact, the U.S.

Congress was prompted to pass (1) legislation in 1992 that charged the Attorney General, through the National Institute, to develop and distribute a constitutional and enforceable antistalking law to serve as a model for the states; (2) the Violence Against Women Act (VAWA) Title IV of the *Violent Crime Control and Enforcement Act of 1994* (Public Law 103–322), which included subtitle F, directing the Attorney General to submit an annual report to Congress providing information about the incidence of stalking and the effectiveness of antistalking efforts and legislation; and (3) a law that prohibited interstate stalking and stalking on federal property and other places within federal jurisdictions (passed as part of the *National Defense Authorization Act of Fiscal Year 1997*, Public Law 104–201, Section 1069, codified at 18 U.S.C. 2261, 2261A, and 2262) (see National Victim Center, 1997; see also Marks, 1997; Monaghan, 1998; U.S. Department of Justice, 1996).

Despite this public attention, systematic research on the extent, nature, and risk factors of stalking lagged behind. As Coleman (1997, p. 421) observed at the time—in an appraisal that still rings substantially true today—"the majority of information is anecdotal because little empirical research has been conducted on stalking." Echoing this view, then-NIJ Director Jeremy Travis (U.S. Department of Justice, 1996, p. 91) noted that "little hard data exist on the incidence of stalking"—an omission that hinders the development of prevention strategies to combat stalking.

In light of the growing interest in, yet limited research on, stalking, we incorporated a section into our National College Women Sexual Victimization Study that attempted to measure the extent, characteristics, and sources of "being pursued"—that is, of being stalked. Other relevant research, of course, is cited in the discussion of stalking that follows. However, the NCWSV Study remains perhaps the most systematic analysis of the stalking of college women. Accordingly, these data provide the main foundation for the conclusions that we present below.

We categorize stalking as a form of *sexual* victimization because it is largely conduct that involves the obsessive behavior of men toward women *on the basis of their gender.* We also suspect that stalking involves a desire for contact, intimacy, and/or sexual relations. We recognize, however, that a variety of motives can underlie stalking (see, e.g., Holmes, 1993; Meloy, 1996). Of course, this can also be said of other forms of behavior typically categorized as sexual victimization, such as sexual harassment and rape (e.g., the desire to control or exert power over women). Lastly, because the definition of stalking usually includes either being physically threatened or fearing for one's safety, stalking has been conceived of as a crime of violence against women (Tjaden & Thoennes, 1998b).

Finally, should we expect stalking to be high or low among female students? We begin our analysis by exploring why campuses offer ample opportunities for stalking. These observations would suggest that similar to other forms of sexual or gender-based victimization, female college students would experience comparatively high rates of stalking. Again, to the extent that college campuses provide a domain in which young women interact extensively with young men, it is plausible to expect that female students would be at risk for becoming objects of stalking by men. The data appear to support this hypothesis. Thus, we examine prior research and in particular the results on stalking from our NCWSV Study. We then explore the nature of stalking and how victims react to being pursued. An important message from this discussion is that stalking is yet another hidden cost that too many female students must face during their college years.

Opportunities for Stalking

Two sizable bodies of interdisciplinary research suggest that certain individuals are more vulnerable to criminal victimization and more likely to commit deviant or criminal acts. Research consistently shows that particular demographic characteristics, as well as lifestyle and routine activities among the public, significantly predict who is at a high risk of experiencing predatory victimization and which are common among predatory offenders in the general population (Cohen, Kluegel, & Land, 1981; Hindelang et al., 1978; Lauritsen, Sampson, & Laub, 1991; Miethe & Meier, 1994). Importantly, college students' demographics, as well as students' lifestyles and routine activities, are similar to those that research reports as creating vulnerabilities for stalking victimization and opportunities to stalk. Below, we explore these factors and how they may facilitate the stalking of female students.

COLLEGE STUDENT CHARACTERISTICS

Over the past decade, researchers developed a better understanding of the demographic characteristics of both stalking victims and stalkers. Age and gender are salient considerations. Thus, studies of the general population have found that over one-half of stalking victims are between the ages of 18 and 29 (Hall, 1998; Tjaden & Thoennes, 1998b). Nobles, Fox, Piquero, and Piquero (2009) reported that the average age at which college women experience the onset of stalking victimization is 20. Further, although both females and males are stalked, females are at a much greater risk. Tjaden and Thoennes (1998b) discovered, for example, that 78% of stalking victims were female. Cupach and Spitzberg (2004) have calculated national estimates of stalking perpetration prevalence across eight studies. They learned that, on average, nearly 15% of males and almost 9% of females reported they had stalked another person. We should note that, although in no way diminishing the salience of male victimization, our interest is confined here to the stalking of females.

Notably, the college population possesses key characteristics that research suggests makes those in the general population vulnerable to being stalked (young and female) or being a stalking perpetrator (young and male). Of the full-time students enrolled at postsecondary institutions in 2004, 77.4% were under age 25, while 57.2% of all students enrolled at postsecondary institutions in 2004 were female (National Center for Education Statistics, 2005). We can also add that the chance of becoming a stalking target or of stalking someone may be enhanced by consumption of alcohol, including binge drinking, and by experimentation with illegal drugs. Substance use and abuse often occur among a substantial portion of college students at parties and social events (Dowdall, 2007).

THE CAMPUS SETTING

The sheer number of young, unmarried women and men who routinely converge in classes and in social settings during their time at college provides a sizable pool of both potential stalking victims and perpetrators. Beyond these considerations, however, another feature of stalking must be understood: unlike other offenses, the behavior is not a onetime event but is a repeated course of action. Therefore, a stalker must (1) have regular access—physical or electronic—to the potential victim and (2) have the time to engage in pursuit behavior continually. Colleges appear to meet these criteria.

From the stalker's perspective, access to campus and its facilities, including dormitories and parking areas, is relatively easy, especially if the assailant is also a student. Ready access to a college campus is evident in its parklike setting with seemingly no physical boundaries other than, perhaps, a public thoroughfare or a sizable body of water (e.g., lake, ocean) that is contiguous. Campuses typically are "open" 24 hours, 7 days a week, 365 days of year to house, educate, employ, and entertain not only students, faculty, and staff, but also daily visitors.

This eclectic campus population easily flows legitimately from building to building or dorm to dorm during all hours of the day or night. Routine locking of many buildings during the school year, especially when classes are scheduled, is uncommon. Even buildings such as dormitories, whose users or residents are supposed to secure the doors, can jimmy them to remain open and go unnoticed. On-campus parking garages and lots are also relatively easy to access. Because of the daily fluidity of the campus population, many parking areas have unrestricted admission and any patron can park and pay a fee, or freely walk in parking areas unnoticed by an attendant or closed-circuit TV.

Students' academic, employment, and social schedules make them easy to communicate with and easily found for several reasons. First, their classes usually occur in the same classroom, at the same day and time over a 10- or 15-week term. Although students' specific classes change from term to term, their schedules are relatively predictable during the course of an academic year. Predictable class schedules, coupled with ease of access to classroom buildings and the larger campus, provide an endless number of opportunities for watching someone, waiting for someone outside or inside a building, and for leaving written notes or objects.

Second, many students live in university-owned or affiliated housing and park their vehicles on campus in assigned areas. One can easily find students' campus and e-mail addresses, and telephone numbers, in printed or electronic directories available from the school. For would-be stalkers, obtaining this information is as easy as going to a school's main Web site, searching an electronic directory for a specific person, and waiting a few seconds for the results to appear on the screen. Many schools assign all their students name-based e-mail accounts, so it is not too difficult to figure out a student's e-mail address even without a Web-based directory. Finding where a student parks her car on campus is just as easy, given that most schools have designated student-parking areas. Stalkers can use this contact and location information to approach the victim by following her to class; waiting outside a classroom or car; communicating through e-mail, social networking sites, or postal service; sending gifts; or damaging the target's property.

Third, students spend much time on campus—a physical space easily monitored by a stalker. For example, a large proportion of students work in the library, as parking attendants, or as lab assistants for their work-study requirements. Students' routine work schedules thus make them easy prey for a stalker once he or she knows the victim's place of employment. Students also frequently participate in regularly scheduled recreational activities on campus that provide another setting for stalking.

STUDENTS' LIFESTYLES AND ROUTINE ACTIVITIES

Opportunities for stalking thus are increased by the presence of young, unattached females and males located in a campus setting. The nature of students' lifestyles or routine activities is an additional factor that contributes to the presence of stalking opportunities.

First, as noted, stalking involves not only having access to the victim but also having the time during the day or night to engage in pursuit behaviors. While at college, students have fairly unrestricted access to campus facilities around the clock, 7 days a week during the academic term. Couple this ease of access with the large amounts of relatively flexible and unsupervised time that most students have, and what arise are ample opportunities to stalk another student.

Second, researchers have shown that stalking occurs throughout the dating continuum from the absence of a relationship (but wanting one to develop), to during the relationship, to after the relationship ends (Williams & Frieze, 2005). Stalking research has established that in well over a majority of incidents, some type of prior relationship—spouse/former spouse, intimate partner (including current/former cohabiting partner, date, girl/boyfriend), or acquaintance—existed between the victim and pursuer (Davis & Frieze, 2000). In fact, the most likely perpetrator of female stalking victims is a current or former intimate partner (through marriage, cohabitation, or dating), whereas men are most likely to be stalked by a stranger or an acquaintance (Tjaden & Thoennes, 1998b).

Third, college students widely use technology—the Internet and cell phones—that provides opportunities for a would-be stalker to easily and repeatedly access them day and night. A poll of Generation 2001 conducted by Harris Interactive (2001) reported that 100% of the sampled college students use the Internet, compared to only two-thirds of the general population. The students' Internet usage averaged from 6 to 11 hours a week, with 9 out of 10 of them sending and receiving e-mail messages on a daily or frequent basis. Furthermore, the annual *360 Youth College Explorer Study* sponsored by Harris Interactive (2004) revealed that 82% of college women and 74% of men own cell phones and are equally likely to use instant messaging daily (43% of women compared to 42% of men), with 60% of students with cell phones sending and receiving text messages on their phones. Market researchers are not the only interested parties to recognize the potential opportunities created by a large proportion of college students frequently using such technology. Stalkers may also take advantage of new technologies to easily and quickly monitor their prey's phone calls or computer use, track their prey using hidden cameras or global positioning systems, or pursue their prey via e-mail or cell phone (Spitzberg & Hoobler, 2002).

Fourth, the college years provide many opportunities for routinely encountering a variety of individuals, including other students and their friends, professors, staff, and visitors. Making acquaintances, developing friendships, initiating and maintaining dating relationships, and experiencing sexual intimacy are popular social activities for most college-aged populations, especially undergraduates who are typically single. Each of these experiences, however, may also be a stalking opportunity waiting to happen. Furthermore, Spitzberg and Rhea (1999) claim that relational mobility (which also suggests relationship termination) might be highest during the college years. Based on a convenience sample of students enrolled in a basic communication course at a large public university in Texas, their study revealed that students had dated an average of five persons since high school. Other studies show a large proportion of stalking occurs among college students within the context of dating and relationship continuums (Cupach & Spitzberg, 2004).

In sum, characteristics ranging from youthfulness and lifestyles to the campus setting provide many opportunities for stalkers to pursue their prey. Combined with students' knowledge of, and willingness to use, technology such as cell phones, instant messaging, and the Internet, one can easily understand why female students are at risk of being a stalking victim. The extent to which college women are, in fact, pursued by stalkers is considered next.

Research on the Extent of Stalking

Although stalking as a salient social issue was discovered about 2 decades ago, research documenting its prevalence, including among college students, is not plentiful. Still, some solid studies have been published (Fisher & Stewart, 2007). Two lines of inquiry are most pertinent to our concerns. First, studies of college students have appeared that furnish insights into the prevalence and nature of stalking among female students. Second, in the most comprehensive investigation to date, Tjaden and Thoennes (1998b) collected national-level data on stalking among women in the United States generally. In the sections that follow, this research is reviewed. As we will see, taken together, the extant empirical literature suggests that younger women—whether on campus or in the general population—are meaningfully at risk of being stalked.

STUDIES OF COLLEGE STUDENTS

Several studies have documented that stalking is a reality that a substantial proportion of college women experience. Estimates suggest that between 12 to 40% of college women reported having been stalked in their lives (see Fisher & Stewart, 2007; Jordan et al., 2007; Nobles et al., 2009). College women are also not immune from experiencing stalking after a dating or marital relationship breaks up. Between 9% and 34% of college women who recently ended a romantic relationship reported that their former partner had stalked them (Coleman, 1997; Logan, Leukefeld, & Walker, 2000; Roberts, 2002).

Three investigations have provided more detailed information and warrant further discussion. Although they have methodological limitations, they confirm the general conclusion that the stalking of female students is common. First, based on a survey of 141 female students in undergraduate psychology classes, Coleman (1997) reports that 29.1% of the sample answered "yes" to the question, "Have you ever ended a relationship that resulted in your former partner giving you repeated, unwanted attention following the breakup?" Further, 9.2% of the students stated that this repeated attention was either malicious, physically threatening, or fear-inducing. The limitations of this study are clear: the use of a small, unrepresentative sample; the lack of a reference period on the response; and the failure to measure stalking by men other than former boyfriends or partners. Still, the general finding that almost 3 in 10 women have received "repeated, unwanted attention" and almost 1 in 10 have experienced attention that threatens their safety is, at the very least, suggestive that stalking is not uncommon. Coleman's results also provide information about the demographic profile of the stalking victim: white, early 20s (mean age 23 years old), a father whose level of education is "some college or more," and a mother whose level of education is "high school or less."

Second, Mustaine and Tewksbury (1999) present the results from a victimization survey, conducted in the fall of 1996, of 861 women drawn from introductory sociology and criminal justice courses at nine postsecondary institutions. Using a 6-month reference period, they report that 10.5% of the females in their sample said that they had been a victim of behavior that the women defined as "stalking." In a multivariate analysis, they also found that the risk of stalking was related to several measures of lifestyle/routine activities. Thus, stalking was higher for women who shopped often at the mall, lived off campus, were employed, bought illegal drugs, and were drunk in public. Women who carried mace and pocket knives also were stalked more often—behaviors that may have been in response to having experienced this victimization.

Third, Jordan et al.'s (2007) study of stalking included 1,010 women enrolled at a large public university in the Southeast. Their results revealed that 18.8% of female students in their sample experienced stalking during their time in college. Further, 11.3% had been stalked within the past year at the university. Again, these findings reveal the prevalence of stalking among college women.

In their study, Jordan et al. (2007) collected additional information on stalking. Thus, half of the women in their sample reported being somewhat to very frightened by the stalking behaviors. Almost an equal proportion experienced one or more instances of a single type of pursuit behavior (e.g., only unsolicited phone calls) or experienced multiple types of pursuit behaviors (e.g., unsolicited phone calls and spying). About 6 in 10 of the victims reported knowing the stalkers. Thus, 43.6% of the victims reported being stalked by an acquaintance and 15.7% reported being stalking by an intimate partner, whereas 40.7% reported a stranger as the perpetrator. Of those stalked by an intimate partner, a majority of them, 85.2%, disclosed that the stalking occurred after the relationship ended. The others stated that they were stalked both during and after the relationship. The majority of victims, 56%, said that they were only stalked, but the remainder reported being victimized beyond the stalking while at the university. Specifically, 25.8% were stalked and raped/sexually assaulted; 10.5% were stalked, physically assaulted, and raped/sexually assaulted; and 7.7% were stalked and physically assaulted only.

TJADEN AND THOENNES'S NATIONAL VIOLENCE AGAINST WOMEN STUDY

Perhaps the most rigorous study of stalking remains Tjaden and Thoennes's (1998b) investigation, which explored this phenomenon as part of their National Violence Against Women Study. As might be recalled from Chapter 2, their survey was conducted in 1995 and 1996, and it included 8,000 women ages 18 and over. What they reported with regard to the extent of stalking was that:

- Eight percent of the women had been stalked at least once in their lives.
- The prevalence for the preceding 12 months was 1.0%.

These results, however, were conditioned by how stalking was defined in the study. To count as a stalking victim, a respondent had to: (1) answer "yes" to one of eight screen questions that described stalking behavior, such as a person spying on or making unsolicited phone calls to the respondent; (2) answer that these behaviors had happened more than once; and (3) answer that the behavior caused the respondent to feel "very frightened" or to "fear bodily harm." This restrictive definition has an important advantage: the incidents qualifying as stalking under this definition would be crimes under the stalking statutes that states passed in the 1990s. The disadvantage is that much of the stalking that women experience is excluded from consideration. Thus, when Tjaden and Thoennes relaxed the definition to include women who felt only "somewhat" or a "little" frightened, their results changed to show that the stalking was far more extensive:

- The lifetime prevalence figure jumped from 8 to 12%.
- The annual prevalence figure jumped from 1 to 6%.

These results suggest that serious incidents of stalking are relatively rare, but that less serious incidents are far more common.

The disparity between annual (1%) and lifetime (8%) figures for the prevalence of stalking also warrants attention. Even taking into account that some women will be victimized more than once and that a single stalking incident can last a lengthy period, it is difficult to see how an annual rate of 1% could result in only 8% of the women being stalked in their lifetime. In part, this can be explained by the concentration of stalking among younger women: 52% of all female stalking victims were ages 18 to 29, with another 22% of the victims being ages 30 to 39. That is, women tend to be victimized while relatively young and then not again. It also is possible that a cohort effect is in place: changes in the status and lifestyle of women have made younger cohorts more susceptible to stalking victimization (see Cohen & Felson, 1979). Still, response bias cannot be discounted: over the course of a lifetime, victims may have recall errors. In particular, they may be most likely to filter out incidents that "did not amount to much" and only report the more serious stalkings that occurred.

Tjaden and Thoennes present additional data on the victimization incidents that met their restrictive definition of stalking (and thus are more likely to be serious in nature). Thus, they found the following:

- Only 23% of the victims were stalked by strangers; less than half the victims were threatened with physical harm.

- Women stalked by former husbands or partners were especially likely to be physically and sexually assaulted.

- Fifty-five percent of the women reported the stalking incidents to the police.

- Stalking victims were more likely than nonvictims to be concerned for their safety and to carry something for self-defense.

- Thirty percent of the women suffered negative psychological and social consequences as a result of their being stalked.

Their results support those reported in a study of 100 stalking victims from a self-selected clinical sample in Australia. In 58% of the cases the stalker made overt threats to the victim; 7% of the victims reported being sexually assaulted and 34% were physically assaulted by their stalker; and the stalking experience had social (e.g., lifestyle changes) and psychological tolls (e.g., post-traumatic stress disorder symptoms) on the victims (Pathé & Mullen, 1997).

Finally, Tjaden and Thoennes present only a limited analysis of the factors that might increase the risk of stalking victimization. They do note that stalking was more common for younger women and for American Indian/Alaska Natives and was less common for Asian women. They do not, however, report multivariate models identifying how lifestyle factors potentially affect the risk of being stalked (see Mustaine & Tewksbury, 1999).

Measuring Stalking in the NCWSV Study

As we have emphasized throughout, a key issue in the study of sexual victimization on campuses is the quality of a study's methodology. We have discussed previously how critics of Mary Koss's classic research have argued that potential limitations in the SES artificially inflate victimization statistics. Regardless of the merits of these critiques, they are valuable in reminding scholars that measurement issues must be addressed carefully if we are to have confidence in any given study's findings.

In this context, the National College Women Sexual Victimization Study was initiated in large part to advance the methodology used to assess the victimization of women. It also meant that when we decided to probe the extent and nature of stalking on college campuses, we had to think carefully about how to measure this type of victimization. Thus, to create our measure of stalking, we examined previous stalking research (e.g., Tjaden, 1997) and various state-level legal definitions of stalking. As noted previously, the legal definition of stalking varies from state to state. In most states, however, to charge and convict a defendant of stalking, three elements must be proven beyond a reasonable doubt: (1) a course of conduct or behavior, (2) the presence of threats, and (3) the criminal intent to cause fear in the victim. First, a course of conduct includes a series of acts, viewed collectively, that present a pattern of behavior. These acts range from specifically defined actions (e.g., nonconsensual communication or lying in wait) to more diffuse types of actions (e.g., harassment). Second, the stalker must pose a threat or act in a way that causes a reasonable person to feel afraid. The threat does not have to be written or verbal to instill fear. For example, the stalker may place a dead animal at the victim's door. Third, the stalker must display a criminal intent to cause fear in the victim (U.S. Department of Justice, 1996).

Given these considerations, we defined a stalking incident as having the same person exhibit repeated behavior that seemed obsessive and made the respondent afraid or concerned for her safety. To measure the extent of stalking, we developed the following screen question that the interviewers asked of all respondents. Thus, they were queried whether, since the school year began in the fall:

> Has anyone—from a stranger to an ex-boyfriend—repeatedly followed you, watched you, phoned, written, e-mailed, or communicated with you in other ways in a way that seemed obsessive and made you afraid or concerned for your safety?

If the respondent answered "yes" to this question, she was then asked this follow-up question:

> How many people exhibited this type of behavior toward you since school began in the fall?

Each respondent was then asked additional questions in a stalking incident questionnaire about the nature of the stalking incident (see below). If the respondent reported that more than one person had stalked her during this time period, the interviewer completed a separate incident report for each of the stalkers. For example, if two different persons stalked one respondent, this would require two separate stalking incidents. The interviewer started with the most recent stalking incident, and then proceeded chronologically until reports were completed for all of the stalkers indicated in the follow-up question.

We developed a stalking incident-level questionnaire to collect detailed information about the stalking incident and its effects on the victim. The questions on the stalking incident report included: the form of stalking (e.g., waiting outside or inside places, watching from afar, sending unwanted letters or cards), duration of the stalking (e.g., length of time in days, weeks, months, and years), intensity (e.g., more than once a day, at least once daily, two to six times a week, once a week, twice to three times a month, and less than twice a month), and location of the stalking (e.g., on campus, off campus, or both, and specific locations—at a social activity, at the library or other building on campus, at your residence, at work). We also asked if the stalker made any threats of harm or attempts to harm the victim, and if the respondent suffered any injuries (e.g., physical ones, including stab wounds, internal injuries, bruises, and/or emotional and psychological ones), and about the characteristics of the stalker (e.g., relationship to the victim and sex). Finally, we asked the respondent about her reporting behavior in terms of reporting the stalking to the police. If the incident was reported to the police, the interviewer asked the respondent to identify the police authority. If the incident was not reported to the police, the interviewer asked the respondent why the incident had not been reported to the police. We also asked if the respondent had told someone else about the incident and who that person was (e.g., a family member, a roommate, a friend, a victim service hotline). Last, we asked the respondent if she had taken any other actions as a result of the stalking (e.g., avoided the person who had stalked her, dropped a class the person was enrolled in, sought psychological counseling, filed civil charges, bought a weapon).

In short, the intent was to collect sufficient data that would allow us to paint a portrait of the extent, nature, and reactions to stalking among college women. The features of this portrait are presented in the following sections.

The Extent of Stalking

Lynch (1987) notes the importance of assessing how victimization varies across different social domains (see also Fisher et al., 1998; Mustaine, 1997). To the extent that college campuses are distinctive domains, we would predict that the nature of victimization would differ from that of other social domains. As noted, the typical lifestyle of college women is such that they come into regular contact with young men—men seeking social and sexual relationships—both in class and in recreational settings, during the day and at night, in public and in private locations, and often without much guardianship. According to routine activity theory, this convergence in time and space of potentially motivated offenders and attractive targets lacking capable guardianship would produce higher rates of sexual victimization than found in other social domains in society. In this context, we should expect elevated rates of stalking on college campuses.

In fact, this appears to be the case. The prevalence of stalking victimization among our national sample of college women is much higher than that reported for the general female population (Tjaden & Thoennes, 1998b) and more similar to that reported in a comparable study of female students (Mustaine & Tewksbury, 1999). Specifically, we found the following:

- Some 13.1% of the women in the sample had been stalked at least once since the academic year had begun—a period that averaged 6.9 months.

- Of those who had been stalked, 12.7% experienced two stalkings and 2.3% experienced three or more stalkings.

- The sample of 4,446 female students experienced 696 incidents of stalking; this is a rate of 156.5 incidents per 1,000 female students.

- The number of victims was 581; this is a victimization rate of 130.7 per 1,000 female students.

- The number of victims was lower than the count of incidents because a considerable proportion, 15% of the women, experienced more than one stalking.

- Finally, consistent with the stalker characteristics research (see Meloy, 1996), nearly all (97.6%) of the stalkers were male.

We do not believe that the comparatively high rate of stalking is a methodological artifact. Recall that our screen question asked the respondents to include as stalking only those incidents in which the attention they received was *repeated and done in a way that seemed obsessive* and *made you afraid or concerned for your safety*. Further, Tjaden and Thoennes (1998b) found that stalking victims tend to be disproportionately young. Beyond the unique risks of being in college, the youthfulness of our college sample also may help to explain the relatively high estimate of stalking we report for female students.

The Nature of Stalking

In this section, we review what our NCWSV Study tells us about the nature of stalking. Thus, we explore the ways in which victims are pursued, the intensity and duration of the stalking, where stalking occurs, and the interaction between victims and offenders.

PURSUING VICTIMS

Types of Pursuit Behavior. What means do stalkers use to pursue their victims? Table 7.1 lists the patterns of pursuit used by perpetrators to stalk the women in the sample. Many stalkers used nonphysically visible means to attract the attention of the victim—that is, means in which they were not physically present. Thus, more than three-fourths of the stalking incidents involved telephone calls, 3 in 10 involved letters, and a quarter involved e-mail messages. The use of text messaging might well be expected to be common today. Further, stalkers were often physically visible to victims. Thus, in almost half the incidents, they were seen waiting for the victim, while in more than 4 in 10 cases they followed the victim or watched the victim from afar. Stalkers also typically had multiple contacts with the victim (see Meloy, 1996). On average, each stalking incident involved 2.9 forms of stalking.

Table 7.1   Types of Pursuit Behaviors

Behaviors	Percentage
Telephoned	77.7
Waited Outside or Inside Places	47.9
Watched From Afar	44.0
Followed	42.0
Sent Letters	30.7
E-mailed	24.7
Sent Gifts	3.3
Showed Up Uninvited	4.9
Other	10.9

SOURCES: Fisher, Cullen, and Turner (1999, 2002).

NOTE: Totals exceed 100% because respondents selected all behaviors that applied.

Duration and Intensity of Stalking. Computing how long the average stalking incident lasted is complicated by outliers in the data (e.g., seven victims reported being stalked for 1 day, and one victim reported being stalked for 10 years). The mean duration for the stalking incident, which is affected by the outlier cases, was 146.6 days; in contrast, the median duration for an incident was 60 days. In any event, the typical stalking incident experienced by college students is not brief but rather persists for

Table 7.2   Intensity of Pursuit Behaviors

Frequency of Stalking	Percentage
More Than Once Daily	9.7
At Least Once Daily	13.3
Two to Six Times a Week	41.0
Once a Week	16.3
Two to Three Times a Month	14.0
Less Than Twice a Month	3.9
Other	1.8

SOURCES: Fisher, Cullen, and Turner (1999, 2002).

about 2 months. Finally, at the time of the survey, in 18.1% of the incidents, the stalking behavior was still ongoing.

The intensity of the stalking also can be assessed by how frequently the forms of stalking transpired (see Table 7.2). Thus, those who were pursued were asked, "During this period, how often did these events occur?" Notably, 4 in 10 respondents reported two to six times a week, while almost another fourth of the sample stated that the incident occurred either daily (13.3%) or more than once daily (9.7%). Taken together, these results indicate that almost two-thirds of the victims experienced stalking that was not only repeated but also consistently present in their lives. In contrast, only one-third of the sample stated that the stalking incidents took place once a week or less, and of these victims less than 4% reported that the stalking incidents occurred less than twice a month.

Where Stalking Takes Place. More than two-thirds of the incidents happened either on campus or both on and off campus; 31.4% of the stalking incidents occurred exclusively off campus. Most often, victims were stalked at their residence. Other common locations of stalking were over the telephone or through e-mail, in a classroom, at work, or going to and from some place.

VICTIM–STALKER INTERACTION

Do They Know Each Other? Similar to other types of sexual victimization, female students typically are not stalked by strangers. Thus, four in five victims reported knowing their stalker. In half of those incidents in which the stalkers were known, the respondent stated that the stalker was "well known" to them. Further, when stalkers were known, there was a link to an established or previously established relationship. Thus, more than 4 in 10 were a boyfriend or ex-boyfriend. Almost a quarter of the known stalkers were classmates, about 2 in 10 were either a friend or an acquaintance (9.3% and 10.3%, respectively), and 1 in 20 was a coworker. College women generally were not stalked by college professors or graduate assistants, by employers/supervisors, or by relatives.

Are Victims Harmed? The majority of the stalking incidents did not appear to have involved explicit physical threats or lasting injuries. Still, in 15.3% of the incidents, the victim reported that the stalker either threatened or attempted to harm them. With regard to the types of injuries, in 30.3% of the incidents the stalking victims suffered some type of emotional or physical harm. Thus, in 95.1% of the incidents involving harm, the respondents stated that they were "injured emotionally or psychologically." Further, physical harm was also experienced: 1.5% of the incidents involved a "knife or stab wound"; 1% had "broken bones or had teeth knocked out"; 1.5% involved the victim being "knocked unconscious"; and 14.8% involved "bruises, black-eye, cuts, scratches, swelling, or chipped teeth." Finally, we also should note that in 10.3% of the incidents, the victim reported that the stalker "forced or attempted sexual contact."

We should note that our study was not structured to probe the full emotional toll that stalking might entail, especially among those expressing that they had been harmed. Previous clinical and self-report studies of stalking victims have concluded that stalking causes an array of negative psychological and emotional problems (Hall, 1998; Pathé & Mullen, 1997). Feelings of fear, anger, and stress at not being able to control one's privacy can be pervasive (Davis & Frieze, 2000). Studies of college students echo these findings. Westrup, Fremouw, Thompson, and Lewis (1999), for example, reported that female victims suffered significant negative psychological effects due to stalking. Stalking victims reported more psychological symptoms than harassed or control groups of students. Victims of stalking also reported significantly higher levels of post-traumatic stress disorder symptoms relative to the harassed and control groups. Bjerregaard (2000) found that female victims were more likely to seek counseling than males. In our NCWSV Study, only 3.9% of the stalking victims sought counseling. Close to 6% of the women, however, stated that due to stalking, they had become less trustful or more cynical of others.

Who Is at Risk of Being Stalked?

Earlier discussions explored why attending college might increase the likelihood of being stalked. As we have seen, it does appear that college is a social domain that is conducive to stalking. Not all female students, however, are equally at risk of being pursued. What, then, differentiates students who are or are not stalked?

Lifestyle or routine activities appear to play a role. Thus, in the NCWSV Study, we found that women were more at risk of stalking who

- frequented places where alcohol was served (i.e., exposure to crime),
- lived alone (i.e., absence of guardianship),
- were involved in dating relationships (i.e., close proximity to a motivated offender), especially less than a year in duration.

Women who frequently go to parties, bars, or clubs where alcohol is served may come in contact with sexually predatory people (Schwartz & Pitts, 1995). Women who live alone may be more vulnerable to stalkers because they are suitable targets; namely, there are fewer barriers for the stalker, including someone other than the victim to witness the obsessive behavior. Dating provides a means to meet and over time to become intimate with a person who is or may become obsessive with regard to the person the stalker is or was dating (Meloy, 1996). The literature on the characteristics of stalkers and stalking victims both suggests that there is a link between stalking and intimate relationships (Meloy, 1996; Tjaden & Thoennes, 1998b). We note, however, that marriage or cohabitation lowered the odds of being a stalking victim. Being married or having a significant other might depress stalking by increasing guardianship (a partner is present) and making the target—the female student—less attractive due to her unavailability.

Consistent with the results from several sexual victimization studies (Crowell & Burgess, 1996), including findings reported in earlier chapters, women who were previously sexually victimized were more likely to be a stalking victim. We have no firm data on why this relationship exists, but some insight might be drawn from Finkelhor and Asdigian's (1996, p. 6) work on "target congruence." In an extension of the routine activity theory's concept of target attractiveness, Finkelhor and Asdigian note that "personal characteristics" might "increase vulnerability to victimization, independent of routine activities, because these characteristics have some *congruence with the needs, motives or reactivities* of offenders" (p. 6: emphasis in the original). Such congruence may be exacerbated by a victim's target vulnerability—a situation in which a personal characteristic "may compromise the potential victim's capacity to resist or deter victimization . . . the prototypical risk factors . . . would be attributes like small size, physical weakness, emotional deprivation, or psychological problems" (p. 67). In this context, prior sexual victimization may increase a woman's vulnerability in relationships with men and decrease her capacity to deter men with propensities to engage in stalking. These, speculations, of course, warrant further empirical investigation.

We also found significant that the risk of stalking varied among different types of women. Two findings are of interest. First, stalking is higher among undergraduate students than graduate or other students. It is possible that undergraduates may place themselves in a wider diversity of social situations and then increase their exposure to the types of people who sexually prey on women. Further, undergraduate women may have schedules that are more predictable and routine (e.g., a political science class three days a week at 11:00 a.m., followed by a criminal justice class at 12:20 p.m., a daily work-study job that begins at 3:30 p.m., dinner between 5:00 p.m. and 6:30 p.m., and studying in the library from 7:00 p.m. to midnight) than graduate students or other adult students and thus they are easier to stalk. Further, they may frequently attend parties and bars and date more than other students and, as a result, increase their risk of being stalked because they put themselves in different types of vulnerable situations and increase their exposure to those who sexually prey on women.

Second, women who attended schools located in small towns or rural areas were more likely to be stalked. We would typically expect such schools to be safer. It may be, however, that female students who attended schools in a small town or rural area physically live and socialize in a confined geographical area that makes them easier to stalk.

How Do Victims React?

When college students are stalked, how do they react? We address this question in two parts. First, we examine whether victims take actions to deal with the stalking and, if so, what these measures involve. Second, we explore the extent to which victims report stalking and, if so, to whom.

ACTIONS TAKEN BY VICTIMS

In nearly three-fourths of the incidents—73.1%—victims reported that they had taken "actions as a result of their stalking." These actions were diverse and are presented in Table 7.3. Several conclusions are warranted.

Of those who took action, the most common strategy was to avoid or to try to avoid the stalker (43.2%). Alternatively, the second most frequent response was to confront the stalker (16.3%). Although not in high percentages (under 5% of the incidents), victims stated that they had taken such actions as getting caller ID, improving the security on their residence, moving their residence, and/or dropping a class. Respondents were very unlikely to use the legal system to address stalkers. Thus, in a little less than 4% of the incidents a respondent sought a restraining order, in only 2% of the incidents the respondent filed criminal charges, and in a little over 1% of the incidents the respondent filed civil charges. They were also not likely to use formal disciplinary processes available at the respective institution; only 3.3% of the incidents involved a respondent filing a grievance or initiating disciplinary action.

REPORTING STALKING

The survey also explored whether stalking victims reported being stalked to the authorities and, if so, to whom. Overall, 83.1% of the incidents were not reported to

Table 7.3   Preventative Actions Taken by Victims as a Result of Being Stalked

Type of Action	Percentage
Avoidance Actions	
Avoided or Tried to Avoid Stalker	43.2
Did Not Acknowledge Messages or E-Mail	8.8
Moved Your Residence	3.3
Dropped a Class the Person Was In or Taught	1.4
Filed Civil Charges	1.2
Quit Your Job	0.8
Changed Colleges or Universities	0.4
Changed Majors	0.2
Confrontation	
Confronted the Stalker	16.3
Self-Protective Action	
Got Caller ID	4.9
Improved Security System of Residence	4.1
Traveled With a Companion	3.9
Bought a Weapon	1.9
Took a Self-Defense Class	0.4
Judicial Actions	
Sought a Restraining Order	3.9
Filed a Grievance or Initiated Disciplinary Action With University Officials	1.9
Went Forward With Criminal Charges	1.9

SOURCES: Fisher, Cullen, and Turner (1999, 2002).

NOTE: Percentages do not add up to 100 because more than one action could be reported.

police or campus law enforcement officials. Of those incidents that were reported, on-campus stalking was most often reported to campus police or security, while stalking that occurred off campus (wholly or in part) was most often reported to the police. Note that although only 16.9% of stalking incidents were reported, this is higher than for completed and attempted rape.

As we found for rape and other victimizations in Chapter 6, common answers for not reporting stalking included not thinking the incident was serious enough to report (72%), not being clear that the incident was a crime or that harm was intended (44.6%), and not believing that the police would think it was serious enough (33.6%). The victims, however, also noted that they did not report the stalking because of lack of proof (24.4%), because they did not want their family (9.0%) or other people (8.5%) to know, because they did not know how to report the incident (10.8%), and because they were afraid of reprisals (15.3%).

Further, in nearly all the incidents (93.4%), the respondents in the survey confided to someone that they were being stalked. Most often, they reported their victimization to a friend (69.5% of the incidents), to a parent (32.1%) or other family member (15.2%), or to a roommate (21.9%). A small number of stalking victims reported that they were being stalked to resident hall advisors (3.2%) or to college professors or other university officials (3.5%).

Conclusion

Among college women, stalking appears to be a common form of victimization. As reported, 13.1% of the women in our NCWSV Study were pursued by a stalker during the academic year. Because the reference period for the study averaged 6.9 months, it seems likely that the annual prevalence of stalking would be higher, especially if women spent their summers on campus as well. Over the course of their higher education career—which now averages about 5 years—it seems likely that a substantial minority of the over 6.2 million college women will experience stalking, some repeatedly (Snyder, Dillow, & Hoffman, 2009; U.S. Department of Education, 2003).

The proposal that stalking is a common form of victimization that college women endure undoubtedly will be subject to scrutiny by more conservative, antifeminist commentators who view claims of high prevalence rates for sexual victimization as an ideologically inspired social construction of reality. They legitimately could point to the fact that stalking incidents with less serious consequences are far more widespread; about 85% of the incidents resulted in no threatened or attempted physical harm to victims. Further, over 8 in 10 incidents were not reported to the police, with the main reason being given that the stalking was "not serious enough to report." Taken together, these findings could be used to suggest that many of the stalkings in the sample may not qualify as crimes, since most states require either an explicit threat or the requirement that a "reasonable person" would interpret the behavior of the stalker as threatening (U.S. Department of Justice, 1996).

While these considerations are useful in guarding against the conclusion that an epidemic of life-threatening criminal stalking grips the nation's ivory towers, other findings in our study caution against seeing the high rate of stalking as inconsequential. Thus, in designing our study, we endeavored to avoid Gilbert's (1997) concern that bias is introduced when researchers use an overly broad definition of what counts as a sexual victimization. Instead, we employed a screen question that specifically asked if the stalking behavior had been "repeated," "obsessive," and "made you afraid or concerned for your safety." We relied on this definition to rule out truly petty forms of attentive behavior which, though rude or bothersome, were not repeated and salient enough to induce fear or concern. Response errors are possible, but it seems likely that our measure detected mainly patterns of behavior that would be widely regarded as stalking.

This conclusion gains credence when the nature of the stalking incidents is examined. As reported, victims were typically stalked for 2 months, with two-thirds indicating that offenders contacted them in some way at least two to six times a week. Again, we cannot say what proportion of these stalking incidents formally crossed the line into criminal behavior or, more pragmatically, would be prosecuted by a district attorney as criminal. More detailed information would have to be collected to discern whether the nature of the stalking would be reasonably seen as "threatening"—even if it did inspire fear or concern for safety in the victims. Regardless, the duration of and the frequency of contact in these incidents obviate any claim that the offenders' conduct somehow was misinterpreted or misunderstood by our female respondents.

In fact, the measurement of stalking may be less open to methodological bias than that of other sexual victimizations precisely because stalking is a repeated pattern of behavior. We did not ask whether the single act of a person following a respondent was obsessive and made her concerned for her safety. If we had, it might have been difficult to discern whether the behavior was really stalking or just an awkward attempt to get the attention of the female student. However, when the acts continue again and again over time—that is, when victims have numerous *empirical observations* of the offender's conduct—it is unlikely that female victims do not know what is occurring in their lives and are erroneously reporting that they have been stalked. Accordingly, we can have a commensurate level of confidence that the prevalence of stalking reported in our study is not somehow widely inflated by the wording of the question we have used.

We would also be cautious about assuming that stalking incidents are merely petty simply because the respondents justify not reporting their victimization with the reasoning that the stalking was "not serious enough" (an issue we also addressed in Chapter 6 on reporting generally). Stating that a stalking incident is not serious *enough* to call in the police is not identical to saying that the incident is not serious or otherwise consequential. Reporting a victimization to the police or to campus authorities must be balanced against the costs that such action incurs (e.g., time, anticipated anxiety over going to court, publicity). On college campuses, victims would also have to overcome norms against "turning in" or "snitching on" one's fellow students. Most salient perhaps is that in four in five cases, the victims knew their stalkers. It may very well be that stalking would have to pass a high threshold—to have imminent or completed physical harm—before it would be seen as serious enough to warrant having a classmate and/or ex-boyfriend arrested. Consistent with this view, the victims in our sample were less likely to report a stalker if they knew the person and were more likely to report their victimization if the stalking persisted for a longer period of time, if they were followed by the stalker, and if they were injured.

Relatedly, although victims did not often summon authorities to exercise formal social control, the data suggest that they did engage in "self-help" to cope with their victimization (see, more broadly, Black, 1983; Smith & Uchida, 1988). There is no evidence, for example, that the victims perceived their stalking to be so minor that they dealt with it as a purely private matter. Instead, in more than 9 in 10 incidents, the respondents stated that they confided in someone they knew—most often friends, family members, and roommates—about being stalked. In turning to those close to them, it is likely that they were seeking social support to help them cope with their stalking. Further, in nearly three-fourths of the incidents, victims took some action in response to their victimization. Most often this involved avoiding the stalker or, in a smaller but not insignificant number of cases, confronting the stalker directly.

Taken together, this discussion suggests that the prevalence of stalking in our study is not due to methodological artifacts and that most stalking incidents—even if not physically harmful—result in victims exercising coping responses. But let us assume for the moment that conservative, antifeminist critics are correct and that most of what our respondents report is relatively minor—certainly not life-threatening or criminal, mostly just aggravating male behavior—and thus is not deserving of sustained social intervention. The danger in this reasoning is that in their contentious efforts to deconstruct supposed feminist claims that sexual victimization occurs in epidemic proportions, these critics make the opposite error of *normalizing* the unwanted intrusion of males into the lives of women in private and in public. That is, why should women have to endure the persistent, if not obsessive, violation of their lives? Even if only mildly and episodically unnerving—only enough to cause a female to avoid the stalker and to seek out of friend's ear—why should this level of victimization be minimized? Why the sympathy for "men acting badly"?

We recognize, of course, that constitutional rights may expose citizens of any gender to a certain level of uncivil behavior. It may also be a reality that the criminal law will have a role in controlling only the more extreme forms of stalking. Still, on college campuses, administrators will have to wrestle with the question of the extent to which stalking is a problem that diminishes the quality of female students' lives. The relatively high prevalence of stalking found in our data would seemingly suggest that this form of sexual victimization should not be ignored. Instead, it is perhaps time for colleges and universities to design comprehensive strategies for protecting women whose days are punctuated by the obsessive intrusions of male stalkers.

8

Creating Safe Havens

Preventing Sexual Victmization

"But was it rape?" This question was the bold-print headline in a recent special report in the *Cincinnati Enquirer* (Kurtzman, 2009, p. F1). The story recounted the allegations by a female student at a local university that she was raped by a fellow student. She was about to leave a party alone, after drinking some alcohol, late on a cold winter night. The alleged assailant offered to give her a ride home, but stopped his car during the drive. By her account, he started to kiss her and they crawled into the back seat of the vehicle. "That's when he pressed her down on her shoulders, she said. That's when he swore at her, told her to shut up, tore at her pants and forced himself onto her. She was frozen in fear, paralyzed by what was happening" (p. F1). A passing police car prompted him to stop. He drove back to the party and disappeared. She was "frantic. Tears ran down her face. She bent over and vomited. Then she ran home, down the dark street she feared, all alone" (p. F1). In the end, she was traumatized and left school, only to return the next year—still not the same person. She had reported the act to the university police 2 hours after the encounter; it was a case of rape to her. He claimed that the act was consensual. No criminal charges were filed, but he was eventually disciplined by the university and left for another college.

This account is a reminder of the continuing salience of the issue of acquaintance rape and, more generally, of sexual victimization on college campuses. Despite more than 2 decades of research, reports in newspapers and magazines, activism, and programs on college campuses, there is little evidence that female students are less at risk of sexual assault. Victims still struggle to prove their victimization; alleged assailants still claim consent. These considerations suggest that the daunting task of creating safe havens for female students remains to be addressed with continued vigor and efficacy. In this context, this chapter offers thoughts on avenues that might be pursued, arguing eventually that situational crime prevention—reducing opportunities for victimization—provides the best prospects for protecting college women. Before turning to this issue, we reiterate two themes that inform this book and thus are messages that we trust readers will take with them.

Two Themes

BEYOND IDEOLOGY: THE IMPORTANCE OF METHODOLOGY

Beginning in the 1980s, there was increasing recognition of the sexual victimization of college women (and of women in general). This "discovery" of acquaintance and date rape and other sexual victimizations necessitated advocacy on the part of those concerned with the protection of female students. The impetus for these advocacy campaigns often came from feminists who saw the victimization of female students as another form of gender inequality that marks colleges and the larger society. Unfortunately, this issue became wrapped up in a culture war, as those who rejected a feminist interpretation of life on campus and beyond attacked claims of the extensiveness and seriousness of victimization made by feminist scholars and activists. They argued that feminist researchers used flawed methods and biased interpretations of the data to artificially inflate estimates of the true amount of sexual victimization, especially rape. Critics accused feminists of advocacy research that was inspired by ideology, not science. It is ironic that these antifeminist scholars criticized extant investigations but rarely conducted studies of their own to refute the empirical results offered by scholars such as Mary Koss.

Regardless, some of the critics' arguments had a point—specifically, that methodological choices can affect studies' results. The methods used within any scientific field should not remain static but, where possible, should evolve. With regard to sexual victimization, as newer studies are undertaken with more refined measurement, one would hope that ideology can increasingly be set aside. Better measurement helps to undermine claims of methodological artifact and to increase confidence that the results presented more closely capture empirical reality. Our National College Women Sexual Victimization Study was born in this spirit—in the belief that science rather than ideology was the conduit to truth. To a large extent, it is important that our results were mostly consistent with the findings of previous research that pointed to sexual victimization being a meaningful problem among college women. Koss and others like her were substantially correct.

We recognize, of course, that no study is sacrosanct—including ours. Further research, using more sophisticated designs and completed on national samples, is clearly called for. The lives led by female students—their safety, the quality of their collegiate experience and beyond—are certainly worthy of further investigation.

HIDDEN INEQUALITY: THE COST
OF BEING A FEMALE STUDENT

Based on our National College Women Sexual Victimization Study and other extant research, it is clear that female college students do not exist in an ivory tower that insulates them from sexual victimization. Instead, there appears to be mounting evidence—added to by our research—that college women are targets for rape and sexual assault, for stalking, and even more frequently for minor forms sexual victimization (e.g., verbal harassment).

The parameters of this victimization can be grasped by reviewing some of the central findings of our NCWSV Study. First, the analysis revealed that during the 7-month reference period since the start of the academic year (about 6.9 months), 1.7% of the college women sampled reported that they had experienced a completed rape, while the corresponding figure for attempted rape was 1.1%. The percentage of the respondents experiencing either completed rape or attempted rape was 2.8%. These statistics suggest that, on an absolute level, the risk of rape victimization *during any given academic* year is about 1 in 40 female students. Still, taken by itself, this one finding can be misleading. Indeed, the risk of rape victimization may be seen as disquieting when it is calculated over a longer time period and/or over a larger population.

Thus, if our half-year (6.9-month) victimization figure is extended to cover a year's time, it would appear that, in a crude estimate, about 1 in 20 college women experience an attempted or completed rape in this period. If this figure is in turn extended over the time women typically spend securing a college degree, then it would appear that perhaps a fifth to a quarter of these women will experience a rape victimization. Relatedly, if these yearly and college-career figures are calculated over the population base at a given college or university, it can be seen that tens, if not hundreds, of female students will experience rape during a year or over several years. From this vantage point, our rates of victimization can pose important policy concerns for university administrators seeking to ensure an educational experience that is physically safe and nurturing of intellectual growth.

Second, beyond rape, college women are likely to experience other forms of sexual victimization. Across the 12 types of victimization measured in the main part of our survey, including rape, 15.5% of the women experienced at least one victimization during the reference period. When analyzed by the presence or absence of force, almost 8% of the sample were sexually victimized in an incident that involved force or the threat of force, while 11% were subjected to an unwanted sexual victimization that did not involve the threat or use of force.

The data on verbal and visual forms of sexual victimization are further instructive. In general, visual victimization was not widespread, although instances of being viewed naked without one's consent and of being exposed involuntarily to pornographic pictures and to sexual organs did occur (with victimization figures ranging from 2.4 to 6.1%). In contrast, verbal victimizations were commonplace among college women. Half of the female students experienced sexist comments and sexually tinged catcalls and whistles; about 1 in 5 experienced obscene telephone calls and intrusive questions about their sex lives; and about 1 in 10 had false rumors spread about their sex lives. Though some observers may consider these acts mainly to be minor and often as reflecting merely bad taste that must be tolerated in a democratic society, the extensiveness of these experiences in a relatively short reference period raises the question of how these victimizations impact the quality of life female students have on a college campus. Again, how to achieve more civility and to spare women students such harassment are issues that campus administrators arguably, in light of these results, should address proactively.

Third, it appears that stalking is relatively widespread. Thus, in the current academic year, 13.1% of the female college students indicated that they had been stalked. Again, when this figure is projected over time and across a college's entire female student population, the dimension of the stalking problem would seem to warrant attention from officials in higher education institutions.

Despite the limitations of our study and the differential interpretations that our data might inspire, we believe that the following conclusion is warranted: There is little doubt that sexual victimization is sufficiently pervasive that college women will repeatedly encounter sexist and harassing comments, will likely receive an obscene phone call, will have a good chance of being stalked and of enduring some type of coerced sexual contact, and will be at some risk—especially over the course of a college career—of experiencing an incident in which someone she knows will attempt to use force, against her will, in the pursuit of sexual intercourse. Taken together, these observations suggest that sexual victimization—in its minor and more serious forms—is a high cost that, compared to their male counterparts, is endured disproportionately by college women and that may diminish the quality of their lives on and off campus.

Much of this cost, moreover, remains hidden from public view. Although victims often tell friends when incidents occur, they rarely report their victimizations to authorities or seek help. These victim secrets mean that female students often receive few services and that campus officials have little capacity to respond. It seems clear, therefore, that the hidden costs experienced by college women must be anticipated and, where possible, prevention efforts proactively implemented.

Three Approaches for Preventing Victimization

Creating safe havens for female college students is a daunting task. There are no easy answers, in large part because most sexual victimizations are embedded in routine activities and lifestyles that are common among many college students. Further, preventing sexual victimization is not cost free. Universities must invest money in programs and in security personnel; legal action at times must be taken. Potential victims must shoulder an inherent and unfair cost: the advice that, by the sheer virtue of being a female, they should curtail "risky" behavior even though male students do not face such admonitions. Is this "victim blaming" or the realities of avoiding sexual victimization? In short, at the beginning of any discussion, it is prudent to understand that no panaceas exist and that different approaches will entail different costs and, we might add, generate different benefits.

We begin our assessment by first conveying in this section three prevention approaches. These have been distilled from the existing research. Some scholars and advocates might embrace parts of each model. However, these approaches offer distinct ideas on how best to approach the prevention of sexual victimization and, as such, deserve to be presented as competing visions on prevention. In the next section, we present a fourth approach—one that emphasizes the reduction of victimization opportunities as a means of creating safe, or at least safer, havens for female students. We believe that this latter approach offers the most promising prospects for preventing the sexual victimization of college women.

CONSERVATIVE APPROACH

We have used to the term *conservative* to describe those who believe that feminist scholars—exemplified by Mary Koss—have used flawed empirical estimates to create a "rape crisis" that does not exist. In fairness, it is not clear that all of these commentators would be politically right-wing on all social issues. What they do have in common, however, is that at least when it comes to sexual victimization on college campuses, they are decidedly antifeminist (Gilbert, 1997; Mac Donald, 2008; Roiphe, 1993).

There is general agreement, of course, that rape is a serious offense that deserves intervention. But conservatives depart from others in their view on the extent of sexual victimization. "Everyone agrees that rape is a terrible thing," notes Roiphe (1993, p. 54), "but we don't agree on what rape is. There is a gray area in which someone's rape may be another person's bad night." In the conservatives' view, nearly all sexual transgressions that occur on college campuses are, in fact, "bad nights." Young love—or at least young lust—is marked by misinterpreted cues, clumsy advances, decision making blurred by alcohol or drugs, and remorse over liaisons that were exploitive or not fully welcomed. Feminists, the argument goes, are simply trying to criminalize heterosexual relationships—to sanitize them of their human qualities under threat of a prison sentence.

Implicit in the "bad night" view is that the only rape to be concerned about is "real rape"—physically brutal assaults, typically committed by strangers, that can be proven in criminal court (see Estrich, 1987). Only a tiny fraction of the events counted as sexual victimization by Koss and others, it is argued, are such real rapes; the rest can be comfortably ignored. In fact, focusing on these mythical rapes leads to poor social policy—to resources being poured into social problems that do not really exist. "It is difficult to criticize advocacy research [of the feminists] without giving the impression of caring less about the problem under consideration than do those who are engaged in magnifying its size," observes Gilbert (1997, p. 142). But reality should trump ideology. As Gilbert continues, "the few impose their definition of social ills on the many—seeking to incite moral panics. This type of advocacy research invites social policies that are likely to be neither effective nor fair" (p. 142).

What, then, should be done about sexual victimization on college campuses? Conservatives offer three pieces of advice. First, they assert that it is important to debunk the idea that rape is widespread. This involves a rejection of feminist ideology and its supposed hold on academic institutions. Second, when real rapes occur, victims should call the police. Campus officials should not be in the business of policing and adjudicating sex crimes. This task is better left to the criminal justice system. And third, women should take responsibility for their well-being and not put themselves in situations where they are likely to have undesired sex. Mac Donald (2008, p. 5) articulates this last point in a blunt way, suggesting that feminists—whom she calls "the rape industrialists"—might give this advice to college women:

> Above all, they could persuade girls not to put themselves into situations whose likely outcome is intercourse. Specifically: don't get drunk, don't get into bed with a guy, and don't take off your clothes or allow them to be removed. Once you're in that situation, the rape activists could say, it's going to be hard to halt the proceedings, for lots of complex emotional reasons. Were this advice heeded, the campus "rape" epidemic would be wiped out overnight.

There is an element of truth in Mac Donald's observation, which is that risky routines increase the likelihood of victimization—regardless of whether the crime is sexual in nature or involves being robbed or having one's laptop computer stolen. (We return to this issue later in this chapter.) The difficulty in this context, however, is that Mac Donald and other conservatives treat males as silent partners in sexual victimizations. In their unstated view, men are a bunch of impulses, driven by evolutionary development to take sex when it is within reach. After all, as the saying goes, "what is a man to do when a woman is drunk and naked?" Males are excused from having any moral compass or exercising any responsibility *for their sexuality*. There are "bad nights" but not "bad men"—males who either episodically or repeatedly are predatory.

As we have stated, we do not propose that the extent and seriousness of the sexual victimization of college women should be treated as a closed empirical issue. But we believe that the extant data, from our national-level research and from other studies, show that rape and other forms of sexual victimization are not ideological creations but comprise an empirical reality to be addressed. Unfortunately, in denying that any problem exists, conservative commentators have little insight to add on how best to create safe havens that reduce the risk of sexual victimization for female students.

FEMINIST APPROACH

Believing that there is a rape epidemic on college campuses, feminist scholars propose a multifaceted, concerted effort to combat the risks posed by sexual victimization to female students (see, e.g., Belknap & Erez, 2007; Warshaw, 1988). These diverse efforts can be grouped into three main categories.

First, feminists argue that the *traditional culture of the campus must be changed*. As in society at large, they observe, patriarchal values still infuse college campuses. Particularly troubling for campuses are the numerous male peer support groups that, through long-established traditions, encourage and sustain these values and their victimizing behaviors (Schwartz & DeKeseredy, 1997). As a result, it is essential to mandate that students and staff take rape awareness seminars that reveal the nature and inappropriateness of various types of sexual victimization. Rape myths and cognitions that demean women and excuse their victimization must be targeted for change. It is important to establish expectations about the right of students to be free from untoward incursions on their bodies and about the disciplinary consequences that will greet wayward conduct.

Second, feminists assert that female students must be *protected against sexual predators*. In the evening hours, for example, escorts should be provided to walk students from their classes to their cars or residence halls. Access key cards or security control at residence halls are needed to deny predators access to female coeds. Call boxes might be located strategically across campuses in "hot spots," such as parking garages or along green space walkways, to ensure that campus police or security officers can readily respond to the call for help. Extra lighting may be needed to guard against the dangers that loom in the darkness as well as the need for better landscaping that could provide refuge to the would-be offender. It might be warranted to urge students to use call whistles or mace to fend off an attack. Efforts should be made to teach students how to resist verbally and through self-defense so as to thwart the coercive physical advances of a perpetrator.

Third, feminists state that *survivors of sexual victimization must be helped*. All students should be aware that victim services are available on campus that will provide psychological counseling and medical care while ensuring privacy. Victim advocates should be—and in most schools are—available 24 hours, 7 days a week to assist victims with their needs. Campus police and security personnel, including resident assistants at dormitories, should be trained in how to respond effectively to the occurrence of a sexual victimization. Survivors of assaults also must be protected against their assailants who remain students on campus either because no formal criminal justice action is being taken or because judicial proceedings have yet to be conducted. In short, a culture that is characterized by a continuum of support should be constructed that furnishes survivors with both the medical and social support and the legal protections that will minimize the harms these women have experienced. This support is needed to allow victimization survivors to continue their education at the university.

Taken together, this multifaceted approach most likely has increased awareness of sexual victimization on college campuses nationwide. The critical issue is whether these initiatives "work" to diminish the incidence of female sexual victimization. Especially important is to prevent a student's first incident at college, since many women come to college already having been sexually victimized and hence are at an elevated risk of revictimization.

Most campus sexual victimization prevention programs aimed at changing the culture of campus are designed to increase awareness and knowledge by educating college men and women about the extent and nature of different forms of rape (e.g., forcible, intoxicated). They challenge as well prevailing rape myths and rape-supportive attitudes. Many programs also include some combination of various topics, such as characteristics of the victims and perpetrators, the risk associated with rape, the health effects of rape on the victim, and the availability of criminal justice and health resources (see Lonsway et al., 2009).

In their review of educational programs, Fisher, Daigle, and Cullen (2008) concluded that it is not readily apparent what works to reduce the incidence of sexual victimization because the results from the evaluation of these programs have been somewhat mixed at best. On one hand, the research documents positive results of these education programs (for a review, see Breitenbecher, 2000). On the other hand, the positive effects are very limited in scope. Any success these programs do find is usually based on increases in knowledge or changes in attitudes among the female participants, not the males—the population that commits almost all the rapes (see Schewe, 2006). Support for the effectiveness of these programs is further compromised by the lack of long-term stability of attitude changes (see Lonsway et al., 2009). The duration of improved attitudes is often brief, rebounding to preprogram levels within 2 to 5 months following program completion (see Breitenbecher, 2000). Few studies have included rape victimization or perpetration measures to determine if attitudinal changes affected these behaviors and to assess if a reduction in rape subsequently occurred (see Lonsway et al., 2009).

Protecting students against predators by limiting their access to college women in their residence halls and by providing access to immediate responses that are linked to campus law enforcement have been a mainstay of the campus response to sexual victimization. In part, these campuswide environmental responses aimed at a specific situation are "easy fixes" because they are visible responses to sexual victimization meant to ease students' worries primarily about predators who are strangers as opposed to the more typical assailants who are known to the victims. This focus is not too surprising because most colleges' sexual victimization prevention efforts are guided by what "makes sense" rather than by a theoretical model grounded in empirical research (Yeater & O'Donohue, 1999).

The effectiveness of these campuswide responses is questionable at best for several reasons. First, few studies have evaluated the effectiveness of these programs, and those that have been done are not rigorous in terms of research design (e.g., lack of a control group or a panel design) (Cass, 2007; Fisher et al., 1998). Second, although exceptions exist, much of this research has examined the effectiveness of only one or a few strategies on a single campus (Day, 1995). Third, this limited body of research suggests that these strategies do not reduce the incidence of sexual victimization. In one of the very few national studies to incorporate the theoretical framework of routine activities theory in predicting rape victimization, Cass (2007) reported that *none* of the institution-level interventions aimed at protecting college women from rapists or other attackers were significant predictors.

These campuswide protective responses are not without their critics within the feminist community. Schwartz, DeKeseredy, Tait, and Alvi (2001), for example, have argued that these strategies place the burden of responsibility foremost on women themselves and thereby encourage women to blame themselves for their victimization. Considering that these strategies focus on preventing sexual victimization assaults against one woman at one location in time instead of changing the underlying conditions favorable to sexual assault, they are unlikely to reduce the incidence of campus sexual victimization (Day, 1995).

Instead of focusing on changing the behavior of women, addressing the emotional and physical well-being and safety needs of survivors of sexual victimization continues to top the advocacy agenda within the feminist community. These altruistic goals are to be applauded, yet the research evidence in terms of survivors' help-seeking behaviors is somewhat mixed regarding their experience and subsequent actions. Research has well documented that women are often physically and psychologically injured during the course of being sexually victimized, especially raped, with some injuries having a long-term negative toll on women's health. College women are not immune from such injuries and their effects (see Logan et al., 2006). Our NCWSV Study reported that about one in five women experienced an injury in addition to the attempted or completed penetration during the rape (21.9%), most often citing "bruises, black-eye, cuts, scratches, swelling or chipped teeth." Of those completed rape victims who reported experiencing an injury, 41% cited "emotional or psychological" injuries (Fisher et al., 1999). Interestingly, just over a quarter (27.3%) sought medical care for their injuries. Within this context, the feminist approach to helping survivors can be seen as much needed by those who have been sexually victimized.

Despite their need for physical and psychological health care, survivors do not readily report their victimizations to those who are in positions to help these women. Recall the discussion on reporting figures presented in Chapter 6. Very few women who were sexually victimized—in fact less than 5% of those raped—reported their experience to law enforcement, and only half of these incidents were reported to campus police or enforcement officials (Fisher et al., 1999; Fisher et al., 2003a). But if these women disclosed their victimization to anyone, they were most likely to tell somebody close to them—a friend or someone they were living with such as a roommate. Our NCWSV Study reported that none of the rape survivors who reported their experiences to someone shared their experiences with a women's program or service staff, with a victim service hotline, or with a counselor or a therapist not from a victim hotline (Fisher et al., 1999; Fisher et al., 2003a). Only a very small percentage, about 1%, of survivors of the other forms of sexual victimization reported their experience to a counselor or a therapist not from a victim hotline; none of these women disclosed their victimization to a women's program or service staff or victim service hotline. The point is quite simple: feminists want to help and have created opportunities to supply support to survivors of sexual victimization, but few college women survivors take advantage of these opportunities.

More generally, although we see value in specific recommendations, we are not persuaded that feminist theory per se is sufficiently specific to direct the most effective crime prevention efforts. In the long run, it may prove more fruitful to draw on knowledge gained in the broader crime prevention literature to help inform attempts to reduce sexual victimization. We return to this issue later when we discuss the potential relevance of the approach of situational crime prevention for making campuses safer havens.

LEGAL APPROACH

A third prevention approach has been to address the problem of sexual victimization through the law—whether through civil lawsuits, the passage of statutes, or the expansion of judicial proceedings on campus. Taken together, these initiatives have served to highlight the salience of sexual victimization. More questionable, however, is whether these efforts have meaningfully improved female students' safety or have served more as a symbolic reform that has been more show than substance.

The legal issue of colleges incurring civil liability for students' victimization, including rape, arose from a number of students or their families suing schools for injuries suffered during criminal incidents (see Burling, 2003; Fisher, 1995). State courts have used the doctrine of foreseeability, as well as the duty to provide students with adequate security protection, as the standard for establishing liability in lawsuits filed by victimized students. Because this doctrine is prone to subjective interpretation, the courts have not always agreed on the interpretation of foreseeability or set consistent standards for adequate security protection. Although foreseeability has become the touchstone of university liability for the criminal victimization of students, the courts have not consistently ruled in favor of the students and their families. Some rape victims won their lawsuits against schools while others lost; other cases were settled out of court. The outcome of these lawsuits was that by the late 1980s and early 1990s, colleges across the country were systematically responding to these lawsuits, or to the threats posed by them, by upgrading security and by warning the campus community about crime occurring on campus.

This was the eventual outcome of Connie and Howard Clery's lawsuit against Lehigh University for the rape and murder of their daughter, Jeanne Ann Clery, in her dorm room in 1986. They settled out of court for an undisclosed amount of money. Then, inspired by their daughter's murder, the Clerys initiated lobbying efforts during the late1980s, first in Pennsylvania and then at the federal level. After successfully prompting the Pennsylvania legislature to enact legislation requiring colleges to report campus crime statistics publicly, the Clerys then turned their attention to the U.S. Congress. The Clerys' activism—coupled with testimony (including from rape victims) in the 1990 hearings on campus crime, court decisions in favor of victims, and the media's increased coverage of rape among college women—moved Congress to pass The Crime Awareness and Campus Security Act of 1990 (Title II of Pub. L. 101–542; 20 U.S.C § 1092). This act was later renamed The Jeanne Clery Disclosure of Campus Security Policy and Campus Crime Statistics Act in 1998.

A key provision of the Clery Act was that it mandated that colleges publish an annual security report. In this document, the Clery Act requires that all Title IV–eligible colleges publicly disclose "official" crime statistics on and around campus for the three most recent calendar years. (They also must describe their crime prevention and security policies and procedures.) Sexual offenses are included in these statistics. Both forcible offenses (e.g., forcible rape) and nonforcible offenses (e.g., statutory rape) that have been reported to campus police or security departments or to university administrators must be included in the report. This information is contained in the annual security report that schools disseminate yearly to all currently enrolled students and employees. Prospective students and employees also must be made aware that this information is available and that they are entitled to request a copy of the annual security report.

Connie and Howard Clery envisioned laudable goals for the Clery Act. They wanted to ensure that currently enrolled college students and prospective students had accurate, official crime statistics about how much criminal offending occurred on and around each and every campus. The underlying presumption is that dangerous campuses would be pressured to improve students' safety or risk losing enrollments to other institutions. The difficulty, however, is that official statistics—crimes known to law enforcement authorities—vastly underestimate the extent of crime, including the sexual victimizations of female students. As discussed in Chapter 6, a number of investigations—including our NCWSV Study—have repeatedly shown that very few women report their sexual victimization experience to law enforcement or campus officials. For example, the NCWSV Study reported that less than 3% of forcible rapes were reported to campus authorities. Relatedly, as also discussed in Chapter 6, many women whose experience meets the legal definition of rape do not acknowledge that they have been raped. These unreported incidents would not be counted in the Clery Act statistics; thus, the rapes that are included in Clery Act statistics are but a small percentage of all the rapes that occur to college women.

Other considerations also undermine reporting by sexual victims to campus officials. In their national study of how campuses respond to the report of a sexual victimization, Karjane, Fisher, and Cullen (2001) identified institutional barriers to sexual victimization reporting. Their results showed that only 74.8% of the colleges had confidential reporting options, even though nearly 94% of the schools' administrators perceived that this type of reporting would encourage reporting. Less than half (43%) of the schools stated that they had anonymous reporting, despite 90% of the administrators perceiving that it would encourage reporting. These reporting limitations and barriers most likely result in the Clery Act statistics grossly underestimating the true amount of sexual victimization on and near campuses and hence distort the safety of these places.

Although not yet documented empirically, it is also possible that official statistics might distort which colleges are, in fact, safer. Institutions that are invested in the prevention of sexual victimization actively encourage the reporting of incidents. Ironically, the very policies and practices that increase reporting behavior and make students safer might produce official statistics that depict such colleges as unsafe. In any event, it is doubtful that the nationwide effort at collecting and disseminating crime statistics year after year has had more than a marginal impact in reducing female students' risk of sexual victimization.

The Clery Act also included the requirement that all Title IV schools implement policies and programs to address sexual victimization prevention. This is a commendable goal. Because colleges now have to do something to address sexual victimization on their campuses, there has been a proliferation of new programs and policies. Unfortunately, the act did not require that these programs and policies be evaluated to determine how effective, or ineffective, they are in reducing sexual victimization. This omission, in part, may explain why there are so few published rigorous evaluations of campus programs aimed at reducing the incidence of sexual victimization and revictimization (for exceptions, see Banyard, Moynihan, et al., 2007; Gidycz, Layman, et al., 2001; Gidycz, Rich, Orchowski, King, & Miller, 2006; Gidycz, Lynn, et al., 2001; Marx et al., 2001).

The purpose here is not to cynically criticize the efforts of the Clerys. Again, they called attention to college students' victimization and created pressures for institutions to take steps to address this issue. But legal reform in the absence of science produces outcomes that may be more symbolic than substantive in their effects (see also Fisher, Hartman, Cullen, & Turner, 2002). In this context, beyond the publicity it generated, the Clery Act must be seen as a legal reform effort whose effects at best are uncertain and at worst have diverted limited resources into areas of questionable value.

Another legal approach also appears to be of questionable value. Thus, many colleges now use "disciplinary procedures," "judicial systems," "grievance procedures," or some similarly named process to address sexual victimization among students. Sexual victimization is processed under these procedures because it is viewed by college administrators as a violation of the school's student code of conduct and falls under their jurisdiction—just as academic dishonesty might. In their national study of 2,438 randomly selected higher education institutions, Karjane and her colleagues (2001) reviewed each college's annual security reports and the faculty and student codes of conduct/university rules. Their content analysis of these materials revealed that overall, most schools are not equipped to adjudicate sexual victimization cases. For example, only about a third (33.5%) of the schools even mentioned having a judicial or disciplinary process. Of these schools, less than half (45.8%) provided a written description of the hearing process. Between 37.2% and 52.9% of the colleges mentioned (1) the accuser and the accused could have others present during the hearing, (2) evidence could be presented, (3) testimony would be given, (4) witnesses could be called and testify, (5) cross-examination was possible, (6) the burden of proof used, and (7) the type of vote (e.g., majority, unanimous) used in a hearing. By contrast, only 3.4% of the schools mentioned that hearing participants might be subject to training or education concerning violence against women. Further, a mere 8.7% of the institutions mentioned the existence of *rape shield* provisions—that is, a procedure that protects victims from the irrelevant use in a hearing of their past sexual history.

This variability makes campus hearing procedures problematic on at least two grounds. First, putting aside the normative question of whether colleges should be adjudicating sexual victimization claims, there is a more fundamental question: Are schools equipped to process sexual victimization cases in such a way that all parties are aware of the process and are treated with fair due process? Second, are these hearings effective on any criteria relating to reducing sexual victimization or stopping perpetration? Campus administrators have not satisfactorily addressed either question (see Karjane et al., 2001). The issues raised by both questions should not be overlooked; they are central to comprehensively addressing sexual victimization on campuses.

In sum, the legal approach to crime prevention generally suffers an inherent limitation: it typically does not address the underlying sources of people's victimization. The law can provide justice, inspire attention to a given criminal offense, and, under specific circumstances, achieve a measure of deterrence. Nonetheless, an effective strategy for the prevention of students' victimization—including their sexual victimization—must also appreciate that the law is rarely a solution to society's ills, including those on its campuses and that touch the lives of college students. Creating safe havens for students requires a more detailed understanding of their lives and of the situational contingencies that increase or decrease their risk of victimization.

Opportunity-Reduction Approach: Situational Crime Prevention

Preventing sexual victimization among college students presents unique challenges because events often occur between those who know one another and in a private setting. In tackling this difficult issue, we believe that the most fruitful strategy is to draw from the broader theory and research on crime prevention and, in particular, from the model known as *situational crime prevention.* Thus, we begin by discussing this approach and then probe how it might be applied to sexual victimization. Much of what we propose is speculative. Even so, we are persuaded that this way of thinking offers the most promising prospects for making campuses safer for female students.

SITUATIONAL CRIME PREVENTION

The commission of any given criminal act depends on two elements: first, the presence of someone willing to commit the act (a *motivated offender*) and, second, the presence of the opportunity for the offender to carry out the act (a *performance structure*) (see Cloward, 1959). Most criminological theories provide insight into why some individuals are motivated to break the law or feel constrained from taking advantage of criminal temptations. However, until the emergence of several perspectives now grouped under the umbrella of *environmental criminology* (Bottoms, 1994), relatively little attention was paid to the opportunity side of offending (see also Wilcox, Land, & Hunt, 2003).

Writing 3 decades ago, Ronald Clarke (1980, 1982) decried this disproportionate emphasis on offenders as opposed to opportunity. His main concern was in preventing crime, and he had an important point to make: to stop a criminal act from taking place, it was easier to knife off opportunity than it was to remove criminal motivation from an offender. The willingness to offend was often wrapped up in complex risk factors that may have accumulated since birth and that are reversed only with evidence-based, systematic interventions (Cullen & Gendreau, 2000). By contrast, the opportunity to offend is in the here and now, and it may be reduced or eliminated by relatively simple means—perhaps a lock on a door, a dog at home barking, an alarm system turned on, a security guard on duty, or a store constructed so that the cashier is visible to passersby. Clarke termed these and similar measures as *situational crime prevention* (see also Clarke & Felson, in press).

Importantly, the concept of opportunity was elaborated by Cohen and Felson (1979; see also Felson, 2002) in their routine activity theory. In this pathbreaking work, they divided opportunity into two elements: the presence of an *attractive target* (which could be a person or property) and the absence of *capable guardianship*. A criminal act could occur when a *motivated offender* intersected in time and space with an attractive target that lacked capable guardianship. In terms of crime prevention, the opportunity to offend could be decreased either by making potential targets less attractive or by providing targets with guardianship capable of warding off a motivated offender.

Many criminologists dislike or are wary of the situational crime prevention approach for two reasons. First, they see it as a brand of "administrative criminology"—as a perspective that implicitly acquits the larger social structure from its role in breeding crime (Clarke & Felson, in press). Larger sources of inequality, including patriarchy, are ignored while attention is paid instead to seemingly mundane issues such as where to place security cameras, whether attendants at building doors discourage crime, and how rerouting traffic might divert offenders away from a neighborhood now suffering a high incidence of burglary. The obvious response of Clarke and his fellow scholars is that situational crime prevention admittedly does not solve the larger ills gripping society but does save people's bodies and property from victimization. Theories that illuminate crime's root causes may be scientifically correct and ideologically comforting, but they typically have little or no utility in preventing crime (see also Wilson, 1975). They are distant from crime events and do not give concrete guidance on what factors can be manipulated to stop victimization. By contrast, a situational crime prevention is just that—situational! It focuses on the microelements of a situation to see what can be altered to eliminate the opportunity for the criminal event to take place.

Second, situational crime prevention focuses on the behavior of targets and how their choices might expose them disproportionately to motivated offenders and decrease their guardianship. This attention to how people might contribute to their own victimization risk can incite charges of victim blaming. This is especially the case in the area of sexual victimization where, in an ideal world, one would hope that a woman's beginning exploration of sexual intimacy would not be viewed as an invitation to unwanted touching or penetration. Further, given the privacy of most crime events, sexual assault victims are often twice victimized when they have to prove that they "were not asking for it." Even so, from a situational crime prevention approach, potential victims are an integral component to understanding differential exposure to risk and, in turn, to developing opportunity-reduction strategies. In a crude way, Mac Donald (2008) captured this point when, as noted above, she said that women who were inebriated, naked, and in bed with a man increased their risk of rape. From a scientific standpoint, this is an empirical reality and not a moral judgment.

In this context, we suggest that the next stage in creating safe havens for female students is to draw on the insights of situational crime prevention theory and research in hopes of reducing the victimization opportunities faced by women on and off campuses. Some beginning strides have been made in this direction (see, in particular, Sampson, 2002). Still, much of what we offer here is not proven fact but more of a way of thinking about the prevention of sexual victimization. Although this is speculative, we are convinced that this approach—focusing on crime-specific means of reducing opportunities for rape and other sexual assaults—furnishes the most promising future approach to limiting female students' victimization. We hold this view because situational crime prevention is theoretically grounded in environmental criminology and has been shown empirically to reduce other types of offenses in diverse social domains (Felson, 2002). Accordingly, below we outline three interrelated ways of creating safer havens that are informed by a situational crime prevention approach: discourage offenders, decrease target attractiveness, and increase capable guardianship.

DISCOURAGE OFFENDERS

Traditionally, the advocates of situational crime prevention ignored potential criminals. They were all lumped into the category of motivated offenders and their presence was largely taken for granted. Recently, however, more attention had been placed on offenders. There is still no attempt to probe individuals' bodies, minds, or social circumstances to discover why some are, and some are not, predisposed to offend. But there is a recognition that motivated offenders are less likely to break the law when others are around that discourage them from doing so. Sometimes, those who discourage crime are called offenders' *handlers* (Cullen, Eck, & Lowenkamp, 2002; Felson, 1995).

Advocates of situational crime prevention generally do not believe that the threat of criminal justice sanctions does much to prevent crime. Such threats are uncertain and their consequences distant from the immediate gratifications a criminal act yields. Rather, they believe that efforts to discourage crime should be part of informal social control. The key with attempting to prevent any crime—whether rape or burglary—is to think about how best to exert pressure not to offend. Part of this effort should target "excuses" or techniques of neutralization that make crime possible (see Sykes & Matza, 1957). In the area of sexual victimization, this would mean attempting to debunk rape myths. Another part of the effort is to apply informal sanctions to those whose behavior violates shared expectations.

Rape awareness seminars comprise one means of discouraging sexual victimization. But it would seem that this broad-brush approach relies on education not backed up with informal social controls. An alternative approach might be to look for organized groupings on campus that are capable of exercising control over at least some portion of the student population. For example, athletic departments and head coaches could be mandated not only to provide awareness seminars to athletes but also to remind student-athletes about their sexual responsibilities. The goal would be to elevate the salience of this issue and to require team captains to keep other players "in line." In a similar way, fraternities might be put on notice that instances of sexual victimization will cause the organization to lose its university affiliation. In this way, responsibility for "handling" potential sexual victimizers would be placed in the hands of those closest to them—their fraternity brothers.

Finally, Felson (2002, p. 41) warns about the importance of attending to "cues" in a setting that "communicates temptations and controls." The temptations for sexual victimization in a residence hall room might be strong. To counterbalance these enticements, universities might post signs in dormitory rooms (e.g., on the back of doors) defining and cautioning against untoward sexual conduct. This recommendation—and the others shared above—admittedly are suggestive at best. Even so, the principle they embody is worthy of further exploration: the more those close to potential perpetrators can be moved to discourage sexual victimization, the fewer women will be victimized.

DECREASE TARGET ATTRACTIVENESS

In the situational crime prevention model, victims are an essential ingredient in the degree to which opportunities for victimization exist. Potential victims may enter a risky situation differentially prepared to avoid or deter a perpetrator and thus be more or less attractive as a target for victimization. Accordingly, the prevention of sexual victimization should be taken seriously, making college women less vulnerable to assailants.

In this regard, Rozee and Koss (2001) have described a process by which women decrease their attractiveness to would-be offenders who view them as suitable sexual victimization targets. They used the acronym AAA for the three key components of their approach: assess, acknowledge, and act. Thus, the AAA model is based on women first assessing a specific situation as potentially dangerous, then acknowledging a situation as dangerous, and finally acting with effective resistance strategies.

Of further relevance, research suggests that sexually victimized women are less able to identify risky situations that provide opportunities for sexual victimization. Women's situational risk perception—their ability to identify cues and certain contexts as risky and respond to the threat by protecting themselves—is one possible reason that women are sexually victimized. Researchers have reported that sexually victimized women have longer response latencies in identifying dangerous or risky situations (Marx et al., 2001) and that revictimized women have longer response latencies than women who experienced a single incident (Wilson, Calhoun, & Bernat, 1999; for an exception, see Breitenbecher, 1999). Also, victimized women need more cues to feel uneasy or on guard (Norris, Nurius, & Graham, 1999). It is possible, then, that college females who may be inclined to take risks or who do not identify risks are more attractive targets than women who are not risk takers or who identify risky cues. Potential offenders may sense a vulnerability in these women that they do not in others.

Research needs to be undertaken that examines risk heterogeneity—individual factors that place individuals at risk of being sexually victimized, such as risk recognition. To date, more attention has been given to situational factors that influence risk, but it is likely that other individual characteristics, such as risk-seeking and self-control, also increase the likelihood that a woman will be sexually victimized. Although not specific to sexual victimization risk, research on victimization suggests that having low levels of self-control increases victimization risk (Schreck, 1999). It remains to be seen whether self-control or risk-seeking impacts sexual victimization. Identifying additional individual factors that similarly influence college women's risk of being sexually victimized will be instructive in the development of risk-reduction programs.

The ability to recognize risk may be compromised by alcohol consumption and drug use. Should women choose to frequent bars and parties and consume alcohol and/or drugs, they should do so with attention to the accompanying risk. It is likely that substance use impairs women's ability to recognize dangerous situations and to react quickly and possibly more effectively to such danger (Abbey et al., 2004). Would-be offenders may also view women who are under the influence of alcohol and/or drugs as being more attractive in that they may be perceived as being more easily victimized.

Also important is the context in which female students often drink or use drugs. The college experience is commonly characterized by attending parties and frequenting bars or clubs at which alcohol is widely available to everyone. As noted in our NCWSV Study and in other research, college women who spend time in places that are predominantly male (such as fraternity parties and parties with male college athletes) and who have a greater propensity to drink alcohol and use drugs are at a higher risk of being sexually victimized than other college women (Fisher et al., in press; Schwartz & Pitts, 1995). Although women can and should spend their time in situations of their choosing without fear of assault, recognizing the stubborn reality that certain contexts make them more vulnerable to being sexually victimized is imperative. One way women may reduce risk and decrease their target attractiveness is to make sure that someone they trust goes with them and checks in with them when at bars, clubs, and parties. Such a buddy system, in which women have friends look out for their well-being, while simplistic, may interrupt a sexual victimization that is about to occur. We return to this issue of guardianship below.

Even if adept at risk recognition, college women may not be fully insulated against sexual victimization. Thus, using effective self-protective actions is a way in which women may further reduce their attractiveness as targets. Self-protective actions are typically classified as being one of four types: forceful physical, nonforceful physical, forceful verbal, and nonforceful verbal. Forceful physical actions are active and aggressive behaviors, such as punching and biting an offender, while nonforceful physical actions are more passive, such as trying to flee. Forceful verbal actions are used to scare an offender or attract outside assistance and include yelling and screaming. Pleading, talking, and begging are examples of nonforceful verbal protective actions (Ullman, 1997, 2007).

Research on the context of sexual victimization events shows that the majority of college women use some type of self-protective action during the incident (Fisher, Daigle, Cullen, & Santana, 2007). Using self-protective action is important for college women because doing so has generally been linked to the reduction in the likelihood that an incident will be completed without increasing risk of injury (Fisher et al., 2007; Ullman, 1997, 2007). Not all self-protective actions, however, are likely to stop the victimization from occurring. Research shows that self-protective actions are most useful when they are in parity with the level of force that the offender uses. That is, if the offender is using physical force, then the victim should use forceful strategies in order to thwart the victimization attempt (Fisher et al., 2007). Women who use self-protective actions are thus less vulnerable to having a victimization be completed. Research also indicates that women who use self-protective action during an initial incident are less likely to experience a subsequent sexual victimization (Daigle et al., 2008). Given this body of research, risk-reduction programs have begun to include components of risk recognition and teaching self-defense. Although not yet evaluated thoroughly enough to draw conclusions about their effectiveness, such programs likely hold promise in prompting women to attune themselves to risky cues in their environment and to use self-protective actions that reduce the risk of sexual victimization occurring.

INCREASE CAPABLE GUARDIANSHIP

Reducing sexual victimization of college women may be tied to facilitating social guardianship—the presence of supportive individuals who serve as protection against sexual victimization. Social guardianship can be provided by simply having another person, such as a friend or roommate, either present or in close proximity. Not being alone can be enough to protect a person from a potential offender who may choose to target individuals who are alone without guardianship.

Simply having another person present may not be enough, however, to provide sufficient social guardianship. Building on this idea, recent efforts have been made to design and implement programs to address the context or culture of support for sexual victimization of women as a means to prevent its occurrence. The notion that bystanders may play an active role in the prevention of sexual victimization is a relatively new theoretically grounded strategy. Bystander intervention is a community approach to guardianship with the objective of involving men and women in changing the environment that may be supportive of sexual violence of women. It involves empowering bystanding students with skills to recognize and confidently intervene in risky situations with the intent of preventing sexual victimization and supporting survivors who might disclose (see Banyard, Plante, & Moynihan, 2005; Lonsway et al., 2009). The role of bystanders is to proactively interrupt situations that could lead to sexual victimization or to intervene during risky or dangerous situations for sexual victimization, to speak out against social norms that promote sexual victimization, and to possess the skills and knowledge to be effective and supportive allies of survivors (Banyard et al., 2005).

These bystander education programs include discussions about how community members can provide prevention when observing risky situations such as an intoxicated person being led to a bedroom at a party (Banyard, Moynihan, et al., 2007). Role playing and other exercises are used to teach skills about how to intervene successfully and safely and how to respond to the victim, including using formal support services such as the police and rape crisis centers. Although not plentiful, evaluations of these programs provide promising findings (Schewe, 2006).

Thus, using a sample of college students enrolled at a single campus who were randomly assigned to bystander training and a control group, Banyard, Moynihan, and Plante (2007) provided the first empirical evidence that bystander intervention may be effective for sexual victimization prevention. They reported that the program participants evidenced positive changes in increased knowledge of sexual assault, reducing adherence to rape myths, confidence in being an active bystander and employing actual bystander behaviors (e.g., having walked a friend home from a party who has had too much to drink). Moynihan and Banyard (2008) also completed an exploratory pilot study of bystander intervention for sexual victimization prevention with members from one fraternity, one sorority, and a men's and women's intercollegiate athletic team—all of which research has reported place female students at high risk for either sexual victimization or perpetration. The results indicated that, in general, the bystander intervention was effective in changing knowledge, attitudes, and bystander efficacy (e.g., confidence to ask a stranger at a party who looked upset if he or she is okay or needs help). Based on Banyard's evaluations of bystander programs, it is possible that sexual victimization may be reduced on college campuses if more individuals were active and effective interveners.

In addition to teaching skills to intervene during the antecedents to sexual victimization that people may witness, these programs also emphasize how to appropriately respond to victims who disclose their experiences to them. As noted in Chapter 6, although most college women who are sexually victimized do not report to the police, they most often do tell a friend about their experience. It is important, then, that these individuals to whom a victim discloses respond in a way that is supportive, informative, and empowering to the victim. Research shows that many women do not receive supportive or helpful responses from those to whom they disclose (Dunn et al., 1999) and that many college women are not advised by their confidants to report to the police (Pitts & Schwartz, 1993). These unsupportive responses may discourage women from seeking help after being sexually victimized. They also may contribute to a culture in which sexual victimization is perceived as unserious and as being the victim's fault rather than the perpetrator's responsibility.

Disclosure is also important in that if made soon after the initial victimization, it may create an opportunity to prevent revictimization. As mentioned in Chapter 5, women are at a heightened risk of experiencing a subsequent sexual victimization immediately following the initial incident. As such, women are particularly vulnerable for revictimization in the days and weeks following the initial sexual victimization. If a woman discloses her experience to a friend, the friend has a chance to potentially knife off additional sexual victimizations if the friend takes particular effective actions. Initially, the friend may encourage the victim to report to the police, thus increasing the likelihood that the offender may be identified and arrested. To the extent that revictimization is perpetrated by the same offender, doing so may reduce future victimization risk for the victim (and possibly other women, too). In addition, the friend may recommend to the victim that she seek assistance from a counseling center, health clinic, or rape crisis center. Doing so may enable a victim to better cope with being victimized and to utilize available help resources. In turn, the victim may not only minimize the harm from the incident but also reduce her risk of future sexual revictimization—an event, we have noted, that can occur shortly following an initial incident.

Finally, just having a friend provide support and advice may help empower the victim. Friends may be able to help the victim process the events and help the victim "make sense" out of what transpired. In addition, the friend may be able to point out signs of risk that occurred prior to the event and help the victim assess, recognize, and successfully act to avoid and manage risk in the future. In this way, friends may provide a type of effective guardianship.

Preventing Stalking

The prevalence of stalking among college women—13.1% in a single academic year according to our NCWSV Study—suggests that this type of victimization is a public policy issue that warrants recognition and prevention. At this point, however, there is little evidence that college officials recognize the seriousness of stalking or the need for a systematic response. As we have seen, over the past 2 decades, college campuses have had to come to grips with their responsibility to address the sexual victimization of college women. Despite this raised consciousness, stalking has largely fallen outside the formal concerns of college and university administrators. Thus, recall Karjane et al.'s (2001) national-level study of the official sexual assault security reports and documents of postsecondary institutions. Notably, in the colleges' sexual assault policies, only 1.5% of the institutions had a separate stalking policy and another 1.5% merely mentioned stalking in their reports. That is, 97% ignored stalking in their sexual assault materials (Karjane et al., 2001, pp. 52–53).

Stalking, of course, can occur not only on campus but also off campus. As with higher educational institutions, it appears that law enforcement departments also have "marginalized" the subject of stalking (Farrell, Weisburd, & Wyckoff, 2000, p. 167). Even in a department that had begun to implement "a new stalking protocol" to respond more effectively to women's victimization, Farrell et al. found that two-thirds of the officers surveyed either did not know that a written stalking policy existed or said that their department had no such policy. As Farrell et al. conclude, these results were not surprising because even in the 21st century, "stalking is not a priority issue for police departments" (p. 164).

If the first step in effective public policy is recognizing that stalking is a genuine risk for college women, the second step is devising strategies for preventing this victimization. Stalking presents unique prevention challenges because it is not a single episode but rather a victimization that is repeated over time and space. Still, as with sexual victimization generally, useful insights into possible prevention strategies might be drawn from the perspective of routine activity theory and situational crime prevention. Specifically, as in our discussion above, three strategies are suggested.

First, efforts should be made to *discourage* offenders from continuing their repeated pursuit behaviors. Building on informal control theories, Felson (1995) contends that misconduct can be discouraged if offenders are monitored by handlers—people whose social bond to an offender constitutes a "handle" that can be "grabbed" and used to exert social control (see also Cullen et al., 2002). Handling in stalking is particularly important because the activity is not a discrete event but ongoing and thus likely to come to the attention of those close to the offender. In this context, colleges might wish to explore ways of creating a wider awareness on campus of the need for males to prevent their peers from inappropriate pursuit behavior. Education programs might seek to develop specific skills in how friends might effectively persuade or shame offenders from continued stalking. Another possibility, however, is to assign campus employees (e.g., counselors, ombudsmen) the task of confronting stalkers about their behavior (Felson, 1995). In doing so, they might exercise direct social control and/or provide a conduit for offenders to seek counseling.

A certain portion of cases, however, might well require formal intervention by institutions. In such cases, college administrators will have to face the daunting challenge of developing clear guidelines to incorporate into student disciplinary codes as to when stalking conduct violates a female student's right not to be harassed and when it warrants formal hearings and punishments. Already, many postsecondary institutions are grappling with their disciplinary role when accusations of sexual misconduct are made. Further, as noted, few university codes of conduct contain either specific prohibitions of stalking or clearly articulated procedures for how violations of this sort would be processed (Karjane et al., 2001). In part, this omission reflects the fact that codes of conduct regarding sexual victimization are relatively recent inventions, whose quality and comprehensiveness vary considerably across postsecondary institutions (Karjane et al., 2001). A cultural lag of sorts will have to be surmounted before stalking becomes incorporated systematically into these codes and provides a formal basis for intervening with stalkers.

Second, efforts should be made to *decrease the target attractiveness* of stalking victims. One approach might be to advise female students what to do if a stalking incident emerges. Such *coping strategies* should involve equipping students with strategies on how to send clear messages that continued advances are unwelcome. It might also provide insights on how to thwart opportunities for contact (e.g., unlisted telephone number, change e-mail address). Further, college women should receive explicit information on the support or counseling services on and off campus that might be accessed in a stalking situation. These services may be of particular importance because of the finding that women who have been sexually victimized in the past are more at risk for a stalking victimization. Their cumulative vulnerability to victimization may require special intervention to ensure that their college careers are not derailed by the long-term presence of a stalker in their lives.

Third, efforts should be made to *increase guardianship.* Importantly, a first step is in persuading college women of the necessity of reporting their stalking either to campus authorities or, if that is not desirable, to trusted friends. Reporting is a prerequisite to victims receiving guardianship. In this regard, as with rape prevention programs, one possibility for increasing protection would be to supply females with escorts on and near campus. They might not only serve as guardians in the situation but also carry videotapes to record evidence of stalking conduct. Another possibility would be to have residence hall personnel, professors, staff, and campus security function as *place managers* who are trained in how to discourage stalkers who are looming in a location (Eck, 1994; Felson, 1995). Such place managers might be particularly important in providing guardianship for female students who live alone. Further, when stalking occurs via the telephone or Internet, it might be possible to *harden the target* to block unwanted contacts and/or to devise methods to collect evidence for future legal intervention (e.g., printing a hard copy of the e-mail message and creating a separate directory for unwanted e-mail messages).

In any case, we would urge that college administrators take a proactive approach in dealing with stalking victimization. From a pragmatic standpoint, the very prevalence of stalking may expose institutions to considerable legal liability if they have taken no procedural or substantive steps to address this problem and a stalking incident turns tragic. From an educational standpoint, administrators should be concerned that so many of their female students have the quality of their college experience diminished by lengthy periods of unwanted pursuit behaviors by males. This victimization is a price of going to college that students should not have to bear or, if experienced, should not have to bear alone and without the support of campus administrators, law enforcement, advocates, and health providers.

Conclusion

How is it possible to measure something that is as complex as sexual victimization? This is the daunting challenge that, building on the research of previous scholars, we have taken up. We trust that our efforts have advanced knowledge and provided a basis for fashioning more effective policies and practices. Still, we see our work as part of a line of inquiry that remains in its beginning stages. Given the significance of the issue, the sexual victimization of college women has received insufficient attention. It is clear that systematic, national-level studies are needed to explore in more detail not only the extent but also the situational dynamics of rape and other forms of sexual assault and their short-term and long-term effects on students' well-being. Further, there is a collateral need to undertake theoretically informed experimental studies of programs aimed at preventing and minimizing the harms stemming from female students' victimization.

We are persuaded that rigorous science should guide this collective effort to unravel the sources of, and design the most effective prevention programs for, sexual victimization (see also Daigle, Fisher, & Stewart, 2009; Fisher et al., 2008; Jordan, 2009; Logan et al., 2006). Social policy, including on college campuses, cannot fully escape political ideology; our cherished values guide what we see as important and wish to give priority to in the allocation of scarce resources. Even so, wanting the world to be a particular way does not make it so. The special utility of science is that it produces knowledge by following rules that anyone—regardless of political ideology—is free to use. If disputing a finding, then the implicit expectation is for critics to undertake a study and determine if their results confirm their view of the world. In the end, the quality of the data, not the party with the loudest voice, settles the matter.

Of course, science and the data it produces are not ends in and of themselves. Science can invite a sense of detachment as statistics are compiled and published. But as David Brodeur (1985, p. 355) notes, "statistics are human beings with the tears wiped off." As the account opening this chapter illustrates, sexual victimization touches students' lives. Sometimes it only aggravates or is minimally disruptive, but on other occasions it harms women psychologically and physically to the extent that they are never the same. Pain is felt and tears are shed that tarnish the ivory tower in which they are pursuing their education. This very human side of what we study should provide extra incentive in our quest to conduct research that furnishes sound insight and inspires evidence-based interventions. Even if utopian, our goal should be to make campuses safe havens that allow all college women to reach their potential without the risk of sexual victimization that disrupts their daily lives and damages their psychological and/or physical well-being.

References

Abbey, A., McAuslan, P., Ross, L. T., & Zawacki, T. (1999). Alcohol expectancies regarding sex, aggression, and sexual vulnerability: Reliability and validity assessment. *Psychology of Addictive Behaviors, 13,* 174–182.

Abbey, A., Ross, L. T., & McDuffie, D. (1994). Alcohol's role in sexual assault. In R. R. Watson (Ed.), *Drug and alcohol abuse reviews, Volume 5: Addictive behaviors in women* (pp. 97–124). Towota, NJ: Human Press.

Abbey, A., Zawacki, T., Buck, P. O., Clinton, A. M., & McAuslan, P. (2004). Sexual assault and alcohol consumption: What do we know about their relationship and what types of research are still needed? *Aggression and Violent Behavior, 9,* 271–303.

Ageton, S. S. (1983). *Sexual assault among adolescents.* Lexington, MA: Lexington Books.

Ahrens, C. E., Campbell, R., Ternier-Thames, N. K., Wasco, S. M., & Sefl, T. (2007). Deciding whom to tell: Expectations and outcomes of rape survivors' first disclosures. *Psychology of Women Quarterly, 31,* 38–49.

American College Health Association. (2000a). *National College Health Assessment: Reference Group Executive Summary, Spring.* Baltimore: American College Health Association.

American College Health Association. (2000b). *National College Health Assessment: Reference Group Executive Summary, Fall.* Baltimore: American College Health Association.

American College Health Association. (2001a). *National College Health Assessment: Reference Group Executive Summary, Spring.* Baltimore: American College Health Association.

American College Health Association. (2001b). *National College Health Assessment: Reference Group Executive Summary, Fall.* Baltimore: American College Health Association.

American College Health Association. (2002a). *National College Health Assessment: Reference Group Executive Summary, Spring.* Baltimore: American College Health Association.

American College Health Association. (2002b). *National College Health Assessment: Reference Group Executive Summary, Fall.* Baltimore: American College Health Association.

American College Health Association. (2003a). *National College Health Assessment: Reference Group Executive Summary, Spring.* Baltimore: American College Health Association.

American College Health Association. (2003b). *National College Health Assessment: Reference Group Executive Summary, Fall.* Baltimore: American College Health Association.

American College Health Association. (2004a). *National College Health Assessment: Reference Group Executive Summary, Spring.* Baltimore: American College Health Association.

American College Health Association. (2004b). *National College Health Assessment: Reference Group Executive Summary, Fall.* Baltimore: American College Health Association.

American College Health Association. (2005a). *National College Health Assessment: Reference Group Executive Summary, Spring.* Baltimore: American College Health Association.

American College Health Association. (2005b). *National College Health Assessment: Reference Group Executive Summary, Fall.* Baltimore: American College Health Association.

American College Health Association. (2006a). *National College Health Assessment: Reference Group Executive Summary, Spring.* Baltimore: American College Health Association.

American College Health Association. (2006b). *National College Health Assessment: Reference Group Executive Summary, Fall.* Baltimore: American College Health Association.

American College Health Association. (2007a). *National College Health Assessment: Reference Group Executive Summary, Spring.* Baltimore: American College Health Association.

American College Health Association. (2007b). *National College Health Assessment: Reference Group Executive Summary, Fall.* Baltimore: American College Health Association.

American College Health Association. (2008a). *National College Health Assessment: Reference Group Executive Summary, Spring.* Baltimore: American College Health Association.

American College Health Association. (2008b). *National College Health Assessment: Reference Group Executive Summary, Fall.* Baltimore: American College Health Association.

Bachman, R. (1998a). The factors related to rape reporting behavior and arrest: New evidence from the national crime survey. *Criminal Justice and Behavior, 25,* 8–29.

Bachman, R. (1998b, October). *A comparison of annual incidence rates and contextual characteristics of intimate perpetrated violence against women from the National Crime Victimization Survey (NCVS) and the National Violence Against Women Survey (NVAW).* Background paper for Workshop on Building Data Systems for Monitoring and Responding to Violence Against Women, U.S. Department of Justice, National Institute of Justice and Bureau of Justice Statistics, and U.S. Department of Health and Human Services, National Center for Injury Prevention and Control and National Center for Health Statistics, Arlington, VA.

Bachman, R., Paternoster, R., & Ward, S. (1992). The rationality of sexual offending: Testing a deterrence/rational choice conception of sexual assault. *Law and Society Review, 26,* 401–432.

Bachman, R., & Taylor, B. (1994). The measurement of family violence and rape by the redesigned National Crime Victimization Survey. *Justice Quarterly, 11,* 499–512.

Banyard, V. L, Moynihan, M. M., & Plante, E. G. (2007). Sexual violence prevention through bystander education: An experimental evaluation. *Journal of Community Psychology, 35,* 463–481.

Banyard, V. L, Plante, E. G., & Moynihan, M. M. (2005). *Rape prevention through bystander education: Bringing a broader community perspective to sexual violence prevention.* Washington, DC: U.S. Department of Justice, National Institute of Justice.

Banyard, V. L., Ward, S., Cohn, E. S., Plante, E. G., Moorhead, C., & Walsh, W. (2007). Unwanted sexual contact on campus: A comparison of women's and men's experiences. *Violence and Victims, 22,* 52–70.

Barberet, B., Fisher, B. S., & Taylor, H. (2004). *University student safety in the East Midlands.* London: Home Office.

Basile, K. C. (1999). Rape by acquiescence: The ways in which women "give in" to unwanted sex with their husbands. *Violence Against Women, 5,* 1036–1058.

Basile, K. C., & Saltzman, L. E. (2002). *Sexual violence surveillance: Uniform definitions and recommended data elements.* Atlanta, GA: National Center for Injury Prevention and Control, Centers for Disease Control and Prevention.

Baum, K., & Klaus, K. (2005). *Violent victimization of college students, 1995–2002.* Washington, DC: U.S. Department of Justice, Office of Justice Programs, Bureau of Justice Statistics.

Belknap, J. (1996). *The invisible woman: Gender, crime, and justice.* Belmont, CA: Wadsworth.

Belknap, J., & Erez, E. (2007). Violence against women on college campuses: Rape, intimate partner abuse and sexual harassment. In B. S. Fisher & J. J. Sloan III (Eds.), *Campus crime: Legal, social, and policy perspectives* (2nd ed., pp. 188–209). Springfield, IL: Charles C Thomas.

Belknap, J., Fisher, B. S., & Cullen, F. T. (1999). The development of a comprehensive measure of the sexual victimization of college women. *Violence Against Women, 5,* 185–214.

Best, J. (1990). *Threatened children: Rhetoric and concern about child-victims.* Chicago: University of Chicago Press.

Biaggio, M. K., Brownell, A., & Watts, D. L. (1991). Reporting and seeking support by victims of sexual offenses. *Journal of Offender Rehabilitation, 17,* 33–42.

Bjerregaard, B. (2000). An empirical study of stalking victimization. *Violence and Victims, 15,* 389–405.

Black, D. (1983). Crime as social control. *American Sociological Review, 48,* 34–45.

Bondurant, B. (2001). University women's acknowledgment of rape: Individual, situational, and social factors. *Violence Against Women, 7,* 294–314.

Boney-McCoy, S., & Finkelhor, D. (1995). Prior victimization: A risk factor for child abuse and for PTSD-related symptomology among sexually abused youth. *Child Abuse and Neglect, 19,* 1401–1421.

Botta, R. A. & Pingree, S. (1997). Interpersonal communication and rape: Women acknowledge their assaults. *Journal of Health Communication, 2,* 197–212.

Bottoms, A. E. (1994). Environmental criminology. In M. Maguire, R. Morgan, & R. Reiner (Eds.), *The Oxford handbook of criminology* (pp. 585–656). New York: Oxford University Press.

Brady, T. V. (1996). *Measuring what matters: Part 1. Measures of fear, crime, and disorder.* Washington, DC: U.S. Department of Justice, National Institute of Justice.

Breitenbecher, K. H. (1999). The association between the perception of threat in a dating situation and sexual victimization. *Violence and Victims, 14,* 135–146.

Breitenbecher, K. H. (2000). Sexual assault on college campuses: Is an ounce of prevention enough? *Applied and Preventive Psychology, 9,* 23–52.

Breitenbecher, K. H. (2001). Sexual revictimization among women: A review of the literature focusing on empirical investigations. *Aggression and Violent Behavior, 6,* 415–432.

Brener, N. D., McMadon, P. M., Warren, C. W., & Douglas, K. A. (1999). Forced sexual intercourse and associated health-risk behaviors among female college students in the United States. *Journal of Consulting and Clinical Psychology, 67,* 252–259.

Broach, J. L., & Petretic, P. A. (2006). Beyond traditional definitions of assault: Expanding our focus to include sexually coercive experiences. *Journal of Family Violence, 21,* 477–486.

Brodeur, P. (1985). *Outrageous misconduct: The asbestos industry on trial.* New York: Pantheon Books.

Brownmiller, S. (1975). *Against our will: Men, women, and rape.* New York: Simon & Schuster.

Budz, D., Pegnall, N., & Townsley, M. (2001). *Lightning strikes twice: Preventing repeat home burglary.* Queensland, Australia: Criminal Justice Commission.

Bureau of Justice Statistics. (1994a). *Criminal victimization in the United States, 1992.* Washington, DC: U.S. Department of Justice.

Bureau of Justice Statistics. (1994b). *National Crime Victimization Survey: Questions and answers about the redesign.* Washington, DC: U.S. Department of Justice.

Bureau of Justice Statistics. (1997). *Criminal victimization in the United States, 1994.* Washington, DC: U.S. Department of Justice.

Burgess, A. W., & Holmstrom, L. L. (1975). Rape: The victim and the criminal justice system. In I. Drapkin & E. Viano (Eds.), *Victimology: A new focus* (Vol. 3, pp. 101–110). Lexington, MA: D.C. Heath.

Burling, P. (2003). *Crime on campus: Analyzing and managing the increasing risk of institutional liability* (2nd ed.). Washington, DC: National Association of College and University Attorneys.

Burt, M. R. (1980). Cultural myths and supports for rape. *Journal of Personality and Social Psychology, 38,* 217–230.

Campus Awareness and Campus Security Act of 1990, Title II of Pub. L. 101–542 (1990).

Canadian Urban Victimization Survey. (1988). *Multiple victimization* (Bulletin No. 10). Ottawa, ON: Ministry of the Solicitor General.

Canter, D., & Lynch, J. P. (2000). Self-report surveys as measures of crime and criminal victimization. In D. Duffee (Ed.), *Criminal justice 2000: Vol. 4—Measurement and analysis of crime and justice* (pp. 85–138). Washington, DC: U.S. Department of Justice.

Carter, S. D., & Bath, C. (2007). The evolution and components of the Jeanne Clery Act: Implications on higher education. In B. S. Fisher & J. J. Sloan (Eds.), *Campus crime: Legal, social, and policy perspectives* (2nd ed., pp. 27–44). Springfield, IL: Charles Thomas.

Cass, A. (2007). Routine activities and sexual assault: An analysis of individual- and school-level factors. *Violence and Victims, 22,* 350–366.

Catalano, S. M. (2004). *Criminal victimization, 2003* (NCJ 210674). Washington, DC: U.S. Department of Justice, Office of Justice Programs.

Chapleau, K. M., Oswald, D. L., & Russell, B. L. (2003). Male rape myths: The role of gender, violence, and sexism. *Journal of Interpersonal Violence, 23,* 600–615.

Clarke, R. V. (1980). Situational crime prevention: Theory and practice. *British Journal of Criminology,* 20, 136–147.

Clarke, R. V. (1982). Situational crime prevention: Its theoretical basis and practical scope. In M. Tonry & N. Morris (Eds.), *Crime and justice: An annual review of research* (Vol. 4, pp. 225–256). Chicago: University of Chicago Press.

Clarke, R. V., & Felson, M. (in press). The origins of routine activity theory approach and situational crime prevention. In F. T. Cullen, C. L. Jonson, A. J. Myer, & F. Adler (Eds.), *The origins of American criminology: Advances in criminological theory* (Vol. 16). New Brunswick, NJ: Transaction.

Classen, C. C., Palesh, O. G., & Aggarwal, R. (2005). Sexual revictimization: A review of the empirical literature. *Trauma, Violence, and Abuse, 6,* 103–129.

Cloward, R. A. (1959). Illegitimate means, anomie, and deviant behavior. *American Sociological Review, 24,* 164–176.

Cohen, L. E., & Felson, M. (1979). Social change and crime rate trends: A routine activity approach. *American Sociological Review, 44,* 588–608.

Cohen, L., Kluegel, J., & Land, K. (1981). Social inequality and predatory criminal victimization: An exposition and a test of a formal theory. *American Sociological Review, 46,* 505–524.

Coid, J., Petruckevitch, A., Feder, G., Chung, W., Richardson, J., & Moorey, S. (2001). Relation between childhood sexual and physical abuse and risk of revictimisation in women: A cross-sectional survey. *Lancet, 358,* 450–454.

Coleman, F. (1997). Stalking behavior and the cycle of domestic violence. *Journal of Interpersonal Violence, 12,* 420–432.

College Alcohol Study. (2009). Retrieved October 1, 2009, from http://www.hsph.harvard.edu/cas/About/index.html

Combs-Lane, A. M., & Smith, D. W. (2002). Risk of sexual victimization in college women: The role of behavioral intentions and risk-taking behaviors. *Journal of Interpersonal Violence, 17,* 165–183.

Core Institute. (2009). Retrieved October 1, 2009, from http://www.core.siuc.edu

Crawford, E., Wright, M. O., & Birchmeier, Z. (2008). Drug-facilitated sexual assault: College women's risk of perception and behavioral choices. *Journal of American College Health, 57,* 261–272.

Crowell, N. A., & Burgess, A. W. (Eds.). (1996). *Understanding violence against women.* Washington, DC: National Academy Press.

Cullen, F. T., Eck, J. E., & Lowenkamp, C. T. (2002). Environmental corrections: A new paradigm for effective probation and parole supervision. *Federal Probation, 66*(2), 28–37.

Cullen, F. T., & Gendreau, P. (2000). Assessing correctional rehabilitation: Policy, practice, and prospects. In J. Horney (Ed.), *Criminal justice 2000: Vol. 3. Policies, processes, and decisions in the criminal justice system* (pp. 109–175). Washington, DC: National Institute of Justice.

Cupach, W. R., & Spitzberg, B. H. (2004). *The dark side of relationship pursuit: From attraction to obsession and stalking.* Mahwah, NJ: Erlbaum.

Daigle, L. E., Fisher, B. S., & Cullen, F. T. (2008). The violent and sexual victimization of college women: Is repeat victimization a problem? *Journal of Interpersonal Violence, 23,* 1296–1313.

Daigle, L. E., Fisher, B. S., & Guthrie, P. (2007). Experiencing more than one criminal victimization: What researchers know about its terminology, reoccurrence and characteristics, and causes. In R. C. Davis, A. J. Lurigio, & S. Herman (Eds.), *Victims of crime* (3rd ed., pp. 211–232). Thousand Oaks, CA: Sage.

Daigle, L. E., Fisher, B. S., & Stewart, M. (2009). The effectiveness of sexual victimization prevention among college students: A summary of "what works." *Victims and Offenders, 4,* 309–404.

Davis, K. E., & Frieze, I. H. (2000). Research on stalking: What do we know and where do we go? *Violence and Victims, 15,* 473–487.

Day, K. (1995). Assault prevention as social control: Women and sexual assault prevention on urban college campuses. *Journal of Environmental Psychology, 15,* 261–281.

DeKeseredy, W. S., & Schwartz, M. D. (1998). *Women abuse on campus: Results from the Canadian National Survey.* Thousand Oaks, CA: Sage.

Desai, S., Arias, I., Thompson, M. P., & Basile, K. C. (2002). Childhood victimization and subsequent adult revictimization assessed in a nationally representative sample of women and men. *Violence and Victims, 17,* 639–653.

Dowdall, G. W. (2007). The role of alcohol abuse in college student victimization. In B. S. Fisher & J. J. Sloan (Eds.), *Campus crime: Legal, social and policy perspectives* (2nd ed., pp. 167–187). Springfield, IL: Charles C Thomas.

Dunn, P. C., Vail-Smith, K., & Knight, S. M. (1999). What date/acquaintance rape victims tell others: A study of college recipients of disclosure. *Journal of American College Health, 47,* 213–222.

Eck, J. E. (1994). *Drug markets and drug places: A case-control study of the spatial structure of illicit drug dealing.* Unpublished doctoral dissertation, University of Maryland.

Eigenberg, H. M. (1990). The National Crime Survey and rape: The case of the missing question. *Criminology, 7,* 655–671.

Estrich, S. (1987). *Real rape: How the legal system victimizes women who say no.* Cambridge, MA: Harvard University Press.

Farrell, G. (1992). Multiple victimization: Its extent and significance. *International Review of Victimology, 2,* 85–102.

Farrell, G., & Pease, K. (2006). Preventing repeat residential burglary. In B. C. Welsh & D. P. Farrington (Eds.), *Preventing crime: What works for children, offenders, victims, and places* (pp. 161–178). Dordrecht, Netherlands: Springer.

Farrell, G., Phillips, C., & Pease, K. (1995). Like taking candy: Why does repeat victimization occur? *British Journal of Criminology, 35,* 384–399.

Farrell, G., Sousa, W., & Weisel, D. (2002). The time-window effect in the measurement of repeat victimization: A methodology for its examination, and an empirical study. In N. Tilley (Ed.), *Crime prevention studies: Vol. 14—Analysis for crime prevention* (pp. 15–27). Monsey, NY: Criminal Justice Press.

Farrell, G., Weisburd, D., & Wyckoff, L. (2000). Survey results suggest need for stalking training. *Police Chief, 67,* 162–167.

Feldman-Summers, S., & Ashworth, C. D. (1981). Factors related to intentions to report a rape. *Journal of Social Issues, 37,* 53–70.

Felson, M. (1995). Those who discourage crime. In J. E. Eck & D. Weisburd (Eds.), *Crime and place* (pp. 53–66). Monsey, NY: Willow Tree Press.

Felson, M. (2002). *Crime and everyday life* (3rd ed.). Thousand Oaks, CA: Sage.

Fiebert, M. S., & Tucci, L. M. (1998). Sexual coercion: Men victimized by women. *Journal of Men's Studies, 6,* 127–133.

Fienberg, S. (1980). Statistical modeling in the analysis of repeat victimization. In S. Fienberg & A. Reiss (Eds.), *Indicators of crime and criminal justice: Quantitative studies* (pp. 54–58). Washington, DC: U.S. Department of Justice.

Finkelhor, D., & Asdigian, N. L. (1996). Risk factors for youth victimization: Beyond a lifestyles/routine activities theory approach. *Violence and Victims, 11,* 3–19.

Finkelhor, D., & Yllo, K. (1985). *License to rape.* New York: Holt, Rinehart and Winston.

Fisher, B. S. (1995). Crime and fear on campus. *The Annuals of the American Academy of Political and Social Science, 539,* 85–101.

Fisher, B. S., & Cullen, F. T. (1999). *Violent victimization against college women: Results from a national-level study* (Final Report). Washington, DC: U.S. Department of Justice, Bureau of Justice Statistics.

Fisher, B. S. & Cullen, F. T. (2000). Measuring the sexual victimization of women: Evolution, current controversies, and future research. In D. Duffee (Ed.), *Criminal justice 2000 Volumes: Vol. 4—Measurement and analysis of crime and justice* (pp. 317–390). Washington, DC: National Institute of Justice.

Fisher, B. S., Cullen, F. T., & Turner, M. G. (1999). *The extent and nature of sexual victimization among college women: A national-level analysis* (Final Report). Washington, DC: U.S. Department of Justice, National Institute of Justice.

Fisher, B. S., Cullen, F. T., & Turner, M. G. (2000). *The sexual victimization of college women.* Washington, DC: U.S. Department of Justice, Bureau of Justice Statistics.

Fisher, B. S., Cullen, F. T., & Turner, M. G. (2002). Being pursued: Stalking victimization in a national study of college women. *Criminology and Public Policy, 1,* 257–308.

Fisher, B. S., Daigle, L. E., & Cullen, F. T. (2008). Rape against women: What can research offer to guide the development of prevention programs and risk reduction interventions? *Journal of Contemporary Criminal Justice, 24,* 163–177.

Fisher, B. S., Daigle, L. E., & Cullen, F. T. (in press). What distinguishes single from recurrent sexual victims? The role of lifestyle-routine activities and first-incident characteristics. *Justice Quarterly.*

Fisher, B. S., Daigle, L. E., Cullen, F. T., & Santana, S. (2007). Assessing the efficacy of the protective action-sexual victimization completion nexus. *Violence and Victims, 22,* 18–42.

Fisher, B. S., Daigle, L. E., Cullen, F. T., & Turner, M. G. (2003a). Reporting sexual victimization to the police and others: Results from a national-level study of college women. *Criminal Justice and Behavior, 30,* 6–38.

Fisher, B. S., Daigle, L. E., Cullen, F. T., & Turner, M. G. (2003b). Acknowledging sexual victimization as rape: Results from a national-level study. *Justice Quarterly, 20,* 535–574.

Fisher, B. S., Hartman, J. L., Cullen, F. T., & Turner, M. G. (2002). Making campuses safer for students: The Clery Act as symbolic legal reform. *Stetson Law Review, 32,* 61–89.

Fisher, B. S., & Sloan, J. J. (Eds.). (2007). *Campus crime: Legal, social, and policy perspectives* (2nd ed.). Springfield, IL: Charles C Thomas.

Fisher, B. S., Sloan, J. J., III, & Cullen, F. T., with the assistance of Lu, C., & Nasar, J. L. (1995). *Understanding crime victimization among college students: Implications for crime prevention* (Final report). Washington, DC: U.S. Department of Justice, National Institute of Justice.

Fisher, B. S., Sloan, J. J., III, Cullen, F. T., & Lu, C. (1998). Crime in the ivory tower: The level and sources of student victimization. *Criminology, 36,* 671–710.

Fisher, B. S., & Stewart, M. (2007). Vulnerabilities and opportunities 101: The extent, nature, and impact of stalking among college students and implications for campus policy and programs. In B. S. Fisher & J. J. Sloan III (Eds.), *Campus crime: Legal, social, and policy perspectives* (2nd ed., pp. 210–230). Springfield, IL: Charles C Thomas.

Fitzgerald, L. F., Schullman, S. L., Bailey, N., Richards, M., Swecker, J., Glid, Y., et al. (1988). The incidence and dimensions of sexual harassment in academia and the workplace. *Journal of Vocational Behavior, 32,* 152–175.

Flack, W. F., Jr., Caron, M. L., Leinen, S. J., Breitenbach, K. G., Barber, A. M., Brown, E. N., et al. (2008). "The red zone": Temporal risk for unwanted sex among college students. *Journal of Interpersonal Violence, 23,* 1177–1196.

Fleming, J., Mullen, P. E., Sibthorpe, B., & Bammer, G. (1999). The long-term impact of childhood sexual abuse in Australian women. *Child Abuse and Neglect, 23,* 145–159.

Frazier, P. A., & Burnett, J. W. (1994). Immediate coping strategies among rape victims. *Journal of Counseling and Development, 72,* 633–639.

Frazier, P. A., & Seales, L. M. (1997). Acquaintance rape is real rape. In M. D. Schwartz (Ed.), *Researching sexual violence against women: Methodological and personal perspectives* (pp. 54–64). Thousand Oaks, CA: Sage.

Gelles, R. J., & Straus, M. A. (1988). *Intimate violence: The definitive study of the causes and consequences of abuse in the American family.* New York: Simon & Schuster.

George, L. K., Winfield, I., & Blazer, D. G. (1992). Sociocultural factors in sexual assault: Comparison of two representative samples of women. *Journal of Social Issues, 48,* 105–125.

Gibbs, N. (1991a, June 3). When is it rape? *Time,* pp. 48–54.

Gibbs, N. (1991b, June 3). The clamor on campus. *Time,* pp. 54–55.

Gidycz, C. A., Coble, C. N., Latham, L., & Layman, M. J. (1993). Sexual assault experience in adulthood and prior victimization experiences: A prospective analysis. *Psychology of Women Quarterly, 17,* 151–168.

Gidycz, C. A., Hanson, K., & Layman, J. L. (1995). A prospective analysis of the relationships among sexual assault experiences: An extension of previous findings. *Psychology of Women Quarterly, 19,* 5–29.

Gidycz, C. A., & Koss, M. P. (1991). Predictors of long-term sexual assault trauma among a national sample of victimized college women. *Violence and Victims, 6,* 175–190.

Gidycz, C. A., Layman, M. J., Rich, C. L., Crothers, M., Gylys, J., Matorin, A., et al. (2001). An evaluation of an acquaintance rape prevention program: Impact on attitudes, sexual aggression, and sexual victimization. *Journal of Interpersonal Violence, 16,* 1120–1138.

Gidycz, C. A., Lynn, S. J., Rich, C. L., Marioni, N. L., Loh, C., Blackwell, L. M., et al. (2001). The evaluation of a sexual assault risk reduction program: A multisite investigation. *Journal of Consulting and Clinical Psychology, 69,* 1073–1078.

Gidycz, C. A., Orchowski, L. M., King, C. R., & Rich, C. L. (2008). Sexual victimization and health-risk behaviors: A prospective analysis of college women. *Journal of Interpersonal Violence, 23,* 744–763.

Gidycz, C. A., Rich, C. L., Orchowski, L., King, C., & Miller, A. K. (2006). The evaluation of a sexual assault self-defense and risk reduction program for college women: A prospective study. *Psychology of Women Quarterly, 30,* 173–186.

Gilbert, N. (1991, Spring). The phantom epidemic of sexual assault. *Public Interest, 103,* 54–65.

Gilbert, N. (1992, May-June). Realities and mythologies of rape. *Society,* pp. 4–10.

Gilbert, N. (1995). Violence against women social research and sexual politics. In R. J. Simon (Ed.), *Neither victim nor enemy: Women's Freedom Network looks at gender in America* (pp. 95–118). Lanham, MD: Women's Freedom Network and University Press of America.

Gilbert, N. (1997). Advocacy research and social policy. In M. Tonry (Ed.), *Crime and justice: A review of research* (Vol. 22, pp. 101–148). Chicago: University of Chicago Press.

Glassner, B. (1999). *The culture of fear: Why Americans are afraid of the wrong things.* New York: Basic Books.

Golding, J. M., Siegal, J., Sorenson, S. B., Burnam, M. A., & Stein, J. A. (1989). Social support sources following sexual assault. *Journal of Community Psychology, 17,* 92–107.

Gross, A. M., Winslett, A., Roberts, M., & Gohn, C. L. (2006). An examination of sexual violence against college women. *Violence Against Women, 12,* 288–300.

Hall, D. M. (1998). The victims of stalking. In J. R. Meloy (Ed.), *The psychology of stalking: Clinical and forensic perspectives* (pp. 115-137). San Diego, CA: Academic Press.

Hamby, S. L., & Koss, M. P. (2003). Shades of gray: A qualitative study of terms used in the measurement of sexual victimization. *Psychology of Women Quarterly, 27,* 243–255.

Harned, M. S. (2004). Does it matter what you call it? The relationship between labeling unwanted sexual experiences and distress. *Journal of Consulting and Clinical Psychology, 72,* 1090–1099.

Harris Interactive. (2001). *Presenting: The class of 2001.* Retrieved October 1, from http://www.harrisinteractive.com/news/printerfriend/index.asp?NewsID=292

Harris Interactive. (2004). *College women close technology gender gap.* Retrieved October 1, from http://www.harrisinteractive.com/news/allnewsbydate.asp?NewsID=773

Hart, T. C. (2003). *National Crime Victimization Survey, 1995–2000: Violent victimization of college students.* Washington, DC: U.S. Department of Justice, Office of Justice Programs, Bureau of Justice Statistics.

Hart, T. C., & Rennison, C. (2003). *Reporting crime to the police, 1992–2000.* Washington, DC: Bureau of Justice Statistics, U.S. Department of Justice.

Hickman, S. E., & Muehlenhard, C. L. (1997). College women's fears and precautionary behaviors relating to acquaintance rape and stranger rape. *Psychology of Women Quarterly, 21,* 527–547.

Hill, C., & Silva, E. (2005). *Drawing the line: Sexual harassment on campus.* Washington, DC: American Association of University Women Educational Foundation.

Hindelang, M. J., Gottfredson, M. R., & Garofalo, J. (1978). *Victims of personal crime: An empirical foundation for a theory of personal victimization.* Cambridge, MA: Ballinger.

Holmes, R. M. (1993). Stalking in America: Types and methods of criminal stalkers. *Journal of Contemporary Criminal Justice, 9,* 317–327.

Humphrey, J. A., & White, J. W. (2000). Women's vulnerability to sexual assault from adolescence to young adulthood. *Journal of Adolescent Health, 27,* 419–424.

Jeanne Clery Disclosure of Campus Security Policy and Campus Crime Statistics Act, 20 U.S.C. § 1092(f) (1998).

Jordan, C. E. (2009). Advancing the study of violence against women: Evolving research agendas into science. *Violence Against Women, 15,* 393–419.

Jordan, C. E., Wilcox, P., & Pritchard, A. J. (2007). Stalking acknowledgement and reporting among college women experiencing intrusive behaviors: Implications for the emergence of a "classic stalking case." *Journal of Criminal Justice, 35,* 556–569.

Kahn, A. S., Jackson, J., Kully, C., Badger, K., & Halvorsen, J. (2003). Calling it rape: Differences in experiences of women who do or do not label their sexual assault as rape. *Psychology of Women Quarterly, 18,* 53–66.

Kahn, A. S., & Mathie, V. A. (2000). Understanding the unacknowledged rape victim. In C. B. Travis & J. W. White (Eds.), *Sexuality, society, and feminism* (pp. 377–403). Washington, DC: American Psychological Association.

Kahn, A. S., Mathie, V. A., & Torgler, C. (1994). Rape scripts and rape acknowledgment. *Psychology of Women Quarterly, 18,* 53–66.

Kalof, L. (2000). Vulnerability to sexual coercion among college women: A longitudinal study. *Gender Issues, 18,* 47–58.

Kanin, E. J. (1957). Male aggression in dating-courtship relations. *American Journal of Sociology, 63,* 197–204.

Karjane, H. M., Fisher, B. S., & Cullen, F. T. (2001). *Campus sexual assault: How America's institutions of higher education respond* (NCJ 205521-Final Report). Washington, DC: U.S. Department of Justice, National Institute of Justice.

Kilpatrick, D. G., Acierno, R., Resnick, H. S., Saunders, B. E., & Best, C. L. (1997). A 2-year longitudinal analysis of the relationships between violent assault and substance use in women. *Journal of Consulting and Clinical Psychology, 65,* 834–847.

Kilpatrick, D. G., Edmunds, C. N., & Seymour, A. K. (1992). *Rape in America: A report to the nation.* Arlington, VA: National Victim Center.

Kilpatrick, D. G., Resnick, H. S., Ruggiero, K. J., Conoscenti, L. M., & McCauley, J. M. (2007). *Drug-facilitated, incapacitated, and forcible rape: A national study* (NCJ 219181-Final Report). Washington, DC: U.S. Department of Justice, National Institute of Justice.

Kirkpatrick, C., & Kanin, E. (1957). Male sex aggression on a university campus. *American Sociological Review, 22,* 52–58.

Koss, M. P. (1985). The hidden rape victim. *Psychology of Women Quarterly, 48,* 61–75.

Koss, M. P. (1988a). Afterword. In R. Warshaw (Ed.), *I never called it rape: The* Ms. *report on recognizing, fighting, and surviving date and acquaintance rape* (pp. 189–210). New York: Harper & Row.

Koss, M. P. (1988b). Hidden rape: Sexual aggression and victimization in a national sample of students in higher education. In A. W. Burgess (Ed.), *Rape and sexual assault* (pp. 3–25). New York: Garland.

Koss, M. P. (1989). Hidden rape: Sexual aggression and victimization in a national sample of college students in higher education. In M. A. Pirog-Good & J. E. Stets (Eds.), *Violence in dating relationships: Emerging social issues* (pp. 145–168). New York: Praeger.

Koss, M. P. (1992). The undetection of rape: Methodological choices influence incidence estimates. *Journal of Social Issues, 48,* 61–75.

Koss, M. P. (1993a). Detecting the scope of rape: A review of prevalence research methods. *Journal of Interpersonal Violence, 8,* 198–222.

Koss, M. P. (1993b). Rape: Scope, impact, interventions, and public policy responses. *American Psychologist, 48,* 1062–1069.

Koss, M. P. (1996). The measurement of rape victimization in crime surveys. *Criminal Justice and Behavior, 23,* 55–69.

Koss, M. P., Abbey, A., Campbell, R., Cook, S., Norris, J., Testa, M., et al. (2007). Revising the SES: A collaborative process to improve assessment of sexual aggression and victimization. *Psychology of Women Quarterly, 31,* 357–370.

Koss, M. P., & Cook, S. L. (1993). Facing the facts: Date and acquaintance rape are significant problems for women. In R. J. Gelles & D. R. Loseke (Eds.), *Current controversies on family violence* (pp. 147–156). Newbury Park, CA: Sage.

Koss, M. P., & Gidycz, C. A. (1985). The sexual experiences survey: Reliability and validity. *Journal of Consulting and Clinical Psychology, 53,* 442–443.

Koss, M. P., Gidycz, C. A., & Wisniewski, N. (1987). The scope of rape: Incidence and prevalence of sexual aggression and victimization in a national sample of higher education students. *Journal of Counseling and Clinical Psychology, 55,* 162–170.

Koss, M. P., & Oros, C. (1982). Sexual experiences survey: A research instrument investigating sexual aggression and victimization. *Journal of Consulting and Clinical Psychology, 50,* 455–457.

Krebs, C. P., Lindquist, C. H., Warner, T. D., Fisher, B. S., & Martin, S. L. (2007). *The campus sexual assault (CSA) study* (NCJ 221153-Final Report). Washington, DC: U.S. Department of Justice, National Institute of Justice.

Kurtzman, L. (2009, February 22). But was it rape? *Cincinnati Enquirer,* pp. F1, F4.

Lane, K. E., & Gwartney-Gibbs, P. A. (1985). Violence in the context of dating and sex. *Journal of Family Issues, 6,* 45–49.

Lauritsen, J. L. (2005). Social and scientific influences on the measurement of criminal victimization. *Journal of Quantitative Criminology, 21,* 245–266.

Lauritsen, J., & Davis Quinet, K. F. (1995). Repeat victimization among adolescents and young adults. *Journal of Quantitative Criminology, 11,* 143–166.

Lauritsen, J. L., Sampson, R. J., & Laub, J. H. (1991). The link between offending and victimization among adolescents. *Criminology, 29,* 265–292.

Lauritsen, J. L. (2009). Safeguarding and improving the nation's statistics on crime and justice. *The Criminologist, 34,* 3–6.

Layman, M., Gidycz, C. A., & Lynn, S. J. (1996). Unacknowledged versus acknowledged rape victims: Situational factors and posttraumatic stress. *Journal of Abnormal Psychology, 105,* 124–131.

Lehnen, R. G., & Skogan, W. G. (Eds.). (1981). *The National Crime Survey: Working papers: Vol. 1—Current and historical perspectives* (NCJ 75374). Washington, DC: U.S. Department of Justice, Bureau of Justice Statistics.

Lehnen, R. G., & Skogan, W. G. (Eds.). (1984). *The National Crime Survey: Working papers: Vol. 2—Methodological issues* (NCJ 90307). Washington, DC: U.S. Department of Justice, Bureau of Justice Statistics.

Littleton, H. L., Axson, D., Breitkopf, C. R., & Berenson, A. (2006). Rape acknowledgment and postassault experiences: How acknowledgment status relates to disclosure, coping, worldview, and reactions received from others. *Violence and Victims, 21,* 761–778.

Livingston, J. A., Buddie, A. M., Testa, M., & VanZile-Tamsen, C. (2004). The role of sexual precedence in verbal sexual coercion. *Psychology of Women Quarterly, 28,* 287–297.

Logan, T. K., Leukefeld, C., & Walker, B. (2000). Stalking as a variant of intimate violence: Implications from a young adult sample. *Violence and Victims, 15,* 91–111.

Logan, T. K., Walker, R., Jordan, C. E., & Leukefeld, C. G. (2006). *Women and victimization: Contributing factors, interventions, and implications.* Washington, DC: American Psychological Association.

Lonsway, K. S., Banyard, V. L., Berkowitz, A. D., Gidycz, C. A., Katz, J. T., Koss, M. P., et al. (2009). *Rape prevention and risk reduction: Review of the research literature for practitioners.* VAWnet: The National Online Resources Center on Violence Against Women. Retrieved October 1, 2009, from http://www.vawnet.org/Assoc_Files_VAWnet/AR_RapePrevention.pdf

Lott, B., Reilly, M. E., & Howard, D. R. (1982). Sexual assault and harassment: A campus community case study. *Journal of Women in Culture and Society, 8,* 296–319.

Lowney, K. S., & Best, J. (1995). Stalking strangers and lovers: Changing media typifications of a new crime problem. In J. Best (Ed.), *Images of issues: Typifying contemporary social problems* (2nd ed., pp. 33–57). New York: Aldine de Gruyter.

Lynch, J. P. (1987). Routine activities and victimization at work. *Journal of Quantitative Criminology, 3,* 283–300.

Lynch, J. P. (1996a). Clarifying divergent estimates of rape from two national surveys. *Public Opinion Quarterly, 60,* 410–430.

Lynch, J. P. (1996b). Understanding differences in the estimates of rape from self-report surveys. In R. J. Simon (Ed.), *From data to public policy: Affirmative action, sexual harassment, domestic violence, and social welfare* (pp. 121–142). Lanham, MD: University Press of America.

Mac Donald, H. (2008, Winter). The campus rape myth: The reality: Bogus statistics, feminist victimology, and university-approved sex toys. *City Journal.* Retrieved October 1, 2008, from http://www.city-journal.org/2008/18_1_campus_rape.html

Marks, C. A. (1997). The Kansas stalking law: A "credible threat" to victims. *Washburn Law Journal, 36,* 468–498.

Marx, B. P., Calhoun, K. S., Wilson, A. E., & Meyerson, L. A. (2001). Sexual revictimization prevention: An outcome evaluation. *Journal of Consulting and Clinical Psychology, 69,* 25–32.

McAnaney, K. G., Curliss, L. A., & Abeyta-Price, C. E. (1993). From imprudence to crime: Anti-stalking laws. *Notre Dame Law Review, 68,* 819–909.

McMullin, D., & White, J. W. (2006). Long-term effects of labeling a rape experience. *Psychology of Women Quarterly, 30,* 96–105.

Meloy, J. R. (1996). Stalking (obsessional following): A review of some preliminary studies. *Aggression and Violent Behavior, 1,* 147–162.

Merton, R. K. (1973). *The sociology of science: Theoretical and empirical investigations* (N. W. Storer, Ed.). Chicago: University of Chicago Press.

Messman-Moore, T. L., & Brown, A. L. (2006). Risk perception, rape and sexual revictimization: A prospective study of college women. *Psychology of Women Quarterly, 30,* 159–172.

Messman-Moore, T. L., Coates, A. A., Gaffey, K. J., & Johnson, C. F. (2008). Sexuality, substance use, and susceptibility to victimization: Risk for rape and sexual coercion in a prospective study of college women. *Journal of Interpersonal Violence, 23,* 1730–1746.

Miethe, T. D., & Meier, R. F. (1994). *Crime and its social context: Toward an integrated theory of offenders, victims, and situations.* Albany: State University of New York Press.

Mohler-Kuo, M., Dowdall, G. W., Koss, M. P., & Wechsler, H. (2004). Correlates of rape while intoxicated in a national sample of college women. *Journal of Studies on Alcohol, 65,* 37–45.

Monaghan, P. (1998, March 6). Beyond the Hollywood myths: Researchers examine stalkers and their victims. *Chronicle of Higher Education,* pp. A17, A20.

Moynihan, M. M., & Banyard, V. L. (2008). Community responsibility for preventing sexual violence: A pilot study with campus Greeks and intercollegiate athletes. *Journal of Prevention and Intervention in the Community, 36,* 23–38.

Muehlenhard, C. L., & Linton, M. A. (1987). Date rape and sexual aggression in dating situations: Incidence and risk factors. *Journal of Counseling Psychology, 34,* 186–196.

Muehlenhard, C. L., Sympson, S. C., Phelps, J. L., & Highby, B. J. (1994). Are rape statistics exaggerated? A response to criticisms of contemporary rape research. *Journal of Sex Research, 31,* 144–146.

Mustaine, E. E. (1997). Victimization risks and routine activities: A theoretical examination using a gender-specific and domain-specific model. *American Journal of Criminal Justice, 22,* 41–70.

Mustaine, E. E., & Tewksbury, R. (1999). A routine activity theory explanation for women's stalking victimizations. *Violence Against Women, 5,* 43–62.

Mustaine, E. E., & Tewksbury, R. (2002). Sexual assault of college women: A feminist interpretation of routine activities analysis. *Criminal Justice Review, 27,* 89–123.

Mustaine, E. E., & Tewksbury, R. (2007). The routine activities and criminal victimization of students: Lifestyle and related factors. In B. S. Fisher & J. J. Sloan III (Eds.), *Campus crime: Legal, social, and policy perspectives* (2nd ed., pp. 147–166). Springfield, IL: Charles C Thomas.

Nack, W. (1992, February 17). A crushing verdict. *Sports Illustrated,* pp. 22–23.

Nagin, D. S., & Paternoster, R. (1991). On the relationship of past and future participation in delinquency. *Criminology, 29,* 153–190.

National Board for Crime Prevention. (1994). *Wise after the event: Tackling repeat victimization.* London: Home Office.

National Center for Education Statistics. (2005). *Integrated Postsecondary Education System, "Fall Enrollment Survey."* Retrieved October 1, 2009, from http://www.nces.ed.gov/programs/digest/2005menu_tables.asp

National Victim Center. (1997). *Stalking and the law.* Arlington, VA: National Victim Center.

Negrusz, A., Juhascik, M., & Gaensslen, R. E. (2005). *Estimate of the incidence of drug-facilitated sexual assault in the U.S., (Final Report).* Washington, DC: U.S. Department of Justice, National Institute of Justice.

Nicholas, S., Povey, D., Walker, A., & Kershaw, C. (2005). *Crime in England and Wales 2004/2005.* London: Home Office.

Nobles, M. R., Fox, K. A., Piquero, N., & Piquero, A. R. (2009). Career dimensions of stalking victimization and perpetration. *Justice Quarterly, 26*, 476–503.

Noll, J. G., Horowitz, L. A., Bonanno, G. A., Trickett, P. K., & Putnam, F. W. (2003). Revictimization and self-harm in females who experienced childhood sexual abuse: Results from a prospective study. *Journal of Interpersonal Violence, 18*, 1452–1471.

Norris, J., Nurius, P. S., & Graham, T. L. (1999). When a date changes from fun to dangerous: Factors affecting women's ability to distinguish. *Violence Against Women, 5*, 230–250.

Paludi, M., & Paludi, C. A., Jr. (Eds.). (2003). *Academic and workplace sexual harassment: A handbook of cultural, social science, management, and legal perspectives.* Westport, CT: Praeger.

Parrot, A. (1991). Institutionalized response: How can acquaintance rape be prevented? In A. Parrot & L. Bechhofer (Eds.), *Acquaintance rape: The hidden crime* (pp. 355–367). New York: Wiley.

Pathé, M., & Mullen, P. E. (1997). The impact of stalkers on their victims. *British Journal of Psychiatry, 170*, 12–17.

Payne, D. L., Lonsway, K. A., & Fitzgerald, L. F. (1999). Rape myth acceptance: Exploration of its structure and measurement using the Illinois rape myth acceptance scale. *Journal of Research in Personality, 33*, 27–68.

Pease, K. (1998). *Repeat victimization: Taking stock* (Crime Detection and Prevention Series Paper 90). London: Home Office.

Perkins, C. A., Klaus, P. A., Bastian, L. D., & Cohen, R. L. (1996). *Criminal victimization in the United States, 1993* (NCJ 151657). Washington, DC: U.S. Department of Justice, Bureau of Justice Statistics.

Peterson, Z. D., & Muehlenhard, C. L. (2004). Was it rape? The function of women's rape myth acceptance and definitions of sex in labeling their own experiences. *Sex Roles, 51*, 129–144.

Pitts, V. L., & Schwartz, M. D. (1993). Promoting self-blame in hidden rape cases. *Humanity and Society, 17*, 383–398.

Pleck, E. (1987). *Domestic tyranny: The making of American social policy against family violence from colonial times to the present.* New York: Oxford University Press.

Polvi, N., Looman, T., Humphries, C., & Pease, K. (1990). Repeat break-and-enter victimization: Time course and crime prevention opportunity. *Journal of Police Science and Administration, 17*, 8–11.

Raghavan, R., Bogart, L. M., Elliott, M. N., Vestal, K. D., & Schuster, M. A. (2004). Sexual victimization among a national probability sample of adolescent women. *Perspectives on Sexual and Reproductive Health, 36*, 225–232.

Rand, M., & Catalano, S. (2007). *Criminal victimization in the United States, 2006.* Washington, DC: U.S. Department of Justice, Office of Justice Programs, Bureau of Justice Statistics.

Randall, M., & Haskell, L. (1995). Sexual violence in women's lives: Findings from the Women's Safety Project, a community-based survey. *Violence Against Women, 1*, 6–31.

Reiss, A. (1980). Victim proneness in repeat victimization by type of crime. In S. Fienberg & S. A. Reiss (Eds.), *Indicators of crime and criminal justice: Quantitative studies* (pp. 41–53). Washington, DC: U.S. Department of Justice.

Rennison, C. M. (1999). *Criminal victimization 1998: Changes 1997–98 with trends 1993–98.* Washington, DC: U.S. Department of Justice, Office of Justice Programs, Bureau of Justice Statistics.

Rennison, C. M. (2002). *Rape and sexual assault: Reporting to police and medical attention, 1992–2000.* Washington, DC: U.S. Department of Justice.

Roberts, K. A. (2002). Stalking following the breakup of romantic relationships: Characteristics of stalking former partners. *Journal of Forensic Sciences, 47,* 1070–1077.

Robinson, M. B. (1998). Burglary revictimization: The time period of heightened risk. *British Journal of Criminology, 38,* 78–87.

Roiphe, K. (1993). *The morning after: Sex, fear, and feminism on campus.* Boston: Little, Brown.

Roodman, A. A., & Clum, G. A. (2001). Revictimization rates and method variance: A meta-analysis. *Clinical Psychology Review, 21,* 183–204.

Rozee, P. D., & Koss, M. P. (2001). Rape: A century of resistance. *Psychology of Women Quarterly, 25,* 295–311.

Ruback, R. B., Menard, K. S., Outlaw, M. C., & Shaffer, J. N. (1999). Normative advice to campus crime victims: Effects of gender, age, and alcohol. *Violence and Victims, 14,* 381–396.

Russell, D. E. H. (1982). The prevalence and incidence of forcible rape and attempted rape of females. *Victimology, 7,* 81–93.

Russell, D. E. H. (1986). *The secret trauma: Incest in the lives of girls and women.* New York: Basic Books.

Rymel, L. (2004). *What is the difference between rape and sexual assault?* School Violence Resource Center, Briefing Paper, College Sexual Assaults. Little Rock: University of Arkansas System, Criminal Justice Institute.

Sampson, A., & Phillips, C. (1992). *Multiple victimization: Racial attacks on an East London estate* (Police Research Group Crime Prevention Unit Series: Paper No. 36). London: Home Office Police Department.

Sampson, R. (2002). *Acquaintance rape of college students.* Washington, DC: Center for Problem-Oriented Policing, U.S. Department of Justice.

Scalzo, T. P. (2007). *Prosecuting alcohol-facilitated sexual assault.* Alexandra, VA: National District Attorneys Association, American Prosecutors Research Institute.

Schewe, P. A. (2006). Guidelines for developing rape prevention and risk interventions. In P. A. Schewe (Ed.), *Preventing violence in relationships: Interventions across the life span.* (pp. 107–136). Washington, DC: American Psychological Association.

Schreck, C. J. (1999). Criminal victimization and low self-control: An extension and test of a general theory of crime. *Justice Quarterly, 16,* 633–654.

Schreck, C. J., Stewart, E. A., & Fisher, B. S. (2006). Self-control, victimization, and their influence on risky activities and delinquent friends: A longitudinal analysis using panel data. *Journal of Quantitative Criminology, 22,* 319–340.

Schwartz, M., & DeKeseredy, W. (1997). *Sexual assault on the college campus: The role of male peer support.* Thousand Oaks, CA: Sage.

Schwartz, M., DeKeseredy, W., Tait, W., & Alvi, S. (2001). Male peer support and a feminist routine activities theory: Understanding sexual assault on the college campus. *Justice Quarterly, 18,* 623–649.

Schwartz, M. D., & Pitts, V. L. (1995). Exploring a feminist routine activities approach to explaining sexual assault. *Justice Quarterly, 12,* 9–31.

Skogan, W. G. (1990). The National Crime Survey redesign. *Public Opinion Quarterly, 54,* 256–272.

Sloan, J. J., Fisher, B. S., & Cullen, F. T. (1997). Assessing the Student Right-to-Know and Campus Security Act of 1990: An analysis of the victim reporting practices of college and university students. *Crime and Delinquency, 43,* 148–168.

Sloan, J. J., & Shoemaker, J. (2007). State-level Clery Act initiatives: Symbolic politics or substantive policy? In B. S. Fisher & J. J. Sloan (Eds.), *Campus crime: Legal, social, and policy perspectives* (2nd ed., pp. 102–124). Springfield, IL: Charles Thomas.

Small, S. A., & Kerns, D. (1993). Unwanted sexual activity among peers during early and middle adolescence: Incidence and risk factors. *Journal of Marriage and the Family, 55,* 941–952.

Smith, D. A., & Uchida, C. C. (1988). The social organization of self-help: A study of defensive weapon ownership. *American Sociological Review, 53,* 94–102.

Smith, M. D. (1987). The incidence and prevalence of women abuse in Toronto. *Violence and Victims, 2,* 173–187.

Smith, P. H., White, J. W., & Holland, L. J. (2003). A longitudinal perspective on dating violence among adolescent and college-age women. *American Journal of Public Health, 93,* 1104–1109.

Snyder, T. D., Dillow, S. A., & Hoffman, C. M. (2009). *Digest of education statistics 2008* (NCES 2009–020). Washington, DC: National Center for Education Statistics, Institute of Education Sciences, U.S. Department of Education.

Sorenson, S. B., Stein, J. A., Siegel, J. M., Golding, J. M., & Burnam, M. A. (1987). The prevalence of adult sexual assault: The Los Angeles Epidemiologic Catchment Area Project. *American Journal of Epidemiology, 126,* 1154–1164.

Spitzberg, B. H. (1999). An analysis of empirical estimates of sexual aggression victimization and perpetration. *Violence and Victims, 14,* 241–260.

Spitzberg, B. H., & Hoobler, G. (2002). Cyberstalking and the technologies of interpersonal terrorism. *New Media and Society, 4,* 71–92.

Spitzberg, B. H., & Rhea, J. (1999). Obsessive relational intrusion and sexual coercion victimization. *Journal of Interpersonal Violence, 14,* 3–20.

Spohn, C., & Horney, J. (1992). *Rape law reform: A grassroots revolution and its impact.* New York: Plenum Press.

Sweet, E. (1985, October). Date rape: The story of an epidemic and those who deny it. *Ms.,* pp. 56–59, 84–85.

Sykes, G. M., & Matza, D. (1957). Techniques of neutralization: A theory of delinquency. *American Sociological Review, 22,* 664–673.

Taylor, B. M., & Rand, M. R. (1995, August). *The National Crime Victimization Survey redesign: New understanding of victimization dynamics and measurement.* Paper presented at the 1995 Annual Meetings of the American Statistical Association, Orlando, FL.

Testa, M. (2002). The impact of men's alcohol consumption on perpetration of sexual aggression. *Clinical Psychology Review, 22,* 1239–1263.

Testa, M. (2004). The role of substance use in male-to-female physical and sexual violence: A brief review and recommendations for future research. *Journal of Interpersonal Violence, 19,* 1494–1505.

Testa, M., & Dermen, K. H. (1999). The differential correlates of sexual coercion and rape. *Journal of Interpersonal Violence, 14,* 548–561.

Testa, M., VanZile-Tamsen, C., Livingston, J. A., & Buddie, A. M. (2006). The role of women's alcohol consumption in managing sexual intimacy and sexual safety motives. *Journal of Studies on Alcohol, 67,* 665–674.

Thompson, M. P., Basile, K. C., Hertz, M. F., & Sitterle, D. (2006). *Measuring intimate partner violence victimization and perpetration: A compendium of assessment tools.* Atlanta, GA: Centers for Disease Control and Prevention, National Center for Injury Prevention and Control.

Thompson, M. P., Sitterle, D. J., Clay, G., & Kingree, J. B. (2007). Reasons for not reporting victimizations to the police: Do they vary for physical and sexual incidents? *Journal of American College Health, 55,* 277–282.

Tjaden, P. (1996). *Violence and threats of violence against women in America: Female questionnaire.* Denver, CO: Center for Policy Research.

Tjaden, P. (1997). *The crime of stalking: How big is the problem?* (National Institute of Justice, Research Preview). Washington, DC: National Institute of Justice.

Tjaden, P., & Thoennes, N. (1998a). *Prevalence, incidence, and consequences of violence against women: Findings from the National Violence Against Women Survey* (Research in Brief, NCJ 172837). Washington, DC: U.S. Department of Justice, National Institute of Justice and U.S. Department of Health and Human Services, Centers for Disease Control and Prevention.

Tjaden, P., & Thoennes, N. (1998b). *Stalking in America: Findings from the National Violence Against Women Survey* (Research in Brief, NCJ 169592). Washington, DC: U.S. Department of Justice, National Institute of Justice and U.S. Department of Health and Human Services, Centers for Disease Control and Prevention.

Tjaden, P., & Thoennes, N. (2000). *Full report of the prevalence, incidence, and consequences of violence against women: Findings from the National Violence Against Women Survey.* Washington, DC: National Institute of Justice.

Tjaden, P., & Thoennes, N. (2006). *Extent, nature, and consequences of rape victimization: Findings from the National Violence Against Women Survey.* Washington, DC: National Institute of Justice.

Ullman, S. E. (1997). Review and critique of empirical studies of rape avoidance. *Criminal Justice and Behavior, 24,* 177–204.

Ullman, S. E. (1999). Social support and recovery from sexual assault: A review. *Aggression and Violent Behavior, 4,* 343–358.

Ullman, S. E. (2007). A 10-year update of "Review and critique of empirical studies of rape avoidance." *Criminal Justice and Behavior, 34,* 411–429.

U.S. Department of Education, National Center for Education Statistics. (2003). *The condition of education 2003* (NCES 2003–067). Washington, DC: U. S. Government Printing Office.

U.S. Department of Justice. (1996). *Domestic violence, stalking, and antistalking legislation: An annual report to Congress under the Violence Against Women Act.* Washington, DC: U.S. Government Printing Office.

Violent Crime Control and Enforcement Act of 1994, Pub. L. 103–322 (1994).

Ward, D., & Lee, J. (2005). *The handbook for campus crime reporting.* Washington, DC: U.S. Department of Education, Office of Postsecondary Education.

Warshaw, R. (1988). *I never called it rape: The* Ms. *report on recognizing, fighting and surviving date and acquaintance rape.* New York: Harper & Row.

Weis, K., & Borges, S. (1973). Victimology and rape: The case of the legitimate victim. *Issues in Criminology, 8,* 71–115.

Weisel, D. L. (2005). *Analyzing repeat victimization: Problem-oriented guides for police problem-solving tool* (Series Guide No. 4). Washington, DC: U.S. Department of Justice, Office of Community Oriented Policing Services.

Weisel, D. L., Clarke, R. V., & Stedman, J. R. (1999). *Hot dots in hot spots: Examining repeat victimization for residential burglary in three cities, (Final Report).* Washington, DC: U.S. Department of Justice.

Westrup, D., Fremouw, W. J., Thompson, R. N., & Lewis, S. F. (1999). The psychological impact of stalking on female undergraduates. *Journal of Forensic Sciences, 44,* 554–557.

White, J. W., & Smith, P. H. (2001). *Developmental antecedents of violence against women: A longitudinal approach, executive summary.* Washington, DC: U.S. Department of Justice.

White, J. W., Smith, P. H., & Humphrey, J. A. (2001). A longitudinal perspective on women's risk perceptions for sexual assault. In M. Martinez (Ed.), *Prevention and control of aggression and the impact on its victims* (pp. 255–260). New York: Kluwer Academic/Plenum.

Wilcox, P., Land, K. C., & Hunt, S. A. (2003). *Criminal circumstances: A dynamic multicontextual criminal opportunity theory.* New York: Aldine de Gruyter.

Williams, L. S. (1984). The classic rape: When do victims report? *Social Problems, 31,* 459–467.

Williams, S. L., & Frieze, I. H. (2005). Courtship behaviors, relationship violence, and breakup persistence in college men and women. *Psychology of Women Quarterly, 29,* 248–257.

Wilson, A. E., Calhoun, K. S., & Bernat, J. A. (1999). Risk recognition and trauma-related symptoms among sexually revictimized women. *Journal of Consulting and Clinical Psychology, 67,* 705–710.

Wilson, J. Q. (1975). *Thinking about crime.* New York: Vintage.

Wolf, N. (1991). *The beauty myth: How images of beauty are used against women.* New York: William Morrow.

Wyatt, G. E., Guthrie, D., & Notgrass, C. M. (1992). Differential effects of women's child sexual abuse and subsequent sexual revictimization. *Journal of Consulting and Clinical Psychology, 60,* 167–173.

Yeater, E., & O'Donohue, W. (1999). Sexual assault prevention programs: Current issues, future directions, and the potential efficacy of interventions with women. *Clinical Psychology Review, 19,* 739–771.

Zorza, J. (2001). Drug-facilitated rape. In A. J. Ottens & K. Hotelling (Eds.), *Sexual violence on campus: Politics, programs, and perspectives* (pp. 53–75). New York: Springer.

Index

About the Authors

Bonnie S. Fisher is Professor in the School of Criminal Justice and Research Fellow in the Center for Criminal Justice Research at the University of Cincinnati. Professor Fisher received her Ph.D. (1988) in Political Science from Northwestern University. She is a nationally recognized expert in the areas of sexual, violent, and stalking victimization of college women, including repeat victimization, self-protection effectiveness, and fear of crime, and how postsecondary schools respond to reports of sexual victimization. She has authored more than 150 publications in national and international peer-reviewed criminology, criminal justice, crime prevention, gerontology, legal, medical, methodological, nursing, urban planning, public administration, psychology, security, and victimology periodicals. She also has edited several volumes that focus on victimization issues, including *Encyclopedia of Victimology and Crime Prevention* (with Steven P. Lab), *Campus Crime, Legal, Social and Political Perspectives,* 2nd edition (with John Sloan III), *Violence Against Women and Family Violence,* and *Developments in Research, Practice, and Policy.* She has been the coeditor of the *Security Journal* since 1998. She has served as the Deputy Editor of *Justice Quarterly* and since 2008 has been the Associate Editor of the *Journal of Research Crime and Delinquency.* She has been the Principal Investigator or Co-PI on several U.S. Department of Justice grants examining a range of college student victimization issues and on a grant from the British Home Office to examine college student victimization in the East Midlands, United Kingdom. Currently she is a Co-PI on a National Institute of Health grant examining forensic sexual examinations and the use of digital images and staining techniques to enhance the detection of injuries and the use of digital images in decision making among the police, prosecutors, defense attorneys, judges, and juries in the criminal justice process.

Leah E. Daigle is Assistant Professor in the Department of Criminal Justice at Georgia State University. She received her Ph.D. in Criminal Justice from the University of Cincinnati in 2005. Her most recent research has centered on repeat sexual victimization of college women and the responses that women use during and after being sexually victimized. Her other research interests include the development and continuation of offending over time and gender differences in the antecedents to and consequences of criminal victimization and participation across the life course. She is coauthor of *Criminals in the Making: Criminality Across the Life Course* and has published numerous peer-reviewed articles that have appeared in *Justice Quarterly, Journal of*

Quantitative Criminology, Victims and Offenders, and the *Journal of Interpersonal Violence.*

Francis T. Cullen is Distinguished Research Professor in the School of Criminal Justice at the University of Cincinnati, where he also holds a joint appointment in sociology. He received his Ph.D. (1979) in Sociology and Education from Columbia University. Professor Cullen has published more than 200 works in the areas of criminological theory, corrections, white-collar crime, public opinion, and the measurement of sexual victimization. He is author of *Rethinking Crime and Deviance Theory: The Emergence of a Structuring Tradition* and is coauthor of *Reaffirming Rehabilitation, Corporate Crime Under Attack: The Ford Pinto Case and Beyond, Criminological Theory: Context and Consequences, Criminology,* and *Combating Corporate Crime: Local Prosecutors at Work.* He also has coedited *Contemporary Criminological Theory, Offender Rehabilitation: Effective Correctional Intervention, Criminological Theory: Past to Present—Essential Readings, Taking Stock: The Status of Criminological Theory, The Origins of American Criminology,* and the *Encyclopedia of Criminological Theory.* He is past president of the American Society of Criminology and of the Academy of Criminal Justice Sciences. Previously, he served as editor of *Justice Quarterly* and of the *Journal of Crime and Justice.* He has been honored as a Fellow of the Academy of Criminal Justice Sciences (ACJS) and of the American Society of Criminology, as the Outstanding Educator by the Ohio Council of Criminal Justice Educators, and with ACJS's Bruce Smith Award and Founder's Award.

Supporting researchers for more than 40 years

Research methods have always been at the core of SAGE's publishing program. Founder Sara Miller McCune published SAGE's first methods book, *Public Policy Evaluation*, in 1970. Soon after, she launched the *Quantitative Applications in the Social Sciences* series—affectionately known as the "little green books."

Always at the forefront of developing and supporting new approaches in methods, SAGE published early groundbreaking texts and journals in the fields of qualitative methods and evaluation.

Today, more than 40 years and two million little green books later, SAGE continues to push the boundaries with a growing list of more than 1,200 research methods books, journals, and reference works across the social, behavioral, and health sciences. Its imprints—Pine Forge Press, home of innovative textbooks in sociology, and Corwin, publisher of PreK–12 resources for teachers and administrators—broaden SAGE's range of offerings in methods. SAGE further extended its impact in 2008 when it acquired CQ Press and its best-selling and highly respected political science research methods list.

From qualitative, quantitative, and mixed methods to evaluation, SAGE is the essential resource for academics and practitioners looking for the latest methods by leading scholars.

For more information, visit **www.sagepub.com**.